Authenticity in and through Teaching in Higher Education

THE UNIVERSITY OF
WINCHESTER

What does
more authe
scholarship
of students

Authent
authenticit
ing toward
each of the

In devel
this book c
nature of t
Other con
'power', 'c

Authent
teaching w
important
towards g
process of
finition a
on assumj
intimately

Rather
works', th
cerned wi
potential
engages w
education

The bo
work on t
tive on th

Carolin Kreber is Professor of Higher Education at the University of Edinburgh, UK.

Authenticity in and through Teaching in Higher Education

The transformative potential of the scholarship of teaching

Carolin Kreber

Routledge
Taylor & Francis Group

LONDON AND NEW YORK

First published 2013
by Routledge
2 Park Square, Milton Park, Abingdon, Oxon OX14 4RN

Simultaneously published in the USA and Canada
by Routledge
711 Third Avenue, New York, NY 10017

Routledge is an imprint of the Taylor & Francis Group, an informa business

British Library Cataloguing in Publication Data
A catalogue record for this book is available from the British Library

Library of Congress Cataloging in Publication Data
Kreber, Carolin.
Authenticity in and through teaching in higher education: the transformative
potential of the scholarship of teaching / Carolin Kreber.
p. cm.
1. College teaching—Philosophy. 2. Authenticity (Philosophy) I. Title.
LB2331.K74 2013
378.125—dc23
2012028917

ISBN: 978-0-415-52007-2 (hbk)
ISBN: 978-0-415-52008-9 (pbk)
ISBN: 978-0-203-07230-1 (ebk)

Typeset in Galliard
by Book Now Ltd

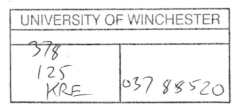

MIX
Paper from
responsible sources
FSC
www.fsc.org   FSC® C004839

Printed and bound by CPI Group (UK) Ltd, Croydon, CR0 4YY

Contents

Illustrations

Figures

Tables

Acknowledgements

I would like to thank Rowena Arshad, Head of the Institute for Education, Community and Society at The University of Edinburgh, for making it possible for me to take a two-month research leave in the spring of 2012 in order to complete this book.

My editor at Routledge, Philip Mudd, and editorial assistant Vicky Parting, were very encouraging of this project, a pleasure to work with, and ensured that the manuscript made the agreed deadline.

In writing this book I obviously was inspired by the work of many philosophers, social scientists and educationalists whose names appear in the references. However, the work of some colleagues in the fields of adult and higher education was particularly helpful to me because they engage with ideas that overlap directly with those discussed in this book. By reading their work my understanding of some of the themes I was analysing was both challenged and deepened. These colleagues include, in alphabetical order, Ron Barnett, Stephen Brookfield, Jon Nixon and Melanie Walker, and I would like to extend my thanks to them simply in appreciation of their scholarship. In addition, Patricia Cranton's work helped me appreciate more clearly the relationship between authenticity and transformative learning.

I am grateful to Ron Barnett for his encouragement when I first mentioned to him the idea for this book following a colloquium in Edinburgh in April 2011. Little did I know at the time that his advice to 'write a page a day' would translate into 'write three, then delete two!' Charles Anderson, Joelle Fanghanel, Jon Nixon and Michael Ross very generously gave up their own time to provide feedback on a full draft of the manuscript. Their astute comments and superb suggestions were most valuable and much enhanced later drafts. I am deeply indebted to each of them.

Andrea Roth showed much tolerance during a week of us visiting in the South of France in September 2011, which I ended up spending mostly in the company of Alasdair Macintyre! Lots of olives, goat cheese, baguettes, Languedoc rosés and your delightful companionship were all imperative for the completion of Chapter 4, but I do owe you a real holiday some day. Throughout the year that I was working on this book Shelley Sikora steadfastly endured weekends that were spent reading, writing and debating the 'meaning of authenticity'! You, also, unfalteringly made yourself available for talking through particularly knotty issues that were causing me a headache and helped me focus my arguments, and your editing suggestions prior to final submission were superb. Any remaining inconsistencies and/or blatantly dubious claims are entirely my own responsibility.

Taylor and Francis kindly granted permission to make use of a forthcoming article in the journal *Studies in Higher Education* ('Empowering the scholarship of teaching and learning: An Arendtian and critical perspective'). Individual sections of this forthcoming article were incorporated into Chapters 7 and 8. The journal website can be found at: www.tandfonline.com.

Carolin Kreber
Edinburgh, June 2012

Preamble

Three case studies

CASE I

Chris

For the past eight years Chris and four of her colleagues have been regular participants at an annual conference on pedagogical research in higher education. They
typically also have three or four students join them. This year they are presenting
the latest findings from a six-year longitudinal study of curriculum change they
carried out in the Department of Materials Engineering at their university in the
United States. Chris and her colleagues have not only been enthusiastically
embracing this change initiative from the start but have also taken leadership in
bringing it about. Asked what motivated them to become engaged with this project Chris mentions among other factors: an absence of community within the
department; a lack of engagement on the part of students and faculty; high drop-
out rates in the first year particularly among women and minority groups; high
numbers of students doing poorly on assignments; negative comments about
students from faculty, including a widely held belief that 'they just don't want to
work hard'; and generally no shared sense that college teaching might actually
matter to and affect people's lives. Chris and her team are excited about the
impact the curriculum change initiative has had on students, colleagues, the
department, the university and themselves. As evidence of change they report:
survey data on student achievement, engagement and satisfaction; interviews
with faculty as well as present and former students; a recent external evaluation
report of the department praising the learning environment and level of community engagement; university documents placing greater emphasis on a shared
vision of teaching; and unsolicited comments from students and colleagues, as in
thank you cards, emails and chats in the coffee room. The most powerful data
they provide include not only personal experiential accounts from the three students who presented with them but also their own stories of change over the past
six years. Although each story is different in terms of the specific experiences that
stand out for them as individual teachers and students, underlying the diversity
in their stories is a common theme of having connected with their true

inner motives for college teaching and learning, and a transformed sense of what is possible for them.

CASE II

Phil

Phil is a member of a reading group on social justice in higher education at his university in the United Kingdom. With nine regular participants the group is rather small, but this also means that the monthly meetings are always characterised by lively discussions. The group began with just three colleagues from the School of Education, but it now includes two from English Literature and one each from the Health Sciences, History, Psychology and Chemistry. Phil is a chemist who started teaching at the university three years ago. Asked what motivated him to join this group he comments that after completing the Postgraduate Certificate in University Teaching at the same university during his first two years he wanted to continue the dialogue but there were no further offerings available. One day he happened to read about this 'social justice in higher education' reading group in an institutional newsletter advertising upcoming events and, although not too convinced by the group's official branding, he was sufficiently intrigued to check it out. At the very first meeting he found the people nice enough, although he had rather strong reactions to the text he had been sent in advance. There were difficult readings on the PG Cert courses too but 'what on earth is "alienation", what if anything have "relations of power" to do with student engagement in the chemistry lab, and who the heck are Lacan and Foucault'? He was not really surprised that after some initial chatting over tea and biscuits other members of the group revealed similar difficulties with this text. As the discussion started, colleagues from English Literature initially intimidated him a little as they tended to speak almost exclusively in five-syllable words, but then he also appreciated the points they raised about the text and delighted in their sense of humour; in particular, their capacity to make fun of their own sheer inability to talk any differently gave cause for a few good laughs within the group. What evolved was a lively exchange of opinions over the meaning of the text, with each person in the group contributing his or her perspective. As the evening unfolded it became apparent that the article had profound relevance to each person's teaching context. As Phil cycled home that evening, still excited by the conversations he had just had, he was thinking about what he would do differently in his class the next morning. Phil has been a member of this group for over a year now and makes it a priority. Asked why he decided to stay with this group he responds that the exchanges with his colleagues make him think about teaching and learning in new ways and he feels he is becoming a better teacher as a result. In particular, he finds that he is more connected to the experiences of different students and aware of how practices that on the surface appear to be fair to all students in reality often serve the interests of only a certain group.

CASE III

Samir

Samir has been teaching philosophy and law for 15 years at two different universities in Canada. When asked to take on the role of mentor for Brenda, a new faculty member in the School of Economics, he happily agreed. When they meet for the first time at a nearby coffee shop, he tells her:

> I'm not what one would call an 'expert teacher'. I'm a philosopher who teaches philosophy and now also law, not an educationalist! I subscribe to a journal called *Teaching Philosophy* although I actually only ever read it when I happen to come across an article that seems directly relevant to what I'm trying to achieve in my course. So I suppose the reason I've been asked over the years to talk to newer colleagues is that I have a strong interest in teaching and am also quite outspoken about teaching issues in department meetings, or whenever I get a chance really [chuckles]. So, while I do not have much academic knowledge to share with you about teaching I find the teaching part of my career immensely enriching and I much value exchanging views about teaching and learning with others.

Asked by Brenda what it is that he most enjoys about his teaching, Samir takes a few seconds stirring his coffee, then looks at her and replies:

> I suppose teaching people about philosophy, an area that not only is of strong personal interest to me but one that matters so hugely to our society, particularly but not exclusively in relation to the law, is not only a privilege but also an enormous responsibility. Over the years, observing the connections students make between the issues we deliberate in class and the choices they make in their immediate and wider communities, watching them learn to distinguish bad from good arguments and in some cases following their careers, I've come to realise that I can actually make a difference in the world through the students who come to our university to study, interpret and practice philosophy or law, and go on to make our world a fairer place. So I've got to say that by being a teacher I feel more connected with my inner self and humanity. And I also like to ruffle a few feathers in department meetings and the like where the student experience is overlooked and increasingly economic imperatives seem to be the driving force.

Brenda shakes her head saying:

> You know, the students in my School just want to pass the courses, some want to do well but it's all extremely marks driven nonetheless. Besides, it was made very clear to me that while teaching matters around here, research

matters even more. I've been here for six months now and I honestly can't get quite as excited about teaching as you seem to be. Moreover, in my School people don't talk much about the student experience. . . .

Samir listens patiently as Brenda goes on a little longer about the conflicting demands of teaching and research and of the current priorities of the university. Eventually he replies: 'How very interesting. That's precisely what I observed when I first started. I suppose the question is whether things could be otherwise.'

***

Chris, Phil and Samir are involved in very different activities. Nonetheless, according to the arguments presented in this book all three of them are engaged in the scholarship of university teaching: through critically reflective inquiry into their own teaching practice, the sharing of insights, a striving for authenticity and a genuine motivation to act in the important interests of students and, ultimately, society.

Introduction

Presenting key concepts and ideas

What does it mean to be authentic? Why should it matter whether or not we become more authentic? How might authenticity inform and enhance the social practice of the scholarship of university teaching and, by implication, the learning and development of students? These are the key questions explored in this book. Four broad constructs emerge from these questions: *teaching*, *scholarship*, *authenticity* and *practice*. The purpose of this introduction is to provide an initial sense of how we might understand the linkages among these.

The university is inconceivable without teaching *and* scholarship. Teaching without scholarship would lack the spirit of curiosity and inquiry that is distinctive of the university and, as one observer put it, 'may at university level simply be called bad teaching' (Elton, 1992, p. 253). Scholarship without teaching would take away a key function of the university, which is its responsibility to provide opportunities for students to learn and develop by inviting them into the scholarly process. Teaching *and* scholarship, together, are therefore vital to the university; but fundamental to both, I argue in this book, is *authenticity*.

Also fundamental to teaching *and* scholarship, I shall argue, is their enactment as a *practice*. By associating teaching *and* scholarship with *practice*, I have in mind not just that they are productive hands-on activities rather than purely theoretical pursuits. Following a less conventional understanding of a *practice* I also want to point to the fact that teaching *and* scholarship are activities in which we, together with other actors, are personally invested and pursue out of an inner motivation and disposition to do good work. Good work carries qualities of excellence, engagement and ethics (Gardner, 2011). I thus suggest that the notion of a practice and that of authenticity are fundamental to teaching *and* scholarship; but because being engaged in a practice, of necessity, involves authenticity (a point I develop more fully in Chapter 4), it is the notion of *authenticity* that is most central. Given that at university level teaching and scholarship always exist together, I will henceforth often employ the term '(scholarship of) teaching' to highlight this relationship; the meaning attached to this specialised term will be elucidated at a later stage. Figure I.1 summarises what has been claimed so far: engagement in scholarship *and* teaching, or the 'scholarship of teaching', when enacted as a practice, is marked by authenticity.

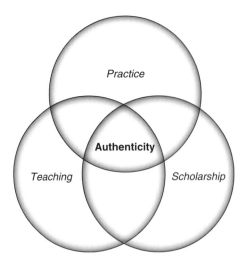

Figure I.1 Teaching, scholarship, authenticity and practice.

Teaching, scholarship, authenticity and *practice*: each of these on its own has generated a considerable body of literature in the fields of philosophy and higher education. In addition, some theorists have identified intriguing relationships between pairs of constructs, specifically between authenticity and teaching (e.g. Barnett, 2007; Cranton, 2001, 2006a,b; Macfarlane, 2007; Palmer, 1998), authenticity and practice (e.g. Nixon, 2004, 2008), authenticity and scholarship (e.g. Rice, 1989), teaching and practice (e.g. Gibbs, Angelides & Michaelides, 2004), scholarship and practice (e.g. Harvey & Myers, 1995; Nicholls, 2005) and also scholarship and teaching (e.g. Cross, 1990; Elton, 1992; Hutchings & Shulman, 1999; Oakley, 1996). The sheer volume of intellectual activity devoted to these themes within the context of academic practice intimates that there is something particularly pressing and compelling about these ideas in our times, which calls for deeper examination and understanding.

Each of these constructs is also marked by a certain degree of ambiguity and complexity. It would not be uncommon for two people employing any one of these notions in a conversation to mean different things by it. What we take *scholarship* to mean, for example, has shifted considerably over time (e.g. Boyer, 1990; Rice, 1989) and several meanings now exist simultaneously. Does scholarship refer to the interpretation of what is known (Elton, 1992), the process of thinking, reading and studying that leads to the final research product (e.g. Braskamp & Ory, 1994), the extension, application or integration of what is known (Boyer, 1990), or do we mean by it the advancement of knowledge through cutting-edge disciplinary or interdisciplinary research? Even university *teaching*, which might strike us as the most straightforward construct of the four, has been shown to be interpretable in a variety of ways (e.g. Fox, 1983; Kember, 1997; Pratt, 1992). Think of the well-known metaphors for teaching such as 'banking', 'gardening', 'coaching' or 'sculpting lives' (Beidler, 1987). Indeed, Ross (2012) recently identified as many as 25 different conceptions of teaching. Speaking to different colleagues also reveals that for some the term 'teaching' means little more than giving lectures and tutorials, while for others it embraces the numerous tasks teachers engage in as organisers of courses, commentators and assessors of student work, supervisors of dissertations or theses, advisors on students' programmes of study, and providers of pastoral support. Again for others, teaching implies being an educator in an even broader sense of wanting to make a difference, not only to the students' learning of subject matter but also to their personal, moral and intellectual development, and, by implication, to the wider world teachers, students and others inhabit. Some see their professional role as academic teachers still more broadly to include having a perspective on the social policy context that influences their work and in engaging with this context. Thus it would appear that although both *teaching* and *scholarship* are traditional functions of the university they do not represent universally construed phenomena.

Authenticity and *practice* are also open to different conceptualisations. What distinguishes *authenticity* and *practice* from *teaching* and *scholarship* is that in construing the former terms we are less limited by our everyday or common-sense understandings but can seek inspiration in formal definitions or theories, often grounded in philosophical literature, that imbue these constructs with a particular meaning. The idea of a *practice*, that I hinted at earlier, for example, is inspired by MacIntyre's (2007) approach to moral philosophy. His conceptuali-sation of a social *practice* as an activity that is situated within a community, with distinct values, standards of excellence, traditions and even qualities or 'virtues', is quite different from how we conventionally understand the term. Formal the-ories of *authenticity* and *practice*, I want to argue, carry the potential to help us think about our academic practice in fresh and perhaps deeper ways, thereby opening up new possibilities for engaging with this work. In this book I apply the ideas of authenticity and practice to a particular domain of academic work: 'the scholarship of teaching'.

Below I briefly review some of the controversies surrounding 'the scholarship of teaching' and discuss why it remains contested. I also outline the particular position on this concept that is taken in this book. Following this I turn to the notion of *authenticity*, discuss what is so compelling about this notion in the con-texts of university teaching and scholarship, and explain how my interest in this notion originated. I conclude by elucidating the book's main title by summaris-ing the three broad perspectives on authenticity that inform later chapters.

'The scholarship *of* teaching' – a contested idea

Over the past two decades, a sizeable literature has been developing internation-ally on the changing nature of academic practice and the academic profession (e.g. Altbach, 2007; Fanghanel, 2011a; Kogan & Teichler, 2007; Locke, 2007) and notably also on a relatively recent concept called 'the scholarship of teaching'. A few years back Nicholls (2005) observed that only a relatively small proportion of academics working in universities in the United Kingdom were familiar with this specialised term. This is likely still to be the case, in the United Kingdom as elsewhere. Nonetheless, the 'scholarship of teaching', now more frequently referred to as 'the scholarship of teaching and learning' in response to an increased focus on learning research and the student experience (e.g. Barr & Tagg, 1995; Tagg, 2003), has undoubtedly grown in popularity. It is for this reason that many have described the 'scholarship of teaching' as a movement of international scope (Asmar, 2004; Bender, 2005; Hughes, 2006; Hutchings, 2004; Kreber, 2005a; McKinney, 2002), and the launch of the International Society for the Scholarship of Teaching and Learning in 2004 and the *International Journal of the Scholarship of Teaching and Learning* in 2007 (the latter independent of the Society and published out of the Center for Excellence in Teaching at Georgia Southern University) bear further testimony to this fact. Growing popularity is perhaps also demonstrated by the 'scholarship of teaching' having achieved an entry into Wikipedia, where the opening sentence reads:

> The Scholarship of Teaching and Learning (SOTL or SoTL; pronounced *so'tl saw'tl* or *S O T L*) is a growing movement in post-secondary education. SOTL is scholarly inquiry into student learning which advances the practice of teaching by making research findings public.
> (http://en.wikipedia.org/wiki/Scholarship_of_Teaching_ and_Learning, accessed in August 2011)

The Wikipedia entry is one plausible way of conceptualising the 'scholarship of teaching' and representative of a widely shared perspective. However, I suggest in this book that the view expressed there is too narrow. In particular, I would like to encourage a broader understanding of the relationships between teaching and scholarship, a less restricted perspective on what counts as relevant inquiry in relation to university teaching and a more creative understanding of 'going public'.

Recently the lead article in the newsletter of the Society for Research into Higher Education (SRHE) in the United Kingdom called for responses to the question: 'Have we been barking up the wrong tree? Should we cherish the scholarship of teaching and learning as special and precious, or is it rather too special, and rather too "precious"?' (Cuthbert, 2011, p. 2). The call reveals that despite its growing popularity and existing definitions, 'the scholarship of teaching' has remained a contested concept. There are at least four interrelated reasons for this: (1) ongoing differences in interpretation over what scholarship means, and hence over what the scholarship of teaching essentially involves; (2) scepticism regarding initiatives that are perceived to separate teaching from a wider integrated notion of academic practice; (3) a sense of disillusionment over the 'scholarship of teaching' not having fulfilled its promise to raise the status of teaching in universities; and (4) an observation that despite increased activity (as demonstrated through funding schemes for pedagogical innovations and investigations, as well as new conferences and journals to share the insights gained from this work) the 'scholarship of teaching' has not adequately taken up the bigger questions of social justice and equality *in* and *through* higher education.

The dominant discourse on the 'scholarship of teaching', according to the fourth reason, is therefore impoverished, that is, not sufficiently engaged with issues of power and concerns beyond immediate classroom processes and activities. The point of the critique is not that examinations of classroom practices do not matter, but rather that they all too often remain under-intellectualised (e.g. Boshier, 2009; McLean, 2006), devoid of insights informed by a range of theories that speak not only to the psychological dimension of university teaching and learning but also to its socio-political purposes. To fulfil its promise of a truly transformational agenda (e.g. Hutchings, 2000), the 'scholarship of teaching' needs to become more *critical,* more concerned with social and political purposes and ideology critique (Kreber, 2005a). Engagement in the 'scholarship of teaching', then, includes revealing the various power dynamics and relationships at work in higher education teaching and bringing to the surface tacit attitudes or assumptions that may work against our own and the students' interests. A review of literature associated with the 'scholarship of teaching', conducted by Gilpin and Liston (2009) (252 journal articles, 8 books and 63 conference proposals published between 1999 and 2008), suggested that about ten per cent of the reviewed publications addressed the transformative potential of the 'scholarship of teaching' and that such work has been increasing in recent years. The aim of this book is to add to this developing literature.

The position taken in this book

This book promotes the view that being a scholar of teaching is an ongoing *transformative learning* process that is intimately bound up with becoming authentic. Construed as an 'authentic practice', the scholarship of teaching emerges as an activity that is guided by certain standards of excellence, virtues and values. Fundamental to the pursuit of certain virtues and values is critical reflectivity, a quintessential aspect of scholarship (Andresen, 2000). Engagement in this practice furthers the authenticity of teachers and ultimately is aimed at serving the important interests of students. The important interest of students, I will argue in Chapter 2, is the students' own authenticity. Both teachers and students are thus implicated in a process of transformative learning, of objective and subjective reframing, of redefinition and reconstruction, in short a process of *becoming*.

This view of the scholarship of teaching is explicitly rooted in a particular value position. Hannah Arendt saw the great challenge for education as offering experiences that help students become prepared 'for the task of renewing the common world' (Arendt, 2007, p. 192). Renewing our common world, I argue, is precisely the great challenge for the scholarship for teaching. Our common world refers to both the particular learning and policy environments that teachers and students are part of *and* the larger world out there that we share with our fellow human beings (and other non-human species). Engagement in the scholarship of teaching involves adopting a critically reflective and inquiring approach not only towards the content we teach but also towards the technical and, most importantly, the moral aspects of teaching, including reflection on the wider goals, social purposes and present policies of higher education (Atkinson, 2001; Cranton, 2011; Kreber, 2005a).

Engagement in the scholarship of teaching, thus construed, implies not only that we work towards a better world in which to learn and teach but ultimately towards a better, that is a fairer, more compassionate and sustainable, *world*. In this way the scholarship of teaching also engages with the bigger questions of social justice and equality *in* and *through* higher education. Moreover, construed as a *practice*, the scholarship of teaching is not merely an activity of the few who carry out empirical studies on student learning and publish their results through conference presentations, articles or books; instead it emerges as an imperative for all academics who teach. We all have a professional responsibility to approach our teaching with the same level of curiosity, knowledge and care we adopt in relation to the other aspects of our academic work. It is for this reason that in the first two chapters I intentionally refrain from distinguishing 'the scholarship *of* teaching' from 'university teaching'. How this view compares to widespread definitions of 'the scholarship of teaching' is discussed in Chapter 3. I add at this stage that I employ a broad understanding of the notion of teaching, one that encompasses not only what teachers do (e.g. course preparation, lecturing, leading seminars, supervising postgraduate students, assessing students' work and so forth) but also the role of universities as providers of higher education opportunities. University teaching is situated within a particular social/policy context. Being engaged in (the scholarship of) teaching also involves being aware of and engaging with this context.

What is so compelling about authenticity?

My interest in the notion of authenticity began by being struck by the outpouring of publications on the theme of authenticity in recent years, both in relation to how we should approach our personal lives and also in relation to *work* (e.g. Arnason, 1994; Fleming, 2009; Giardina, 2002; Gilmore & Pine, 2007; Legere, 2007; Mazutis & Slawinski, 2008; Russ, 2007; Seligman, 2002; Starr, 2008), including *academic practice* (e.g. Nixon, 2008; Vannini, 2007; Vu & Dall'Alba, 2011) and *teaching* (e.g. Barnett, 2007; Brook, 2009; Cranton, 2001; Laursen, 2005; Palmer, 1998). What particularly intrigued me were two issues. The first related to the contested nature of authenticity that was revealed by the texts that were being produced. Different authors seemed to focus their arguments on different ideas or aspects of what it means to be authentic. Some distinguished so-called deviant forms of authenticity from what they recognised as more meaningful interpretations (e.g. Taylor, 1991), while others devoted entire books to arguing against the very idea of authenticity (e.g. Potter, 2010). Authenticity appeared to be a multidimensional notion explored from a variety of philosophical perspectives. This observation led me to want to understand the notion of authenticity at a deeper level and explore the question: *What might authenticity in relation to teaching and academic practice mean once we have disentangled its various features or dimensions?* I report in Chapter 1 on a small series of studies that colleagues and I carried out with the purpose of answering this question. This chapter also offers a more comprehensive discussion of how we might understand the meaning of authenticity generally, drawing on relevant literature from the fields of education and philosophy. I suggest that although authenticity is a contested concept, it is not, as has been claimed at times, pernicious.

The second issue that captured my interest relates to the reason behind this surge of publications on authenticity. The question that formed in my mind was: *What is it about our times, or the world we live and work in, that generates this heightened concern with 'authenticity', particularly in relation to academic practice and teaching?* (e.g. Barnett, 2004a,b, 2007; Brookfield, 2006; Chickering, Dalton & Stamm, 2006; Cranton, 2001, 2006a,b; Cranton & Carusetta, 2004; Dirkx, 2006; Nixon, 2007, 2008; Palmer, 1998; Rogers, 2006; Walker, 2001).

In generating this question I was inspired by Terry Eagleton who, in reflecting on why it is that individuals feel compelled to search for meaning and purpose (and, we might say, *authenticity*) at particular times in their lives, commented: 'Maybe all men and women ponder the meaning of life; but some, for good historical reasons, are driven to ponder it more urgently than others' (Eagleton, 2007, p. 18). I also took inspiration from Martha Nussbaum (2000) who argued that 'to be able to search for an understanding of the ultimate meaning of one's life in one's own way is among the most important aspects of a life that is truly human' (p. 179). Specifically taking into consideration Nussbaum's work, I wondered whether the rising interest in authenticity that could be observed over the past decade might be rooted in a shared sense that aspects of our professional lives have become increasingly separated from this core characteristic of what it means to be truly human (Kreber, 2010a).

Comments made in the recent higher education literature suggest that this might be the case. For example, Astin and Astin (2006) observe that 'academia has for far too long encouraged us to lead fragmented and inauthentic lives' (p. ix), while Nixon (2007) notes that academics are subject to 'conditions of work which are often deeply alienating and inauthentic' (p. 22). Barnett (2004a), referring to students in higher education, suggests that they 'are not always accorded the space and the dignity in which they can be truly authentic' (p. 202). In addition to these statements, one can generally perceive a growing tension between higher education's intellectual, critical, theoretical and moral purposes, and those that are more practical and economic in nature and oriented towards providing a service to society (e.g. Rowland, 2006; Walker, 2006). Perhaps when economic and practical concerns are seen increasingly to define the 'business' of higher education, a felt sense of alienation and 'inauthenticity' arises, due to a disjuncture between what we ourselves regard as meaningful practice and what we are instead expected to comply with. Reaction to this disjuncture may induce a counter tendency, a striving towards greater authenticity (Kreber, 2010a). Chickering and colleagues (2006), for example, argue that their book *Encouraging authenticity and spirituality in higher education* 'grows out of our shared concern about the limits of the heavy emphasis higher education places on rational empiricism and its increasingly narrow focus on professional and occupational training' (p. 5).

However, concerns over a lack of authenticity expressed in the higher education literature are not always explicitly linked to these broad contextual issues characterising the field of higher education. Palmer (1998) implies that a lack of authenticity in university teaching stems from teachers' inability to connect deeply with their subject matter and their role as educators, while Cranton (2001) argues that a lack of authenticity in university teaching comes from being unaware of assumptions guiding our practice that have been uncritically assimilated. A lack of authenticity is then not necessarily something that we are aware of, and can instead be a case of remaining oblivious to how our own views have been shaped by hegemonic forces that operate against our own best interests (a point I will delve into more deeply in Chapter 1 and more specifically in Chapter 6). It seems though that what all colleagues writing about authenticity in the context of higher education have in common is that they are astute observers of certain conditions that promote a sense of alienation, or lack of authenticity, among students and academics, which they then feel a responsibility to respond to.

My own motivation for writing this book grows partially out of a sense that prevailing views of what constitutes engagement with the 'scholarship of teaching' are at risk of promoting a lack of authenticity in this work. Factors that might be seen as contributing to this lack of authenticity include, for example:

> *A prevailing view that to make the scholarship of teaching public means to make the work count by publishing it in conventional ways.*

This view emphasises external rewards for this work, which can distract from the desired internal motivation to enhance teaching and learning and the dialogical public sharing and critiquing of insights on teaching-related practices and policies that can ensue from this internally motivated work.

> *A prevailing view that scholarship is the same as research, or the advancement of knowledge through discovery.*

As discipline-specific research into higher education pedagogy gains increasingly greater currency, there is a tendency to delegitimise other possibilities of engaging with the scholarship of teaching. These possibilities would include, for example, broadening and deepening our knowledge about teaching by integrating different theoretical/philosophical ideas. It might also include addressing societal needs by considering how what our students learn, who they become, and how they choose to make their mark in the world once they graduate, matter to the well-being of our local and wider communities – and using the acquired knowledge to innovate curricula and pedagogies.

> *A prevailing view that the most important knowledge about university teaching (along with expertise in the subject matter) comes from the psychology of learning and instructional design.*

This view tends to undervalue the equally significant contribution that the fields of philosophy, sociology, anthropology or the arts (aesthetics) could make to our understanding of student learning and teaching.

***

The notion of authenticity informs this book on two levels. On a first level (as indicated by the above considerations), I propose that as academics involved in (and/or occasionally charged with) promoting the 'scholarship of teaching', we need to be watchful of possible external constraints on its enactment as an 'authentic practice'. On a second level, I suggest that given its richness and complexity, the notion of authenticity can help us think in fresh and perhaps deeper ways about the kind of teaching and learning that it is particularly desirable to foster in our universities. Such considerations may be especially useful at a time when universities, perhaps more so than ever before in their long history, are expected to make positive contributions to a world marked by massive uncertainty, complexity and inequality. The focus of the next section is on how authenticity informs this book on this second level.

Authenticity *in* and *through* (the scholarship of) teaching

The title 'Authenticity *in* and *through* teaching' requires clarification. 'Authenticity *in* teaching' refers to a particular form of engagement with university teaching, one that is characterised by the teacher's striving for authenticity. 'Authenticity *through* teaching' invites two different readings, both of which are equally relevant. On the one hand 'authenticity *through* teaching' means that through a particular engagement with their teaching teachers become more authentic. On the other hand 'authenticity *through* teaching' highlights that there is a relationship between how teachers engage with their teaching and their students' development towards greater authenticity. The title 'Authenticity *in* and *through* teaching', therefore, is intentionally chosen to intimate that teaching, when characterised by authenticity, may affect students in such a way that they come into their own authenticity. The intimation of a causal relationship between authenticity in teaching and students' authenticity is, of course, contentious. While I will revisit this point in Chapter 2, I note at this stage that this relationship is naturally a potentiality rather that a necessity; however, it is a potentiality that has been claimed on theoretical grounds. Whether this relationship is appropriately thought of as unidirectional, or more plausibly as an interaction, will also be explored in Chapter 2.

Until relatively recently, fostering students' authenticity had not been highlighted as a purpose of higher education. Traditionally, it has been more common to draw attention to the importance of promoting students' autonomy, by which we usually mean their *intellectual* autonomy. Intellectual autonomy refers to the ability to engage in rational decision-making; that is to think, decide and act for oneself rather than accept doctrines uncritically. At the core of intellectual autonomy is the ability to think critically and independently and to be 'free from bias and prejudice' (Gibbs, 1979, p. 121).

Although autonomy and authenticity are related, they are not the same. Authenticity, as we will see later, involves rationality or critical reflection but it goes beyond this. We act authentically, rather than only autonomously, when the choices we make are bound up with our own inner motives (Bonnett, 1976, 1978; Bonnett & Cuypers, 2003). Authenticity involves not just being able to make rational choices; it also implies owning them, being personally invested in them, or feeling a deep inner commitment to them. Investing oneself in this way requires courage but also empathy and compassion. When Nussbaum (1997) suggests that 'we must produce citizens who have the Socratic capacity to reason about their beliefs' (p. 19) she clearly has in mind their ability to think critically and make autonomous decisions; however, her main concern is that university graduates will choose to employ their critical reasoning abilities for the common good. This is why she also argues that 'We must educate people who can operate as world citizens with sensitivity and understanding' (p. 52). Sensitivity and understanding imply an intellectual capacity to be critical but both also require 'narrative imagination' (Nussbaum, 1997). This refers to the disposition, or ability and willingness, to consider a situation from the perspective of someone different from oneself. Together, the capacity for 'narrative imagination', sensitivity and understanding, also motivate personal investment in social, political and environmental issues, commitment to causes and compassion for the plight of others. Being able to feel such personal commitment, finding one's own voice in the midst of other voices, and identifying one's own inner motives are imperative if people are to deal with the challenges and complexities of modern life and to develop 'a care for the world' (Arendt, 2007).

Barnett (2004b, 2005) proposes that universities are places that should develop in students the capacity to live with the challenge of increased epistemological uncertainty due to rapid and continuing changes in knowledge. This challenge is made still more complex by the concurrent rise in specialisations and thus incompatible frameworks by which to interpret this knowledge. In a world marked by such 'super-complexity' (Barnett, 2004b, p. 252), universities should see their role principally as cultivating in students the 'human capacities needed to flourish amid "strangeness"' (Barnett, 2005, p. 794) and thus enact 'a pedagogy of human being' (Barnett, 2004b, p. 247) or 'a pedagogy of affirmation' (Barnett, 2005, p. 795). What is needed, so Barnett argues, are 'human subjectivities that not only tolerate strangeness but can even produce it; for ultimately, the only way, amid strangeness, to become fully human, to achieve agency and authenticity, is the capacity to go on producing strangeness by and for oneself' (Barnett, 2005, p. 794). The capacity to flourish amid strangeness, one would then surmise, involves adopting a critical and *self*-critical attitude but also includes other dispositions such as 'carefulness, thoughtfulness, receptiveness, resilience, courage and stillness' (Barnett, 2004b, p. 258).

Over the past several years, universities have begun to emphasise the need for students to develop so-called 'graduate attributes' (Barrie, 2007; Hounsell, 2011) while pursuing their degree programme. These attributes go beyond the development of intellectual autonomy to include: a capacity for ethical, social and professional understanding; collaboration, teamwork and leadership; global citizenship; and so forth. Although the graduate attribute literature often employs the language of doing or acting rather than being (i.e. what graduates should be able to do with the knowledge acquired) and thus typically does not draw on the notion of authenticity, we nonetheless witness today greater acceptance of the proposition that it is as important to develop a sense of authenticity amongst students as it is to develop their intellectual autonomy. More and more people today tend to buy into an *extended sense* of autonomy (Bonnett, 1978) that institutions of higher education should foster in students, one that is inclusive of students developing academically, intellectually *and* personally.

To sum up, I propose that engagement with (the scholarship of) university teaching is a matter of academic teachers moving towards greater authenticity, with the ultimate goal of promoting the learning, development and, importantly, the authenticity of students. But still, is it possible to say something more concrete about the meaning of 'authenticity'?

Different perspectives on authenticity

Authenticity is a multidimensional concept underpinned by at least three broad philosophical traditions: the *existential*, the *critical* and the *communitarian*. A fourth perspective, at times referred to as the 'correspondence view' of authenticity (Splitter, 2009), I note briefly, as it is frequently evoked particularly in the context of learning and assessment. This perspective suggests that what makes learning experiences authentic is that they are situated within, or correspond to, the 'real world' or appropriate social and disciplinary contexts. As a result of their correspondence to the 'real world', the learning tasks are perceived as relevant by students and, therefore, lead students to become more engaged in their learning (e.g. Herrington, Oliver & Reeves, 2003; Newman, King & Carmichael, 2007).

Newman, Marks and Gamoran (1996), for example, described the features of what they refer to as an 'authentic pedagogy'. To qualify as 'authentic', they argue, pedagogies must encourage students to engage in higher-order thinking, become involved in substantive conversations, develop deep knowledge and make connections to the world beyond the classroom. Assessment tasks characteristic of authentic pedagogy emphasise the students' engagement with disciplinary content and processes. The key distinction between the perspectives on authenticity I concentrate on in this book and the correspondence view just described is that the former focus on the *being* of the students and the *being* of the person engaged in (the scholarship of) teaching, and also have a moral dimension, while the latter refers principally to the technical aspects of the teaching process and the cognitive or intellectual aspects of learning (i.e. how to make learning tasks correspond more closely to the problems one encounters in the real world; how to promote students' intellectual mastery of these learning tasks). Clearly, these perspectives are not incompatible and both are important in higher education. As we will see in the next two chapters, authentic teachers (or more precisely teachers who engage in teaching authentically) will often try to teach in ways that bring about authentic conversations with students but do so not only in order for students to master intellectual skills but also to encourage their personal investment in the learning process and their reflections on the way they make meaning of their experiences. And this reflection on how they make meaning of their experiences, I will argue, certainly includes their reflective thinking in relation to the subject matter they are taught but goes beyond that. I now briefly outline the three broad perspectives on authenticity that inform this book.

Existentialist theories help us to understand authenticity as a process of becoming aware of our own unique purposes and possibilities in life, and emphasise that we are authors of our own life, 'beings-for-themselves', who take responsibility for our actions and stand by our inner commitments (Malpas, 2003; Sherman, 2003a). *Critical theories* suggest that this can happen only through reflective critique, whereby we realise how our ways of thinking and acting are influenced by the assumptions, values and beliefs that we uncritically assimilated at an earlier age and now take for granted (Sherman 2003b). These same normative ways of thinking about and enacting our teaching may not be conducive to our own well-being as academics, let alone the well-being, learning and development of students. Authenticity, understood from this perspective, involves recognising power relations that systematically distort our perceptions. Critical reflection and critical self-reflection are fundamental to the conception of the scholarship of teaching I am proposing. Finally, *communitarian theories* remind us that authenticity is not something to be achieved in isolation from the wider social context one is part of. In contrast to a widespread understanding of authenticity as the expression of what is creative and original in each of us, hence giving us meaning and purpose in life, the communitarian perspective emphasises that only by also acknowledging our social interrelatedness can authenticity become significant to the human condition. Authenticity thus demands recognition of the fact that we

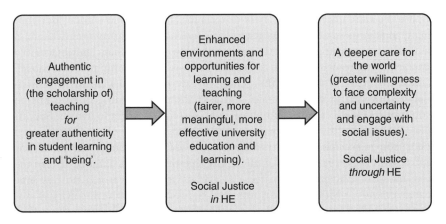

Authentic engagement in (the scholarship of) teaching that fosters authenticity in student learning and 'being', is aimed at contributing to greater social justice *in* higher education (by creating a better world in which to *teach* and *learn*) and *through* higher education (by ultimately creating a better, that is a fairer, more compassionate and sustainable *world*).

Figure I.2 The scholarship of teaching as if the world mattered.

are part of a community by whose socially constructed and historically evolved norms, values and ideals we are already bound and shaped (e.g. Taylor, 1991).

In this book I argue that authentic engagement with (the scholarship of) teaching is inextricably linked to doing what is in the important interests of students (Grimmet & Neufeld, 1994; Kreber, 2007), and this, I propose, involves helping students grow into their own authenticity. Authenticity *in* and *through* (the scholarship of) university teaching is a striving for meaning, purpose and connectedness, aimed at creating a better world in which to *teach* and *learn* and, ultimately, a better, that is a fairer, more compassionate and sustainable, *world*. When we engage in (the scholarship of) teaching authentically we seek to enrich not only the students' academic learning, our repertoire of teaching practices and the knowledge base of teaching. We also have an interest in who we and our students are *becoming* and how, through our work, we can contribute to the common good. Thus, through authentic engagement in (the scholarship of) teaching we demonstrate that the world *matters* to us. Figure I.2 highlights the key points that have been argued.

Structure of the book

The first four chapters set the context for the main argument by offering a more detailed account of how we might understand the linkages among *authenticity*, *teaching*, *scholarship* and *practice*. Chapter 1 explores the complex meaning of authenticity through reference to relevant literature and research. Chapter 2 applies the outcome of this analysis to teaching, learning and student development, and discusses what authenticity *in* and *through* teaching involves. Chapter 3 focuses on the relationship between scholarship and teaching and places the scholarship of teaching within a broader notion of academic professionalism. Chapter 4 explores whether the perspective developed in Chapter 3 satisfies MacIntyre's criteria of 'a practice' and asks whether anything of true import would be lost if the 'scholarship of teaching' did not meet these criteria. Specifically, it considers the role of virtues, values and standards of excellence in the scholarship of teaching. Chapters 5 and 6 move the discussion further forward by focusing on critical reflectivity in the scholarship of teaching. Engagement in the scholarship of teaching is construed as a transformative learning process intimately bound up with becoming authentic and fostering the authenticity of students. Chapter 5 introduces different reflective functions and forms of learning, as well as types and domains of teacher knowledge, and shows how academics, through their engagement in critically reflective inquiry, cultivate the virtues associated with the scholarship of teaching. Chapter 6 suggests that teachers and students encounter the same challenges in their striving for authenticity, which involve recognising power and overcoming hegemonic assumptions. Chapter 7 maintains that the notion of 'evidence-based practice', when interpreted narrowly in terms of a purely instrumental rationality, is inherently conformist. Within such a view important questions regarding the desirability or value of our practices do not arise. The scholarship of teaching, when interpreted as an evidence-based practice, it is argued, is therefore limited in its transformative potential. I suggest that the scholarship of teaching is more appropriately understood as an evidence-*informed* and moral practice. Building on this argument, Chapter 8 proposes that 'making public' in the scholarship of university teaching means more than publishing one's work through articles, books, conferences or websites. This chapter explores the possibility of construing 'making public' as public engagement based on critical reflectivity; Arendt's tripartite categorisation of the *vita activa* (the life of action and speech) and Habermas's theory of communicative action offer useful conceptual tools for this task. The closing chapter offers some final observations on the arguments presented.

Chapter 1

Surfacing the complex meaning of authenticity

Authenticity, teaching, scholarship and *practice* are all open to different concep-tualisations but it is the notion of authenticity that carries the greatest ambiguity and hence is the most resistant to straightforward definition. Indeed, as Vannini (2007) observes, an 'important and widely recurrent criticism of the concept of authenticity is that it is difficult to define and that it suffers from inextricable ties to various ideologies and philosophies' (p. 65). In this chapter I discuss different ways in which the notion of authenticity has been construed, building on our everyday usage of the term. I show why authenticity is a contested notion but argue that dismissing it on the grounds of it being 'pernicious', as at times it has been argued, is misguided. I also show how the three broad perspectives on authenticity outlined in the Introduction – the existential, the critical and the communitarian – emerged from the reading of relevant literature in the fields of education and philosophy as well as recent empirical work exploring lecturers' and students' conceptions of authenticity. Not all of these research findings will be revisited in the chapters that follow; nonetheless, I see merit in offering a more detailed discussion of the multifaceted meaning of authenticity at this stage. Not everyone, therefore, may wish to read the section on empirical work entitled 'Dif-ferent facets or dimensions of authenticity in relation to university teaching'. It is possible to jump this section altogether and reconnect with the discussion in the following chapter, which offers an illustration of authenticity specifically in the contexts of (the scholarship of) university teaching and learning.

Authenticity: a contested notion

Authenticity is a complex concept, a characteristic it shares, for example, with intelligence, wisdom or creativity. Intelligence is a particularly useful case in point given the different perspectives that have informed our understanding of this notion. Is there one general form of intelligence represented by factor g (Spearman, 1904), a two-factor model encompassing crystallised and fluid intelligence (Cattell, 1963), a triarchic model of analytical, creative and practical intelligence (Sternberg, 1985) or an emotional intelligence (Goleman, 1998), or are there multiple intelli-gences, including abilities such as intra and interpersonal intelligence, musical intelligence, spatial intelligence, bodily kinaesthetic intelligence, existential intelligence and so forth (Gardner, 1999)? Given these different conceptualisations, would an acceptable definition of intelligence not need to take account of the fact that the concept has been construed in multiple ways, rather than offer only a partial view? Authenticity, we saw in the Introduction, is likewise informed by different philosophical perspectives. A definition of authenticity would then also need to acknowledge the existence of the various perspectives it is informed by and thus reflect the multilayered meaning of authenticity that these give rise to. The main idea to hold on to here is that a defining feature of authenticity is its conceptual complexity, a characteristic it shares with intelligence and perhaps related constructs such as wisdom and creativity. What I would like to do next is to show that although authenticity shares with these other (otherwise unrelated) concepts the attribute of conceptual complexity, there are two further important attributes that it does *not* share with these concepts. Identifying these attributes, I argue, may explain why authenticity, unlike intelligence, wisdom and creativity, has been slow to enter the educational literature. What are these attributes?

One refers to the extent to which our everyday conceptions of these terms are readily transferable to the realm of education; the other pertains to the degree to which these terms themselves are contested. I address each of these in turn.

Our familiarity with concepts such as intelligence, creativity and wisdom predisposes us differently towards their utility or value in relation to education than does our familiarity with the notion of authenticity. To be more specific, we 'know' that Einstein was intelligent, Van Gogh creative and our grandmother wise, and if she wasn't, we have heard of one who was! When we hear that education should strive to foster these three abilities in students we are less likely to object as we can immediately perceive their value for individuals and society. As I intend to demonstrate in greater detail below, in our everyday lives we also encounter the term authenticity, but our everyday understandings of the term are not always helpfully transferred to the context of education. Think for example of 'the authentic Rembrandt' versus 'its replica'. What could this distinction between the original and its imitation mean in the context of education? Even if we were to perceive an analogy between a 'genuine Rembrandt' and a 'genuine teacher', for example, would we not still find the underlying idea of 'original' versus 'copy' to be unsatisfactory in certain respects? The extent to which our preconceptions, or everyday understandings, of these terms constructively enter into the context of education is therefore the first difference I would like to highlight between authenticity and notions such as intelligence, wisdom or creativity. In other words, I suggest that the attribute of 'perceived/endorsed educational relevance' is shared by intelligence, wisdom and creativity (Sternberg's triarchic theory of intelligence, incorporating aspects of analytical, creative and practical thinking, has long been recognised for its relevance to educational settings, for example) but not necessarily by authenticity. However, the more profound difference lies elsewhere.

I might consider certain behaviours to be intelligent while someone else might not, but it is rather unlikely that anyone would find the behaviours I consider to be intelligent to be objectionable or even distasteful. The idea of emotional intelligence (Goleman, 1998), for example, is perhaps not universally accepted as being part of what it means to be intelligent, but no one would doubt that this ability that we call 'emotional intelligence' is something positive that enhances our lives. Of course, the ability to 'read' the experiences of others could be used for questionable purposes (a torturer can be assumed to empathise with the victim but feel no compassion, for example), but such depravity does not contradict the general claim that emotional intelligence as such is a quality that adds an important dimension to human interactions and well-being. With authenticity, by contrast, such general acceptance cannot be assumed. So while concepts such as intelligence, wisdom and creativity share the attribute that they are widely perceived to carry a positive value in our society, not everyone believes that authenticity carries a positive value. Challenges to authenticity come principally from two directions.

The postmodern critique is essentially a dispute of the humanist ideal of the unified integrated self. Postmodernism challenges the notion that people have a core essence or single and stable identity. Instead, identities are viewed as 'fluid', 'free-floating' and constantly 'shifting'. From a postmodern perspective authenticity emerges as a flawed concept as we can never really know anything with certainty, including ourselves; and more importantly, there is no stable or core self that we can become more 'true' to. As I argued elsewhere (Kreber *et al.*, 2007), the issues emphasised by postmodernist thinkers help us appreciate the complexities associated with the notion of 'authenticity' and see more clearly the tension between viewing the self as an essential core versus an ongoing construction. Taking on board the postmodernist critique of stable identities is helpful in that it leads us to view the notion of 'authenticity' not as something fixed, or something that one has, but rather as a project that one always seeks to strive towards in particular contexts. Although our values may change over time and we assume multiple identities in our lives, we strive to experience congruence between what we do and the values we hold dear. As Vannini (2007) put it: 'authenticity may be a feeling associated with being true to one's self, but we must not rely on assumptions which render such self static and the act of "being true to it" stifling...' p. 67) and later 'Professors change identities...; and often they even become radically different from what they used to value as they receive tenure, age and retire....In a sense professors, like all human beings, derive their uniqueness and complexity precisely from this tension of becoming' (p. 68). The notion of authenticity is therefore not fundamentally incompatible with an understanding of identities as being both shifting and constructed.

The other, and perhaps more profound, challenge to authenticity is associated with the 'malaises of modernity' (Taylor, 1991), especially the increased individualism we can observe in our societies which is coupled with a withdrawal and feeling of alienation from the public sphere. Critics observe that the self-help books (and related DVDs, websites, workshops on how to live the authentic life, etc.) released over the past twenty-some years are partially to blame for the expansion of the 'me culture' that has eroded engagement in public life. The argument goes that these publications and initiatives purport that the path to a happier or more meaningful life lies in focusing on and finding oneself, whereas, in reality, the solution to our most pressing problems cannot lie in promoting further individualism but rather in a strengthening of community life and public engagement. How might one respond to this analysis?

Charles Taylor (1991) argued that it is possible to feel strong sympathy for these observations but still see value in the notion of authenticity. However, for the concept of authenticity to continue to have significance in our times it must be construed dialogically. True authenticity, in Taylor's view, involves recognising and being open to 'horizons of significance' – the various cultural norms, traditions, expectations, purposes or ideals that we as a community agree on and are already bound by. He further explains that horizons of significance offer 'a picture of what a better or higher mode of life would be, whereby terms such as better or higher offer a standard we ought to desire' (Taylor, 1991, p. 16). Horizons of significance thus provide a sense of personal connection with something larger than ourselves, and this 'something larger' is the social and political community we are part of, with its culturally shaped purposes and traditions. This perspective stands in profound contrast to a view that associates authenticity with narcissism, self-centredness and withdrawal from community life, and, consequently, as the cause of many of our social problems (e.g. Potter, 2010).

The negative sense that some people have of authenticity renders it a difficult concept to promote in the context of education. It seems important to emphasise at this stage that the criticism that is typically levelled against authenticity grows not only out of the observation that the public sphere is narrowing but that the underlying self-centredness is seen to be coupled with a potential for the blatant disregard for others. Chickering *et al.* (2006) pick up on this problem. Early on in their book *Encouraging authenticity and spirituality in higher education* they offer a brief definition of what they mean by being authentic: it 'means that what you see is what you get' (p. 8) and 'What I believe, what I say and what I do are consistent' (p. 8). However, aware that according to this definition even the most deplorable atrocities could be labelled as acts of authenticity, they add in the following paragraph: 'History tells us of individuals who were authentically evil. . . . But we strive for an authenticity that is kind, caring and *socially responsible*' (p. 8, emphasis added). That there is not necessarily a direct connection between one's true self and an underlying character of honour, considerateness and compassion, as assumed by Rousseau, was highlighted also by Bernard Williams (2004), who showed that these linkages are, at the very least, not quite as straightforward. By connecting the concept of authenticity with a sense of social responsibility, Chickering *et al.* (2006) turn authenticity into something positive and attach to it a distinctly moral quality. As noted in the Introduction, the individual's external orientation towards community, which is captured in the notion of social responsibility, is central to the *communitarian* perspective on authenticity (Taylor, 1991). Nonetheless, while this recognition of community is clearly a significant dimension of authenticity, we need to ask whether something of equal import to the human condition might be lost if individuals were guided exclusively by that which is external to them. Before we are in a position to answer this question, and gain a sense of what these other, more internal, aspects of authenticity might be, it is helpful to first explore how the notion of authenticity is typically used in everyday language.

What does it mean to be authentic?

We may find it difficult to define authenticity but we all have used or at least heard the term before. Consider the following statements from everyday life:

- I don't know, he just did not come across as authentic in the interview.
- Students need to be given authentic learning and assessment tasks.
- Is this paper based on authentic intellectual work?
- Is this visa authentic?
- Really, he was sporting an authentic Rolex as he was doing the dishes?
- The restaurant is known for its authentic Thai cuisine.
- Please authenticate yourself!
- The authenticity of a Coleridge poem is what makes it so special.
- I just never felt authentic in my previous job.
- I feel I have become more authentic in my research over the years.
- She was authentic when she told the students that she needed to write her book this year and did not think that preparing for the lecture she was going to give would have been a good use of her time.

Many of the above statements associate authenticity with 'being genuine', 'being real' or 'being sincere'. 'He just did not come across as authentic in the interview' suggests that the person making this statement had the impression that the interviewee came across as not quite himself, perhaps was trying to sell himself as someone he was not, and thus was not being real somehow. We typically consider learning and assessment to be authentic when they mirror real-life situations and require the practising of the ways of thinking and problem-solving employed by actual experts in relevant fields. We use the expression authentic intellectual work to refer to the work's originality; what is argued has not been argued before, at least not in quite the same way (hence we note creativity as well), and influencing sources have been properly credited. An 'authentic visa' or an 'authentic Rolex' are obviously objects that are genuine and not a fake. We prefer 'authentic Thai cuisine' over that which is not authentic, as we assume authentic dishes are prepared according to the original recipe that has not yet been contaminated by external influences. When asked to authenticate ourselves on a website we declare our identity by providing a user name and password, thereby making sure that only us, and not someone who is *not* us, can access our account. In these examples the meaning of authenticity seems very straightforward; although it is not necessarily clear how some of these everyday understandings could be relevant to teaching. As one member of staff once said to me:

> I'm not so sure what you mean by 'authentic'. After all, it's me who supervised a doctoral student at 1.00pm, attended a department council meeting at 11.00am, entered the classroom at 9.00am and left the house at 8.00am. It's always me in these situations and I'm not pretending to be someone I'm not.

Thus he was suggesting that it was him and not someone else stepping in for him (as in a 'Doppelgänger' stealing his identity) who fulfilled these various functions. As the quote then reveals, when our aim is to analyse a social practice such as the scholarship of teaching everyday conceptions of authenticity are helpful only to a point. There is some value in these conceptions but they can also mislead us. To arrive at a deeper and possibly more meaningful understanding of authenticity we eventually will need to look for inspiration elsewhere and the field of philosophy offers us a rich resource for this endeavour. But before we go there let us first look at some of the other statements as they already point to some of the deeper meanings of authenticity.

When we speak of the authenticity of a Coleridge poem, usually the point we want to make is not that it was in fact Coleridge who wrote it (we take that much for granted); nor do we mean that for the poem to be authentic we must hold in our hands Coleridge's original handwritten notes from 200 years ago. Instead, what we perceive as the authenticity of a Coleridge poem is the emotional experience it embodies, which genuinely moves us and helps us to connect with something we recognise deep inside ourselves. Here then we encounter a very different meaning of authenticity as an emotional response. Statements such as 'I just never felt authentic in my previous job' and 'I feel I have become more authentic in my research over the years' are in some ways linked to this. Both statements refer to being, or not being, able to connect with one's inner self and to reconcile external demands with one's own inner motives and desires. The final statement 'She was authentic when she told the students that she needed to write her book this year and did not think that preparing for the lecture she was going to give would have been a good use of her time', offers cues as to why talk of authenticity can invite strong resistance from people, particularly, but not only, in relation to a social activity such as teaching. Since scepticism towards authenticity based on the meaning of authenticity implied by the final statement is quite common, as I noted at the beginning of this chapter, it is helpful to first reveal and then deliberate the assumptions underlying this view.

The idea of authenticity is often associated with being true to one's self, or 'knowing oneself', but what we understand this to mean can vary considerably. In ancient Greece, for example, Socrates' famous dictum to 'know thyself' referred to coming to know what is distinct in oneself so that one would be better able to fulfil one's place as it was already determined by the wider cosmic order. At that time, self-knowledge and meaning in life were seen as being attainable by fulfilling one's roles as determined by one's given station in life. By the time Rousseau was writing about 'the true self' this ancient cosmocentric worldview had given way to an entirely different understanding of the world, first to one that was theocentric, and by the eighteenth century to one that was anthropocentric. While both the cosmocentric and theocentric perspectives associated personal meaning with something that was external to the self, the modern or anthropocentric perspective conceives of self-knowledge as being attainable by looking primarily inwardly and identifying one's own deepest personal feelings and desires (Guignon, 2004; Hall, 2004). Today we still interpret authenticity largely in this way, although, as we saw earlier and will return to consider later, 'communitarians' remind us that contemporary perspectives are prone to overlook the social and ethical dimension in what it means to be authentic.

According to the statement 'She was authentic when she told the students that she needed to write her book this year and did not think that preparing for the lecture she was going to give would have been a good use of her time', being authentic is interpreted as stating openly what one feels and thinks in any given moment. However, because the teacher who is open or honest in this way focuses exclusively on her own desires and wants without any consideration of how others are being affected by this, some people warn that authenticity is potentially pernicious. Indeed, in the above example, the allegedly 'authentic teacher', by neglecting her responsibilities, might actually do great harm to students. Those who maintain that the concept of authenticity can usefully inform teaching therefore emphasise that authenticity is not adequately understood as being synonymous to revealing what one feels and thinks in the moment. They argue that authenticity refers to the emotional experience that one's actions are congruent with the values that matter most significantly to one's self (Vannini, 2007). They also suggest that authenticity involves a moral responsibility towards students and their learning (e.g. Cranton, 2001; Grimmet & Neufeld, 1994; Kreber, 2007). In order to move the discussion on the meaning of authenticity forward, it might be helpful at this stage to introduce two points: the first is the difference between authenticity and sincerity (Williams, 2004); the second is the view that authenticity is made up of two distinctive aspects, namely to aspire to live one's life truthfully and to live one's life by pursuing moral aims (Baggini, 2005). I will first explore the distinction between authenticity and sincerity and later incorporate into this discussion the notion of pursuing moral aims.

Authenticity versus sincerity

While authenticity is typically associated with being true to one's self, sincerity may be more adequately described as being true to others. Williams (2004) argued that authenticity goes beyond sincerity and links sincerity with confronting the truth. In making this point Williams drew on the work of the literary critic

Lionel Trilling (2006/1972) who 30 years earlier had argued that with the rise of modernity society witnessed a marked change in what it recognised as its moral ideal. More precisely, Trilling traced a drastic shift from the traditional ideal of sincerity, which meant consistency or congruence between feeling, declaration and action, to the ideal of authenticity, whereby the latter was associated with confronting the truth about oneself. For our purposes, this distinction between free declaration of belief and confronting the truth is a useful one for analysing the case of the above teacher who declared that preparing for teaching was not a good use of her time. The question we need to answer is whether openly announcing what she feels and thinks makes this teacher authentic. Before we turn to this question, let us look at another example from everyday life to clarify the distinction between authenticity and sincerity.

Imagine I am in my car after a stressful day at work and in a hurry to get home to eat my chocolate cake. Am I being authentic when, stuck in rush hour traffic, I honk the horn at every driver who happens to be in front of me? I am probably aware that I am irritated and I act on this self-knowledge as I openly, or genuinely, reveal my irritability to others. But does being genuine in this way make me authentic? Asked differently, are my actions at this moment in harmony with what truly matters to me – with my real values? If authenticity involves confronting the truth, as both Trilling and Williams suggest, would it not entail some form of self-reflection? Imagine now the person in the car ahead of me suddenly stalled the engine, got out of her car and, instead of directing at me an all too familiar gesture requiring an average level of manual dexterity, knocked at my window telling me calmly but determinedly that she had a rough day too and will not be treated by me in this manner! Being confronted with this unexpected event might actually shock me out of my 'habits of irritability' and make me feel rather foolish. In fact, I might even end up apologising to her and really mean it, as, upon reflection, my actions will most likely strike me as utterly self-centred, childish and a plain nuisance to everyone around me. In this case it is perhaps not my initial outburst, or me indulging myself in my irritability by disclosing to the world how I feel, that is appropriately associated with me being authentic but my later regret of precisely this behaviour.

In the earlier example of the teacher the situation might be different. While it is possible that the teacher later regretted having said to students that preparing for the lecture was not a good use of her time, it seems more likely that she made a conscious decision, meaning one that was thought through, to not make teaching a priority this semester. We might then also say that her statement was sincere (i.e. a true statement of what she believes). Equipped with an awareness of the distinction between authenticity and sincerity, and recognising that confronting the truth includes confronting the truth about oneself, we can now ask our earlier question differently: Given that the teacher is sincere, can we therefore assume that she confronts the truth about herself, and thus knows herself? There are two possible responses to this question, one based on Martin Heidegger and one on Theodor Adorno and their respective accounts of authenticity.

Heidegger's (1962/1927) idea of authenticity, as expressed in *Being and time,* moves beyond a simple sense of knowing oneself, as in revealing one's feelings and desires as experienced in the moment, and is deeply grounded in the notion of self-reflection. Heidegger draws a distinction between *authentic existence* and living in the world of *everydayness,* where we basically swim mainstream and do more or less what everyone else does, or what *one* does (which in the original German version he refers to as 'das man', in English often translated as 'the they'). Authentic existence refers to living the examined life. This involves trying to actualise our unique possibilities through identifying and choosing that which is truly important to us in this finite life we own. In developing the notion of 'das man' (what *one* does), Heidegger was presumably influenced by Nietzsche's (1883) notion of 'the herd', although Zimmerman (1986) argues that 'das man' actually refers to a way of being, whereas 'the herd' refers to the masses themselves. From a Heideggerian perspective a person who moves into his or her authenticity breaks free from 'das man', the common unreflected ways of being. In *Being and time* Heidegger conceived of this underlying process as one of resoluteness, that is, a conscious and courageous process of becoming open to one's limited chosen possibilities, or one's true calling. 'As resolute', Zimmerman (1986, p. 76) writes in explaining Heidegger's view, 'I am open to my own particular possibilities'. What could this process of moving towards greater authenticity mean in relation to teaching?

Whenever we seek to apply abstract philosophical ideas to a specific realm of experience, such as university teaching, there will be different interpretations available to us, each highlighting and neglecting particular nuances of the original argument. One plausible way of interpreting what it means to be authentic as a teacher in higher education, argued from a Heideggerian perspective, is to say that what I do when engaged in the process of teaching is experienced by me as strongly resonating with what feels most true or real about me. Such unity between my own values and motives and what the situation demands of me is not always a given, of course. The institution where I teach might expect me to support values that are antithetical to my own; if I comply with this expectation a problem of authenticity arises. As Cooper (1983), arguing from a Nietzschean perspective, once observed:

> When the teacher enters an institution, he not only encounters buildings, classrooms...but policies, beliefs, purposes, and values that permeate its activities.... They are not the ones of his own making; nor is he likely to have much impact upon them. A familiar disturbance felt by a teacher arises when some of these policies, values, or whatever, are not the ones to which he can subscribe.... The disturbance produces a problem of authenticity for unless he resigns or is willing to invite considerable friction at work he must simulate agreement to views that are not his.
>
> (Cooper, 1983, p. 3)

However, authenticity may also be compromised by me not being aware of what it is that I truly value. Heidegger, as we saw earlier, referred to this state of being as living in *everydayness*, or we might say as 'un-authenticity'. If we look at authenticity not as a final state but as a continuous process of becoming, authenticity in teaching might involve the experience of me coming to realise that I would feel incomplete in some way if I could not pursue this particular activity. Involved in teaching, I might connect with something deep inside myself and this experience of connectivity with my own inner motives (Bonnett, 1976, 1978) makes the activity meaningful to me in a profound way.

We encountered this understanding of authenticity earlier in reference to a Coleridge poem. Reading a poem may evoke a particular emotional response in us as it connects us with something that we recognise in ourselves. When engaged in the activity of teaching I might feel that this pursuit perfectly suits me and that it is a good match with my personality (Cranton, 2001). I realise that I want to be a teacher because I feel most at home, or most fulfilled, when I can invite students into the community of truth in my discipline (Palmer, 1998), connect with their experience, and thus make a difference to their learning and development. This does not always happen. But whenever it does I feel that teaching profoundly matters to me and bestows my professional life with meaning it would not otherwise have. I want teaching to be an important aspect of what I *do* because it is part of who I *am*. It is part of my identity. It connects me more deeply with my own inner motives and humanity. Breaking free from 'das man' (or 'the they'), in this sense, means separating from a state of unawareness of my deepest inner motives. Rather than regarding my life as an academic superficially, I become aware of what really matters or has value to me and pursue these unique possibilities. But of course, faced with having to decide how to live my career as an academic I might come to quite a different conclusion about my experiences. I might come to realise that teaching actually matters less to me than I used to think. It is possible that the teacher who told her students that she needed to write her book this year, and did not think that preparing for the lecture she was going to give would have been a good use of her time, had arrived at this conclusion.

Her conclusion might be driven by two different reasons. It is conceivable that she realised that teaching is just not for her and that the experience of teaching had always felt somewhat alienating. It is equally plausible that she decided that her only way to succeed in the academic world was to concentrate on her book and that in order to do that she had no option but to neglect other obligations, at least temporarily. In both instances it might then be suggested that she acted authentically as she made a choice for herself. However, two reservations may be levelled against this interpretation. First, if she did indeed realise that teaching was not a good fit with her personality, and also not a priority for her, perhaps the more authentic response to this realisation would have been to stop teaching altogether (which might mean finding a job elsewhere) rather than hanging in there, possibly being quite unhappy and doing a poor job at teaching. Second, given that her neglect of teaching is hardly in the interests of students, the decision to stop

teaching may also have been the more socially responsible choice. Earlier I emphasised that two points were critical to the discussion. The first was the difference
between authenticity and sincerity (Williams, 2004), which we have been discussing. The second was the dual character of authenticity, implying both aspiring to
live one's life truthfully and living one's life by pursuing moral aims (Baggini,
2005). It is to this second point that I now wish to turn.

Baggini suggests that living one's life truthfully and living one's life by pursuing moral aims are the two defining aspects or criteria of authenticity. Both
sincerity and authenticity inform the first aspect: living one's life truthfully.
According to Baggini's definition, it is perhaps unclear whether our teacher fulfilled this first criterion but she certainly did not meet the second. Some readers
may judge this verdict as crude and insensitive to the wider context in which the
choice was made. 'How can you blame her for not pursuing so-called moral aims
if increasingly more research output is now expected of academics seeking promotion?' some readers may say. 'The whole notion of *teaching as a vocation*
which is seemingly celebrated here, suggesting that we give up everything and
sacrifice ourselves for students and the institution, is a deeply troubling and self-
destructive concept, an incident of self-disciplining that works nicely to ensure
we do more and more with fewer and fewer resources and time! Simply expecting
academics who can't do it all at once to quit their job, face economic hardship
and give up their career hopes and aspirations only because the institution does
not provide an environment that is conducive to doing the various aspects of their
job well is not fair. How can you just say this teacher was *not authentic*? Moreover, maybe this teacher actually likes teaching but felt pressured into adopting
values that are not her own'. Someone else might jump in and add 'Maybe she
does not feel authentic at all actually but rather inauthentic and suffers for it'.

Statements such as these, which I could not agree with more by the way, show
two things: first, they reveal that we value authenticity and second, they bring to
light that it is often the specific external circumstances that drive us into states of
inauthenticity by making us lose sight of that which really matters to us, or possibly worse, make us do things that we know do not matter to us or are antithetical
to our values. The conditions of work for academics have been identified as being
'often deeply alienating and inauthentic' (Nixon, 2007, p. 22) and as encouraging us 'to lead fragmented and inauthentic lives' (Astin & Astin, 2006, p. ix).
The 'self-disciplining' (Foucault, 1980), mentioned above as being associated
with the notion of teaching as vocation, is clearly a self-destructive force that
works within many of us and, in itself, is a good example of living inauthentically.
Recognising the difficult conditions under which many academics pursue their
work, therefore, surely leads us to empathise with this teacher; but these conditions do not challenge the charge of inauthenticity – all we can perhaps say is that
they explain it. I should add that the purpose of this analysis and that which
follows is *not* to show how, from a critical (and postmodern) theory perspective,
the present context of higher education induces a state of inauthenticity. Recognising how context affects authenticity in academic work is imperative but

analysing the relationships between context and consciousness is not the purpose of this present chapter (however, I will return to this important point in Chapter 6). My purpose here is a much plainer and yet equally important one, namely to offer an overview of the multifaceted meaning of authenticity. I therefore would like to return to Heidegger at this point and ask to what extent it can be assumed that the above teacher really separated from 'the they', or in Baggini's language, lived her life as an academic 'truthfully'. Adorno's critique of Heidegger's notion of authenticity is helpful in this regard.

Arguing from a critical theory perspective, Adorno (2003/1964) suggested that Heidegger's notion of authenticity was flawed because it ignored that reflection (and hence the separation from 'the they') must be directed also at aspects that are outside the realm of one's subjective self-awareness. Rather than equating authenticity with pure self-experience, authenticity demanded that persons recognised how their views of the world had been shaped by the conditions or structures inherent in the contexts in which events were experienced. There appears to be a difference in emphasis here between Heidegger's view of separating from 'the they' ('das man'), which is seen in leaving the unexamined life and living in a more conscious manner, and Adorno's sense of 'the they' as the dominant view that is socially constructed, or, to put it differently, 'the they' as an ideology. Seeing consciousness as the product of social situation, Adorno cannot accept a notion of authenticity that presumably fails to consider Being's embeddedness in concrete historical contexts (Kreber & Klampfleitner, 2012). Adorno's perspective on coming into one's authenticity for the above teacher would imply that she explore where her conformity to 'the they' comes from, that is, how her consciousness has been shaped by the social historical context of her work environment. More specifically, it would involve that she examine where her assumptions that research is more important than teaching originated, and whether and how such assumptions or dominant agendas could be challenged and resisted. Although Adorno's criticism of Heidegger has been challenged recently (Macdonald, 2008), for our purposes the distinction is still a useful one as it reveals two different ways of conceptualising authenticity. We will revisit this argument again in Chapter 6.

The point of the above discussion was to show that the meaning of 'being authentic' and 'being true to one's self' has many different facets. We have seen that revealing how one feels in the moment and self-declaration of belief are perhaps aspects of what it means to be authentic, but they do not, in and of themselves, adequately sum up what authenticity refers to. Cranton (2006b) pointed out that being authentic 'is not only being genuine but understanding what genuine means in a deep way for ourselves, and this involves critically questioning the world outside ourselves' (p. 84). Moreover, according to some theorists, authenticity also has a social and, by extension, moral dimension, a point I will revisit towards the end of the chapter. In discussing authenticity, it is helpful to be aware of its various meanings and to be explicit about the particular meaning that is intended.

In order to be able to answer the question of what authenticity in the context of teaching and academic practice might mean once its various features or dimensions have been disentangled, colleagues and I worked with a small group of lecturers (three from Physics, three from Law and three from English literature) and 46 of their students to develop a sense of how they understood the notion of authenticity. It is some of these empirical studies I turn to next.

Different facets or dimensions of authenticity in relation to university teaching

Colleagues and I carried out a small series of studies in which we systematically compared academics' personal conceptions of authenticity in teaching to the conceptions we had identified in the relevant philosophical and higher education literature (Kreber *et al.*, 2007). In following this approach, we took inspiration from Robert Sternberg (1990) who argued that we can gain deeper insight into complex phenomena if, in addition to the formal conceptions developed by experts, we also look at the informal conceptions held by non-specialists, as these can enrich and even lead to reformulations of existing formal articulations. Conceptions of authenticity underlying the relevant literature we thus considered explicit or formal conceptions, and those held by our research participants we considered implicit, informal or everyday conceptions. Implicit conceptions of authenticity in teaching are those that are personally constructed by academics themselves, are not in the public domain and are not (yet) recognised as formal theories. To be clear, our studies principally explored the meaning academics ascribe to the notion of authenticity in teaching (i.e. their personal conceptions of authenticity) and not whether they themselves were being or becoming more authentic. In one study, though, we also investigated whether authenticity played a role in their evolving identities as teachers (Kreber, 2010b).

The educational and philosophical literature we reviewed at the time revealed 13 different features of what it means to be authentic in teaching (Kreber *et al.*, 2007). These are summarised in Table 1.1.

In subsequent work these 13 features were organised in terms of six dimensions of authenticity. Table 1.2 describes these six dimensions (A to F) and the corresponding 13 features. As shown in Table 1.2, the same feature can belong to more than one dimension as each dimension is characterised by a particular *combination* of features. The six dimensions, although each reflecting a distinct conception of authenticity in teaching, are, therefore, not discrete.

We then set out to explore which of these six dimensions of authenticity in teaching were consistent with the ideas or personal conceptions academics themselves had developed. Although at that time the six dimensions were useful for guiding the analyses, I now find it more meaningful to speak not of six dimensions but instead of three broad philosophical perspectives on authenticity – the existential, the critical and communitarian – and will return to these later.

In order to explore academics' informal conceptions of authenticity in teaching, we employed two qualitative data collection methods. The first was an in-depth face-to-face interview with each participant asking how they understood

Table 1.1 Formal features of authenticity in teaching

Feature 1: Care for students

Feature 2: Care for the subject and interest in engaging students with the subject around ideas that matter

Feature 3: Making educational decisions and acting in ways that are in the important interests of students

Feature 4: Presentation of a genuine self as teacher (being candid and genuine)

Feature 5: Practicing a constructive developmental pedagogy

Feature 6: Promoting the 'authenticity' of others (at least their learning and possibly their development in a larger sense

Feature 7: Care for what one's life as a teacher is to be

Feature 8: Reflecting on purposes (and on one's own unique possibilities; those that *matter most*) in education and teaching

Feature 9: Consistency between values and actions

Feature 10: Self-definition in dialogue around horizons of significance

Feature 11: Self-knowledge and being defined by oneself (rather than by others' expectations)

Feature 12: Self-knowledge and confronting the truth about oneself

Feature 13: Critically reflecting on how certain norms and practices have come about

the notion of authenticity and whether, and if so how, they saw authenticity to play a role in their teaching. The second involved the completion of a repertory grid questionnaire (Kreber, 2010b; Kreber & Klampfleitner, 2012; Kreber, McCune & Klampfleitner, 2010). Repertory grids and (focus group) interviews were also employed with 46 students to explore, first, how their personal conceptions of authenticity in teaching would compare to those of their teachers and, second, whether the teacher actions and attributes they perceived as particularly helpful to their learning could be associated with authenticity in teaching, especially with how authenticity is understood in the relevant literature. These findings, however, have not yet been published (Kreber & Klampfleitner, submitted manuscript) and thus will not be reported here.

Completing the repertory grid (Jankowicz, 2004; Kelly, 1955) also involved a face-to-face conversation with each participant. Repertory grids work on the basis of eliciting verbal bipolar statements from respondents about how they perceive the similarities and differences between certain key 'elements' of a particular domain of experience (Kelly, 1955). In this study the domain of experience was university teaching and the key 'elements' in the repertory grid were ten different teacher roles: 'a really good teacher' (twice), 'a really bad teacher' (twice), 'a typical teacher' (twice), 'an authentic teacher', 'an inauthentic teacher' and 'myself as a teacher' and 'my ideal self'. For each role the lecturer was asked to think of a particular teacher he or she knew who, in his or her mind, fitted this role particularly well. On the basis of six different sets of triads (see Figure 1.1), which

Table 1.2 Features and dimensions of authenticity

Formal dimensions of authenticity	Formal features of authenticity
A Being sincere, candid or honest	*Feature 3*: Making educational decisions and acting in ways that are in the important interests of students
	Feature 4: Presentation of a genuine self as teacher (being candid and genuine)
	Feature 9: Consistency between values and actions
B Being 'true to oneself' (e.g. in an individuation or Heideggerian sense)	*Feature 7*: Care for what one's life as a teacher is to be
	Feature 8: Reflecting on purposes (and on one's own unique possibilities; those that *matter most*) in education and teaching
	Feature 9: Consistency between values and actions
	Feature 12: Self-knowledge and confronting the truth about oneself
C Being 'true to oneself' (e.g. in a critical social theory or Adorno sense)	*Feature 11*: Self-knowledge and being defined by oneself (rather than by others' expectations)
	Feature 12: Self-knowledge and confronting the truth about oneself
	Feature 13: Critically reflecting on how certain norms and practices have come about
D Constructing an identity around 'horizons of significance'	*Feature 3*: Making educational decisions and acting in ways that are in the important interests of students
	Feature 10: Self-definition in dialogue around horizons of significance
E Care for the subject, students, and interest in engaging students with the subject around ideas that matter	*Feature 1*: Care for students
	Feature 2: Care for the subject and interest in engaging students with the subject around ideas that matter
	Feature 5: Conceptually linked to constructive developmental pedagogy
	Feature 6: Promoting the 'authenticity' of others (at least their learning and possibly their development in a larger sense)

(Continued)

Table 1.2 (Continued)

Formal dimensions of authenticity	Formal features of authenticity
F A 'process of becoming' sustained through critical reflection on core beliefs and premises	**Feature 8:** Reflecting on purposes (and on one's own unique possibilities; those that *matter most*) in education and teaching
	Feature 11: Self-knowledge and being defined by oneself (rather than by others' expectations)
	Feature 12: Self-knowledge and confronting the truth about oneself
	Feature 13: Critically reflecting on how certain norms and practices have come about

Notes
The same feature related to more than one dimension (see features 3, 8, 9, 11, 12 and 13).
Highlighted rows indicate the dimensions that were identified as most important by respondents.

were determined by the researchers and held constant across all participants, the respondent then created bipolar constructs as in: 'an authentic teacher' and 'a good teacher' both *Are an inspiration to students* while the 'typical teacher' *Does not spark student enthusiasm for the subject* (see Figure 1.1, construct 4). The verbal statement in italics, expressing the meaning the colleague attached to the teacher roles he or she was asked to compare, was the bipolar personal construct (Kelly, 1955). A Likert scale (1–5) was then applied whereby a rating of one or two represented the first pole of the construct and a rating of four or five the second pole. Although the articulation of the construct was based on only three teacher roles, all ten teacher roles were then rated on this scale (see Figure 1.1). Altogether, each participant generated six different constructs following this same procedure, always comparing a different set of three teacher roles. Readers interested in the specifics of the methodology, including how data were analysed, will find this information in the articles referenced above.

   More interesting than these technical details is perhaps the rationale for working with repertory grids in this study, given that they are widely recognised as being quite time-consuming with respect to administration as well as data management and analysis. We decided to work with repertory grids because the theoretical perspective they are informed by, Personal Construct Psychology (Kelly, 1955), offered a particularly meaningful conceptual framework for this study. From the perspective of personal construct theory (Kelly, 1955), implicit theories, defined by Sternberg (1990) as 'constructions by people that reside in the minds of these people' (p. 142), refer to the network of constructs individuals develop over time. These serve as a basis for personal hypotheses that

In what important way are two of these three university teachers (marked by an X) similar in how they engage with teaching that makes them different from the third? (scale 1 to 5)	1: A really good teacher A JP	2: A really good teacher B EJ	3: A typical teacher A JL	4: A typical teacher B GH	5: An authentic teacher NJ	6: An inauthentic teacher TM	7: Myself as a teacher	8: My ideal self as a teacher	9: A really bad teacher A PM	10: A really bad teacher B RS
Construct 1 (generated): Engages with students (1) *versus* is reserved and contained (5)	1 X	1 X	3 X	3	2	4	2	1	5	4
Construct 2 (generated): Well prepared for class (1) *versus* Not well prepared for class (5)	1 X	1	2 X	2	1	3	1	1	3	5 X
Construct 3 (generated): Innovative in relation to methods and assessment (1) *versus* Conservative (tendency to use examinations) (5)	3	1 X	4 X	3	2	4	1 X	1	5	4
Construct 4 (generated): Inspiration to students (regarding engaging them with the subject) (1) *versus* Does not spark student enthusiasm for the subject (5)	1	2 X	3	4 X	1 X	3	2	1	5	5
Construct 5 (generated): Ability to communicate own research in an accessible manner (1) *versus* Research not communicated at relevant level (5)	1	3	2	4 X	2 X	4	3	1 X	4	5
Construct 6 (generated): Passionate about subject and student learning (1) *versus* dispassionate about subject and student learning (5)	2	1	4	4 X	2	4 X	1 X	1	4	4
Construct 7 (supplied): Is aware of and shows respect for where students are at in their thinking (1) *versus* Is not (5)	2	1	2	3	1	4	2	1	4	4
Construct 8 (supplied): Connects with students' experience (1) *versus* Does not (5)	2	1	3	3	3	4	3	1	4	5
Construct 9 (supplied): Models and practices the process of knowledge construction with students (1) *versus* Does not (5)	2	2	3	3	3	5	3	1	5	5
Construct 10 (supplied): Invites students to construct knowledge with him or her (1) *versus* Does not (5)	1	2	4	3	3	4	1	1	5	5
Construct 11 (supplied): Cares about students (1) *versus* Does not (5)	3	1	3	3	2	4	2	1	5	3
Overall construct **Construct 12 (supplied):** Is authentic (1) *versus* Is inauthentic (5)	**1**	**1**	**3**	**3**	**1**	**4**	**2**	**1**	**4**	**5**

Figure 1.1 Example of a completed repertory grid (Nancy, English Literature). All participants thought of specific (real) people in relation to the teacher roles, as indicated by the initials they inserted for each teacher role box.

individuals then test against further experiences and continuously revise in the general direction of increased predictive efficiency (Adams-Webber, 1979). As individual lecturers encounter different teachers over the years, they construct and revise personal conceptions regarding what a 'good', 'poor', 'typical', 'authentic' or 'inauthentic' university teacher is like. In other words, they develop *conceptions* of authenticity in relation to teaching based on their own unique personal experiences. However, teachers are not necessarily aware of the conceptions they hold or may have trouble articulating them. Kelly (1955) developed the repertory grid method to assist in the articulation of people's personal constructs by making explicit what otherwise might remain implicit. The resulting network of personal constructs, or a person's *construct system*, can then be explored for the relationships it reveals between its individual constructs. While the purpose of the first interview we carried out with participants was for them to share with us how they understood the meaning of authenticity, the repertory grid conversation was employed to uncover aspects of their conceptions that they might not have been aware of.

Figure 1.1 offers an example of a repertory grid. As already noted, the first six constructs were generated by the lecturers. The remaining six were supplied by us. Five of these six supplied constructs have their roots in Baxter Magolda's (1999, 2009) principles of a constructive developmental pedagogy. The last construct in the grid, 'is authentic' versus 'is inauthentic', was added as it allowed us to determine which of the six constructs that our participants had generated themselves were, in their minds, most closely associated with authenticity (for a detailed discussion of how including such an 'overall construct' is useful for this purpose, see Jankowicz, 2004). The initials in the top row of Figure 1.1 refer to the specific teachers the lecturer had identified in relation to each teacher role.

The idea behind this research was not to construct an understanding or definition of authenticity in teaching grounded in lecturers' (and students') personal conceptions. The sample size would have been too small for such an effort and the value or *telos* of such an inquiry difficult to see. In order to better understand the meaning of authenticity in teaching it is more sensible to engage in conceptual analysis of the existing educational and particularly philosophical literature relevant to this topic. However, the data we collected from lecturers (and students) were valuable in that they shed light on how authenticity in teaching tends to be understood by non-specialists or practitioners unfamiliar with the theoretical or formal discourse. Our studies showed that there was certainly some overlap between formal conceptions of authenticity in teaching found in the literature and the informal, personal or everyday conceptions held by academics (and students), and that the views held by academics paralleled those of students (Kreber *et al.*, 2010). As can be seen in Table 1.3, based on the interview study with lecturers (Kreber *et al.*, 2010) and the repertory grid study with lecturers (Kreber and Klampfleitner, 2012), 'Being sincere, candid or honest' (Dimension A) appeared as a prominent theme in their conceptions, and the same was observed for 'Care for the subject, students and interest in engaging students with the subject'

Table 1.3 Juxtaposition of formal and personal conceptions of authenticity in teaching

Dimensions of authenticity (derived from philosophical and educational literature)	Specific features of authenticity (formal conceptions and personal conceptions)
A Being sincere, candid or honest	**Formal conceptions** *Feature 3*: Making educational decisions and acting in ways that are in the important interests of students *Feature 4*: Presentation of a genuine self as teacher (being candid and genuine) *Feature 9*: Consistency between values and actions **Personal conceptions** *'admitting gaps in knowledge'* *'not deliberately hiding anything'* *'consistency between values and action',* *'not to hide behind or rest on one's status role'* *'not being a fake'* *'showing the range of possible approaches to a problem but identifying your own'* *'being genuine (also with regards to caring about the subject)'.* 'Engaging seriously and interestedly with students' 'Not minding being on the same level with students (not staying above them or remaining distant)' 'to live and breathe the subject'.
B Being 'true to oneself a' (e.g. in an individuation or Heideggerian sense)	**Formal conceptions** *Feature 7*: Care for what one's life as a teacher is to be *Feature 8*: Reflecting on purposes (and on one's own unique possibilities; those that *matter most*) in education and teaching *Feature 9*: Consistency between values and actions *Feature 12*: Self-knowledge and confronting the truth about oneself **Personal conceptions** *'becoming true to oneself, being yourself (true to one's character, personality)'* *'becoming <u>more</u> true to oneself'* *'not presenting a stage persona'* *'not the same as complete self-disclosure'* *'being genuine (also with regards to caring about the subject)'.* **'Being committed to the subject combined with a sense that teaching it has social value and can make a difference'.**

(Continued)

Table 1.3 (Continued)

Dimensions of authenticity (derived from philosophical and educational literature)	Specific features of authenticity (formal conceptions and personal conceptions)
C Being 'true to oneself b' (e.g. in a critical social theory sense) (the difference to B is that reflection goes beyond one's subjective self-awareness)	**Formal conceptions** *Feature 11:* Self-knowledge and being defined by oneself (rather than by others' expectations) *Feature 12:* Self-knowledge and confronting the truth about oneself *Feature 13:* Critically reflecting on how certain norms and practices have come about **Personal conceptions** *'being defined by oneself rather than other people's expectations (not feeling that one needs to conform to a model'.*
D Constructing an identity around 'horizons of significance' HoS; 'Acting in the important interest of learners' HoS (supporting the flourishing of each student)	**Formal conceptions** *Feature 3:* Making educational decisions and acting in ways that are in the important interests of students *Feature 10:* Self-definition in dialogue around horizons of significance **Personal conceptions** *'teaching only what we are interested in versus teaching what we are interested in plus that which students really need to know about'.* *'Constantly seeking to improve one's teaching'* *'Devoting time to preparing for teaching'* *'Teaching is as important as research'* *'Caring about whether the class enjoys the experience'.*
E Care for the subject, students, and interest in engaging students with the subject around ideas that matter	**Formal conceptions** *Feature 1:* Care for students *Feature 2:* Care for the subject and interest in engaging students with the subject around ideas that matter *Feature 5:* Practicing a constructive developmental pedagogy (dialogical learning situation) *Feature 6:* Promoting the "authenticity" of others (at least their learning and possibly their development in a larger sense) **Personal conceptions** *'bringing one's own true Self into the teaching'* *'being fully invested in the course'*

Table 1.3 (Continued)

Dimensions of authenticity (derived from philosophical and educational literature)	Specific features of authenticity (formal conceptions and personal conceptions)
	'being passionate about the subject' 'sharing the subject one cares about as sharing parts of oneself' 'encouraging authenticity in other' 'promoting student learning' 'teachers care about the subject, show why the subject matters' 'teachers care about their students' learning' 'teachers are themselves, they inspire students to do things themselves' 'teachers are consistent in how they relate to people' 'involves genuine dialogue' 'teachers are truly interested in the questions students ask'.
	'being enthusiastic and stimulating enthusiasm in students' 'engaging students in independent thinking' 'engaging with students' 'being an inspiration to students' 'evidencing interest in subject and concern for student learning' 'the student comes first' 'preparing courses so that students are offered a range of different perspectives' 'engaging the student through socially-contextualising the subject of study'.
F A *'process of becoming'* sustained through critical reflection on core beliefs and premises	**Formal conceptions** *Feature 8:* Reflecting on purposes (and on one's own unique possibilities; those that *matter most*) in education and teaching
	Feature 11: Self-knowledge and being defined by oneself (rather than by others' expectations)
	Feature 12: Self-knowledge and confronting the truth about oneself
	Feature 13: Critically reflecting on how certain norms and practices have come about
	Personal conceptions *'reflecting on why we do what we do'.*

Note
The personal conceptions that are printed in italic type were identified through interviews with university teachers; those that appear in roman type are examples of those that were identified through repertory grid studies.

(Dimension E). There was also some indication that lecturers perceived connections between authenticity in teaching and Dimension D (Constructing an identity around 'horizons of significance'). By horizon of significance we basically meant that these colleagues perceived that authenticity in teaching involved making a conscious decision to act in the important interests of students.

What was particularly striking about the data was that Dimension B: 'Being "true to oneself" in an individuation or Heideggerian sense', Dimension C: 'Being "true to oneself" in a critical social theory sense' and Dimension F: 'A "process of becoming" sustained through critical reflection on core beliefs and premises' did not feature strongly in lecturers' personal conceptions of authenticity (see Table 1.3). It is a distinguishing feature of these three dimensions (B, C and F), compared to the other three (A, D and E), that they open up a view of authenticity as a self-reflective and developmental process. Dimensions A, D and E showed similarity with our everyday usage of the term, emphasising notions such as being sincere, honest or candid, and also genuinely caring about being a teacher and not just faking it (i.e. truly caring about students and caring about one's subject). In contrast, Dimensions B,C and F shed light on an entirely different meaning of authenticity, one that emphasised authenticity not as something one *has* or even *is,* but as a process of *becoming* through self-reflection. Moreover, what became apparent was that Dimensions C and F played an even weaker role in the minds of academics than Dimension B (Kreber & Klampfleitner, 2012). In fact, the idea of *critical* reflection, understood as either reflection on presuppositions and premises (Dimension F) or as ideology critique (Dimension C), featured the least strongly in academics' personal conceptions of authenticity in university teaching.

Here it is interesting to note that based on interviews with 22 academic teachers carried out over three years, Cranton and Carusetta (2004) concluded that there was a strong association between coming into one's authenticity and being reflective. They defined 'being authentic' as 'being conscious of self, other, relationships, and context through critical reflection' (p. 289). The observation that in our study the idea of critical reflection did not seem to feature prominently in lecturers' personal conceptions suggests that there is a need to further clarify the meaning of authenticity in relation to both teaching and learning. Central to this book is the position that critical reflection and self-reflection are at the heart of what it means to move towards greater authenticity.

As noted in the Introduction, I distinguish three broad yet interrelated perspectives on authenticity: the existential, the critical and the communitarian. These map broadly onto the six dimensions (and 13 features) just discussed (see Table 1.4). I should emphasise that the point here is not to allocate each dimension neatly to yet a third category of a higher order (moving from feature, to dimension, to eventually 'perspective'). Instead, the purpose is simply to demonstrate how the dimensions (and features) of authenticity that were identified in previous conceptual and empirical research relate to the three perspectives that underlie this book.

Table 1.4 Dimensions, features and perspectives of authenticity

Dimensions of authenticity	Formal features of authenticity	Perspectives
A Being sincere, candid or honest	*Feature 3:* Making educational decisions and acting in ways that are in the important interest of students	Existential and Communitarian
	Feature 4: Presentation of a genuine self as teacher (being candid and genuine)	
	Feature 9: Consistency between values and actions	
B Being 'true to oneself' (e.g. in an individuation or Heideggerian sense)	*Feature 7:* Care for what one's life as a teacher is to be	*Existential*
	Feature 8: Reflecting on purposes (and on one's own unique possibilities; those that *matter most*) in education and teaching	
	Feature 9: Consistency between values and actions	
	Feature 12: Self-knowledge and confronting the truth about oneself	
C Being 'true to oneself' (e.g. in a critical social theory or Adorno sense)	*Feature 11:* Self-knowledge and being defined by oneself (rather than by others' expectations)	*Critical*
	Feature 12: Self-knowledge and confronting the truth about oneself	
	Feature 13: Critically reflecting on how certain norms and practices have come about	
D Constructing an identity around 'horizons of significance'	*Feature 3:* Making educational decisions and acting in ways that are in the important interest of students	*Communitarian*
	Feature 10: Self-definition in dialogue around horizons of significance	
E Care for the subject, students, and interest in engaging students with the subject	*Feature 1:* Care for students	Existential and Communitarian (and to an extent

(Continued)

Table 1.4 (Continued)

Dimensions of authenticity	Formal features of authenticity	Perspectives
around ideas that matter	**Feature 2:** Care for the subject and interest in engaging students with the subject around ideas that matter	'correspondence view')
	Feature 5: Conceptually linked to constructive developmental pedagogy	
	Feature 6: Promoting the "authenticity" of others (at least their learning and possibly their development in a larger sense)	
F A '*process of becoming*' sustained through critical reflection on core beliefs and premises	**Feature 8:** Reflecting on purposes (and on one's own unique possibilities; those that *matter most*) in education and teaching	***Existential and Critical***
	Feature 11: Self-knowledge and being defined by oneself (rather than by others' expectations)	
	Feature 12: Self-knowledge and confronting the truth about oneself	
	Feature 13: Critically reflecting on how certain norms and practices have come about	

Notes
The same feature related to more than one dimension (see features 3, 8, 9, 11, 12 and 13).
The bold italic font in the right hand column indicates that the highlighted perspectives correspond strongly to the features listed.
Highlighted rows indicate the dimensions that were identified as most important by respondents.

Two factors of authenticity: internal and external

My intent in this chapter was to demonstrate the multifaceted meaning of authenticity, the construct most fundamental to this book. Suggesting that authenticity makes our professional and private lives more meaningful is one thing; explaining what this means is quite another. It became evident that certain popular definitions often leave important aspects of authenticity unacknowledged (as in 'authenticity means being consistent in what you think/feel, say and do') while others tend to underestimate the complexity of certain terms (as in 'authenticity means being true to one's self'). As the previous discussion has shown, sincerity is not the same as authenticity and just what 'to know thyself' means is open to interpretation. I also discussed some of the reasons why authenticity is a contested concept. The strongest critique comes from those who associate the search for authenticity with an extreme individualism, which, in turn, is seen as the cause of the weakening of the public sphere and a lack of social responsibility and engagement. Authenticity, according to this perspective, is equated with narcissism, the selfish pursuit of private ends without consideration of the consequences this pursuit might have for others. Drawing on the Canadian philosopher Charles Taylor, I proposed that it is possible to agree with the social analysis put forward by these critics (e.g. Potter, 2010) and yet not feel obliged to dismiss the notion of authenticity altogether as narcissism, or put differently, on the grounds of it being pernicious. While critics espouse a view of authenticity as a uni-factorial concept that is inward looking and focuses only on the individual, Taylor's (1991) communitarian perspective is both inward and outward looking and stresses also the social dimension of authenticity. Importantly, Taylor acknowledges that authenticity is made up of two factors, one that focuses on the individual and one that emphasises our connectedness with the world around us. He himself puts it this way:

> Briefly we can say that authenticity (A) involves (i) creation and construction as well as discovery, (ii) originality, and frequently (iii) opposition to the rules of society and even potentially to what we recognize as morality. But it is also true . . . that it (B) requires (i) openness to horizons of significance (for otherwise the creation loses the background that can save it from insignificance) and (ii) self-definition in dialogue.
>
> (Taylor, 1991, p. 66)

Earlier I asked whether something equally important to the human condition would be at risk if we were exclusively guided by that which is external to ourselves. Much of the discussion then focused on identifying the internal aspects of authenticity, such as getting in touch with our inner motives, with those possibilities that matter most crucially to us on a deep level, and how and why these might remain concealed from us. In answering the question of what it means to be authentic, both the internal and external aspects need to be taken into account. Both are equally significant to the human condition. In the following chapter I will revisit the three perspectives, the *existential*, the *critical* and the *communitarian*, and explore how each could play out with respect to academic teachers and students; that is, *in* and *through* teaching.

Chapter 2

Focusing on authenticity *in* and *through* teaching

In the Introduction I made four broad claims: first, that authentic engagement in (the scholarship of) teaching promotes authenticity in students (hence the title 'Authenticity *in* and *through* Teaching'); second, that authentic engagement in (the scholarship of) teaching is inextricably linked to doing what is in the important interests of students; third, that through a particular engagement with their teaching teachers themselves become more authentic; and fourth, that by engaging in (the scholarship of) teaching authentically, teachers work towards developing greater social justice and equality not only *in* but also *through* higher education. In this chapter I revisit each of these claims, examining them in depth and explaining their connections. I illustrate what authenticity *in* teaching and authenticity *through* teaching means in reference to the three broad philosophical perspectives identified earlier: the existential, the critical and the communitarian. The claim regarding the relationship between authenticity *in* and *through* teaching, I defend through the notion of 'reciprocity'.

Authenticity *in* (the scholarship of) teaching

The three broad perspectives on authenticity that were outlined in the Introduction, and developed in Chapter 1, are distinct but not unrelated. Authenticity *in* (the scholarship of) teaching will therefore often involve internal processes, experiences and actions assumed by all three perspectives. To start with the *existential* perspective, we might say that academics who engage in (the scholarship of) teaching authentically have a genuine interest in their own development and regularly question the assumptions underlying their personal teaching practice as well as the larger context in which teaching takes place. Reflection concerns the value they attach to teaching in their personal and professional lives but also how they intend to promote the learning and development of students. According to Heidegger (1962), authenticity involves taking into awareness the inevitable fact of our mortality. Importantly, life is not only finite but our lifespan is unknown to us. I may live until I am 95 or 105, but my life might end much sooner. Given that I might only live for one more year, or one more month, I am thrown back on to myself in the here and now and feel compelled to ask: 'What is it that really matters to me?', 'What are my unique possibilities?' and 'How does this aware-ness change what I do *today*?'. The idea that we continue to live in 'everydayness' (Heidegger, 1962), that is, in a superficial and unexamined way that is void of personal meaning and engagement, unless we summon the courage to confront the reality that, ultimately, we are responsible for our choices, has profound implications also for how we engage with our academic practice. Dillard (2006) offers a similar remark:

> As teachers and researchers, ought we not be researching, teaching and writ-ing 'as if we were dying'? Such a standard of rigor would require that we be ever vigilant in examining and tending to our body, mind, and spirit every-day – and that we be absolutely cognizant of our short time on this planet. . . . Such practice would clearly help us to transform the ways we act, talk, and interact with others. And it is a way for us to live in a conscious manner.
>
> (Dillard, 2006, p. 73)

Academics who engage in (the scholarship of) teaching authentically, there-fore, avoid complacency in their professional lives and are willing to challenge themselves. But they also avoid compliance by openly contesting institutional practices or larger policy initiatives they do not agree with. Authenticity *in* (the scholarship of) university teaching therefore implies reflecting on one's own teaching practices, the value one attaches to teaching, and how one's life as a teacher is influenced by social context. As we saw in the previous chapter, authen-ticity also involves breaking away from 'the they'. This breaking away entails examining where our assumptions about what makes for good teaching, and the value we attach to teaching, come from. It also implies considering whether and how these same assumptions, or possibly, dominant agendas, could be chal-lenged and resisted. Such careful considerations of what it is we hope to achieve as university teachers, and challenging of received wisdom and expectations through critical reflection and critical self-reflection, are therefore aspects of both the *existential* and the *critical* perspectives on authenticity.

As noted in the Introduction, the same reflective processes may also lead to an awareness of the importance of inviting students into 'authentic conversations' (Kreber, 2009, p. 15) about the subject, or what Palmer (1998) called the disci-pline's 'community of truth' (p. 122). By this Palmer means the disciplinary com-munity's particular ways of functioning, an idea which has been empirically substantiated through studies that identified disciplinary *ways of thinking and prac-tising* (e.g. Entwistle, 2009; Hounsell & Anderson, 2009; McCune & Hounsell, 2005). *Ways of thinking and practising* include not only disciplinary knowledge and understanding, and subject-specific skills and know-how, but also familiarity with the discipline's values, norms and conventions governing scholarly communi-cation, as well as a meta-understanding of how knowledge in the field comes about. Palmer argues that every academic discipline can be taught by diving deeply into particularity, where the discipline's core ideas, concepts and ways of functioning can be practiced. Rather than trying to tell students as much as possible about what is known in a given field, Palmer suggests focusing on key ideas that exemplify how the discipline works, thereby bringing students into 'the circle of practice in this field, into its version of the community of truth' (Palmer, 1998, p. 122). He proposes that when we teach in this way, 'We honor both the discipline and our students by teaching them how to think like historians or biologists or literary critics . . .' (p. 123).

As we saw in the previous chapter, educators' care for the subject, and their efforts to engage students in genuine dialogue around ideas that *matter* (Kreber *et al.*, 2007), is one integral aspect of authenticity in university teaching. Authenticity, understood as a willingness to avoid complacency and compliance in how we approach our teaching and engage in critique or contestation (Kreber, 2010a), might then also make the actual teaching of the subject and, by extension, the students' learning of the subject, more authentic. When teachers involve students in authentic conversations around significant or unresolved issues in relation to the subject matter, students may become engaged in learning those ways of thinking and practising that are distinctive to the fields they are studying. As they are involved in learning processes required in real world contexts, which often will require not only disciplinary but interdisciplinary solutions or ways of thinking (e.g. Cortese, 2003), they may also perceive learning as more personally relevant and begin to see how these same issues have significance in their own lives. It is in this sense that the three philosophical perspectives on authenticity I focus on this book, which take as their point of reference the *being* of teachers and students, could interact with the 'correspondence view' of authenticity (Splitter, 2009) mentioned in the Introduction.

Viewed from the *communitarian* perspective, authenticity *in* (the scholarship of) teaching involves placing teachers' individual reflective pursuits within a wider horizon of shared ideals in higher education teaching. Questions about what it is that each of us is trying to achieve through our engagement in (the scholarship of) teaching are openly deliberated and negotiated among members of the academic community in the light of, and in order to arrive at, an agreement of fundamental purposes and commitments that could guide us in this work. McLean (2006) noted the limitations of purely individual endeavours to the enhancement of teaching arguing:

> . . . however skilled, creative, inspiring and responsible an individual teacher, individual performance is not enough for genuine pedagogic improvements in universities. What is essential is that relevant actors come to agreement about what counts as good pedagogy, for what purposes and what is to be done to make it happen.
>
> (McLean, 2006, p. 126)

Given the contested nature of the ends and purposes of higher education (Barnett, 1990; Collini, 2012; Furlong & Cartmel, 2009), it might be argued that a horizon of significance of shared values, norms or standards that could serve to guide us in our practice as teachers is an idealistic notion. However, although the aims of higher education are contested and multiple, the literature on higher education *teaching* does point to some shared ideals. The American social critic and educator bell hooks (2003), for example, suggested that the purpose of teachers is *to serve the needs of students*. Similarly, Lewis Elton (2000a), a British (German-born) physicist turned researcher of education and educator, argued that teachers *have a duty towards students*. Elton and hooks do not mean that teachers should respond uncritically to students' expectations, wishes and demands. As we will see later in this chapter, acting in the students' *interests* may at times involve teachers intentionally not meeting the students' expressed needs. What Elton and hooks are saying is that, at the most fundamental level, the teacher's service or duty is to do what is educationally desirable; or, to put this slightly differently, the teacher's duty is to do what is in the *important interests of students* (Grimmet & Neufeld, 1994).

Following Sergiovanni's (1992) moral leadership theory, Grimmet and Neufeld suggest that *doing what is in the important interests of students* is an *authentic* professional motivation for teachers. However, this 'authentic motivation' is subject to constant challenges by two rival motivations. The first competing motivation is to do with what is externally rewarded (which is considered the 'traditional motivation'). The second competing motivation is to do with what is personally rewarding (which is considered the 'alternative motivation'). When the traditional motivation is dominant, teachers may lack the personal investment in their work that makes teaching enjoyable. Assessments are being completed by the deadline, courses redesigned to fit them into yet another required format, and all quality assurance procedures complied with.

Yet, when the alternative motivation is dominant self-love may easily be put above duty towards students (Elton, 2000a). This can be observed, for example, whenever teachers convey enthusiasm only towards those subjects that intrinsically excite them, while showing little genuine engagement with other areas of the same course, or simply avoid teaching those areas altogether. Not engaging with certain content areas, although they might constitute important areas for students to know about, is certainly one way in which the teacher's duty to students is breached; however, putting 'self-love above duty' may take on many other forms as well. We put our own interests ahead of those of students when we manage to carve out periods of time to work on manuscripts and research grants but do not find a moment to respond to a student's email, to provide helpful comments on a thesis chapter, to offer academic and/or emotional support when we see a student is struggling, or simply cannot be bothered with keeping our office hours. We put our own interests ahead of those of students when we approach our teaching as if all students were the same, or if they were all like us, rather than meeting each in his or her uniqueness and being aware of students' different motivations for participation, background knowledge and socio-cultural positioning. We also put our own interests ahead of those of students when we get carried away with the joy of dazzling students with our elegantly articulated and carefully worked out arguments on a complex issue (in the social sciences and humanities often topped off with a good dose of five-syllable words), but never allow them insight into the hard work and effort that was initially required in order to construct such an informed perspective. The same is true when we do not offer students the opportunity to participate in the development and contestation of different arguments on the issue.

According to the *communitarian perspective* teachers should be guided by a horizon of significance of shared values, norms or standards. This led to the argument that we should serve the needs of students (hooks, 2003), do our duty towards students (Elton, 2000a), or, which means the same thing, act in the important interests of learners (Grimmet & Neufeld, 1994). This implies that teachers are guided principally by their caring for the education of students rather than predominantly by either external rewards and/or their own self-interest. Conducting one's life as a teacher in this way inevitably involves continuous negotiation and reflection, leading Grimmet and Neufeld (1994) to observe: '*authentic motivation is … caught up in a struggle to do what is necessary and of value, not just for the organization nor just for oneself, but ultimately in the important interests of learners* [italics added]' (p. 5). Although helpful, it must be acknowledged that these values or norms are also hopelessly vague. The really important task is, therefore, still ahead of us. For if authenticity in (the scholarship of) teaching means serving the important interests of students, then it is imperative that we spell out much more clearly what these important interests are.

One way of answering this question could be to consult the students directly. However, assuming that the students are the best judges of their interests is problematic. For fear of the unfamiliar, students might feel strongly that it is in their important interest that higher education be easy and not challenge their views of the world. A similar observation was offered by Brookfield (2005) who commented from a critical theory perspective:

> Accepting adults' definition of their own needs (their 'felt' needs as they are sometimes called) is clearly premised on the idea that people are always the best judge of their own interests. In practice, learners often express a desire for programs that are familiar and recognizable and decide what to learn by reviewing what others in their peer group are learning. Such an approach to program development certainly expresses [and here Brookfield cites Horkheimer] 'a power of resistance to anything that does not conform'.
>
> (Brookfield, 2005, p. 72)

While accepting learners' definition of their own interests is problematic, simply determining these interests *for* students is equally flawed. To suggest that students (or any group) are so unenlightened that they require us (another group) to identify their 'real interests' for them strikes many of us as utterly conceited and condescending. The very idea of one group determining what is in the real interests of another is blatantly arrogant and often associated with the notion of 'colonisation'. Intuitively most of us could not square such a totalitarian approach with acting in the important interests of students! It is a refreshing thought, therefore, that in our search for an answer to the question '*what are the important interests of students*' another alternative is available to us. This third alternative is an engagement with some of the philosophical literature that is chiefly concerned with highlighting those aspects of our existence that are distinctly human qualities or, by extension, 'human interests'. Unlike the other two alternatives, the philosophical literature not only expresses a third view but identifies and questions the presuppositions underlying this view. Arguments are reasoned arguments, and reasons are made explicit so that readers can engage with them critically. It is because this third alternative is based on reason and also invites further dialogue that I consider it preferable to the other two. So what does this philosophical literature have so say?

Human interests arise from an experience of fundamental needs that must be satisfied for humans to flourish. Heidegger (1962) saw the distinctiveness of human existence in our potential openness to our own particular possibilities. Separating from a state of unawareness of our deepest inner motives and moving closer to our full potential of being he saw as a natural human need. Habermas (1971) identified emancipation, personal growth or self-development as a fundamental human interest (along with the technical interest in controlling one's environment and the practical interest of living in harmony with others). Proponents of the capabilities approach to human development recognise that being able to choose a life one has reason to value is a fundamental human interest (Nussbaum & Sen, 1993). Nussbaum (2000) proposed that 'to be able to search for an understanding of the ultimate meaning of one's life in one's own way is among the most important aspects of a life that is truly human' (p. 179). The question of what is in the important interests of students is answerable in reference to the insights offered by the above philosophers. Drawing on their observations of what constitutes human flourishing, I propose that what is ultimately in the important interests of students is their own striving for *authenticity*. From this premise we can conclude that serving the important interests of students, or promoting their striving for authenticity, is also a moral obligation, and hence a social justice issue. Promoting authenticity, therefore, should be a chief purpose or universal aim of higher education.

Highlighting authenticity as important to student learning is no longer a new idea. As we saw in the Introduction, in more recent years the higher education literature has been emphasising the 'ontological turn' (Barnett, 2004b; Dall'Alba & Barnacle, 2007; Vu, 2012), which brings with it a broader set of purposes for university teaching. Concern lies no longer merely with whether higher education affects what and how students *know*, and what they can *do* with this acquired knowledge, but also, and importantly, who they are *becoming*. Referring back to Heidegger, Brook (2009) analysed the *being* of the process of teaching concluding that it is 'ultimately...for the sake of the formation of authenticity in others' (p. 53). Being a teacher, he infers, means to care authentically for students and also 'to care for the authenticity of students. This is precisely the goal of teaching that characterises the extraordinary task of teaching' (p. 53). In essence, Brook's (2009) position is that the unique purpose of education is to foster the students' becoming, or the formation of their authenticity. Doing so is a matter of true caring. In other words, helping students grow into their authenticity and take responsibility for their choices is in the important interests of students. Other commentators similarly have maintained the view that the purpose of higher education is developing the students' potential of being (e.g. Barnett, 2004b, 2005, 2011; Dall'Alba & Barnacle, 2007) and helping students achieve self-authorship (Baxter Magolda, 1992, 1999, 2009). Self-authorship can be observed when students make meaning of their experiences from inside themselves rather than have their views determined by others. Such self-authorship is a prerequisite for students to cope with uncertainty and complexity in the spheres of work, citizenship, and continued learning throughout life (Baxter Magolda & Terenzini 1999).

Likewise concerned with the formation of students' being, Walker (2006) recommends the application of the capabilities approach mentioned earlier (Nussbaum, 2000, 2011; Nussbaum & Sen, 1993) to higher education pedagogies. Following Nussbaum's (2000) lead, Walker (2006) offers a list of several capabilities that higher education ought to foster. Capabilities are understood as opportunities for human functioning. The goal of nurturing these capabilities is seen in the furthering of greater equality and justice *in* and *through* education. Specifically, Walker advises that university pedagogies should foster the capabilities of '*Practical reason; Educational resilience; Knowledge and imagination; Learning dispositions; Social relations and integrity; Respect, dignity and recognition; Emotional integrity,* and *Bodily integrity*' (p. 127). The list itself, which includes many of Nussbaum's (2000) original suggestions for human and women's development, is suggested for debate and ideally, Walker suggests, is arrived at through public deliberation. Developing these capabilities, I suggest, is in the important interests of students, as they offer them the opportunity to choose a life they have reason to value (Nussbaum & Sen, 1993), and choose certain 'beings' and 'doings' (Nussbaum, 2011). The capabilities thus provide the foundations for students to become authentic. The ancient Greek notion of *eudaimonia*, often translated as 'happiness' but more accurately interpreted as 'living the good life' (i.e. a life that is characterised by its own flourishing), perhaps captures best what is meant by authenticity in this context.

As noted earlier, the *communitarian* perspective on authenticity *in* (the scholarship of) teaching entails that academics pursue their individual reflections and developments within a wider horizon of shared ideals on higher education teaching. 'Horizons of significance' (Taylor, 1991) refer to our socially constructed traditions, cultural views and shared values or standards and, with regards to teaching, stand for the ideals we espouse on what it means to do 'good' and act professionally as academic teachers. I propose that the assumptions that inform the capabilities approach to higher education pedagogies could serve as a meaningful horizon to guide us in (the scholarship of) university teaching. Promoting the students' *practical reason, knowledge and imagination, respect, dignity and recognition, emotional and bodily integrity, educational resilience* and *learning dispositions* in the important interests of students. However, as was observed earlier, the ends and purposes of higher education are contested. In order for 'relevant actors [to] come to agreement about what counts as good pedagogy, for what purposes and what is to be done to make it happen' (McLean, 2006, p. 126), we need more public dialogue and exchange about the purposes of teaching in our times, a point I will return to in Chapter 8.

Part of engaging in (the scholarship of) teaching authentically, I claimed in the Introduction, is for teachers to work towards developing greater social justice and equality *in* higher education. Fostering the capabilities proposed by proponents of the capabilities approach to higher education pedagogies (e.g. Nixon, 2011, 2012; Walker 2006), we provide students with the opportunity to achieve the full potential of their being, which is a social justice issue. This opportunity should exist for each and every student, including those who are marginalised and feel alienated from the higher education environment they have entered (e.g. Haggis, 2003; Mann, 2001; Walker, 2004). Greater opportunity should also exist for those members of our society whose equal participation in higher education (Reay, David & Ball, 2005) and potential for empowerment through higher education (Furlong & Cartmel, 2009; Ross, 2003) have thus far been circumscribed. Critical engagement with widening participation policies and practices, for example, is as important an aspect of (the scholarship of) university teaching, as is inquiry into the particular pedagogies that are employed. Engaging in (the scholarship of) university teaching authentically, therefore, involves working towards providing present, future and potential students with the opportunity to function in ways that support their authenticity, thereby creating a better world *in* higher education.

As well as working towards greater justice and equality *in* higher education, authentic engagement with (the scholarship of) university teaching is also concerned with creating a better world *through* higher education. This involves fostering in our students those dispositions or qualities that eventually motivate them to make a contribution to a reduction of the many problems and inequalities facing our societies (e.g. Atkinson, 2001; Walker, 2010) by being prepared to debate and engage with controversial and difficult social or moral issues. It is in this context too, that theorists like Dillard (2006) and hooks (2003) stress that the purpose of education is to serve the needs of students *and* humanity. Nussbaum (1997, 2010) likewise argued that higher education's main task is to develop democratic and empathetic citizens who have the capabilities to address the complex problems of our times. Our world is rife with issues calling for people's capacity to show both courage and compassion towards those in need. Many of our social problems are those of inequality, where certain groups of the population are deprived of the opportunity to recognise and live their full potential of being. Importantly, acquiring the capabilities of *practical reason, emotional and bodily integrity, respect, dignity and recognition,* and *knowledge and imagination* (Walker, 2006) is in the interests not only of students but also of our wider society. As students are afforded these capabilities (which are always a combination of people's internal ability and their social, political and economic environment), and thus grow into their own authenticity, they may also come to appreciate the importance of recognising and supporting the authenticity of others and, as a result, apply themselves to the many social injustices and problems that characterise our world. In other words, by advancing capability formation in higher education students we may actually advance capability formation more generally within society. Guignon (2004) similarly argued: 'The authentic person takes a stand not just on his or her own life, but on the community's project of achieving a good society' (p. 162). This link between one's own authenticity and that of others will strike some readers as intuitive but others as rather curious. The argument gains purchase through the concept of reciprocity, a notion distinctive of Buber's (1958) *I and Thou* but also highlighted more recently by Brook (2009), Brookfield (2005), Jarvis (1992), Guignon (2004), Nixon (2008), Nussbaum (2004) and Eagleton (2007). All of these theorists suggest that our own striving for authenticity is inextricably linked to us promoting the authenticity of others.

The reciprocal nature of authenticity

Nixon (2008) draws attention to the distinction between the inner-directed and outer-directed aspects of authenticity. When inner-directed, Nixon suggests, authenticity takes on the form of 'courage'. Courage is required when seeking to assert one's own claims to recognition. When outer-directed, authenticity is expressed as 'compassion'. Compassion is required when seeking to assert the claims of others to recognition. Nussbaum (2004) showed that our capacity for compassion for those in need is based on a series of judgements we make. These judgements involve: first, that we understand the situation of these others as serious (which involves being able to imagine a situation from the perspective of someone else); second, that we conclude that they are not to blame for the situation they are in; and third, and importantly, that we recognise their vulnerability as a distinct possibility for ourselves. This implies that we see others as our fellow human beings who are important to our own flourishing or authenticity. If we accept the claims made by Nixon and Nussbaum, we can also assert that by looking out for one another on the basis of compassion we support one another's authenticity. Authenticity thus construed is reciprocal; we work towards our own flourishing, or authenticity, by helping others with their flourishing (Eagleton, 2007; Nussbaum, 2004).

The linkage between students coming into their authenticity and them promoting the authenticity of others is explored also by Brook (2009). Following Heidegger's analysis of Plato's metaphor of the cave, Brook first observes that authentic education, or meaningful learning, involves 'the trans-formation of our (inauthentic) self-understanding' (p. 50), or, we might say, the students' growing into their authenticity. Then he goes on to suggest that those who have been educated eventually become teachers, or carers, for others. Learning, or becoming educated, means that we 'become humans who authentically care for others and the formation of others as authentic human beings' (p. 50). In a similar vein, I propose that students who have been invited into their own authenticity will seek to promote the authenticity of others ('by returning to the cave to care for others – to free others', Brook, 2009, p. 50).

So far my argument has been that by promoting capabilities, such as *practical reason, emotional integrity, respect, dignity and recognition*, and *knowledge and imagination*, we strive to create conditions that allow our students to grow into their own authenticity *in* higher education, whereby it is hoped that through this experience they will eventually become committed to furthering the authenticity of others, or to use Hannah Arendt's (2003) expression, to develop a care for our common world. It is in this sense that authentic engagement in (the scholarship of) university teaching seeks to promote social justice and equality *through* higher education. Suggesting that (the scholarship of) university teaching should be aimed at promoting the students' authenticity, in the sense of fostering their ethical development, is not incompatible with how other commentators have described the purposes of higher education. In *College: The Undergraduate Experience in America*, Boyer (1987) argued that helping students to develop the ethical and moral judgement needed for purposeful civic engagement was an important goal that higher education institutions should foster:

> . . . the college should encourage each student to develop the capacity to judge wisely in matters of life and conduct . . . . The goal is . . . to set them free in the world of ideas and provide a climate in which ethical and moral choices can be thoughtfully examined, and convictions formed.
>
> (Boyer, 1987, p. 284)

In the same year, his fellow American, philosopher Amy Gutman (1987), took a similar position, contending that higher education was particularly suitable to the teaching of moral or ethical reasoning. Specifically she observed that:

> Learning how to think carefully and critically about political problems, to articulate one's views and defend them before people with whom one disagrees is a form of moral education to which young adults are more receptive (than school children) and for which universities are well suited.
>
> (Gutman, 1987, p. 173)

A decade ago, Colby, Ehrlich, Beaumont and Stephens (2003), also arguing from the American context, proposed that preparing students for moral and civic responsibility should be a major aim of undergraduate education in the United

States. In Canada, Martha Piper, when President of the University of British Columbia, declared around the same time that academic study needs to be related to the needs of society, must encourage in students a strong sense of social purpose and instil 'an awareness of one's responsibilities as a citizen and a member of the global community' (Piper, 2002, p. 23). In the United Kingdom, Paterson and Bond (2005) concluded that a certain civic strand of learning could be common to many academic courses offered at university, although this would need to be interpreted differently for different contexts. What is new in the argument underlying some of the texts reviewed earlier, and also in this book, is to link such concerns more explicitly to students achieving their full potential of *being*, or to put it slightly differently, to students moving towards greater authenticity.

At this stage in the discussion I have defended three of the four broad claims made in the Introduction. One claim still requires better substantiation, and this is the idea that teachers themselves become more authentic through a particular form of engagement with their teaching. It is this claim that I address next (and will say more about in Chapters 5 and 6, although I will argue it quite differently there).

Martin Buber (1958) emphasised that the nurturing of growth, development and authenticity crucially depends on genuine dialogue and relationships. At the heart of the 'I–Thou' relationship lies the sincere intent to affirm and foster one another's being, which is achieved by becoming personally invested and bringing oneself into the relationship. The significant point here is the reciprocal nature of the relationship. One person affirms and fosters a second person's being just as this second person fosters the first person's being.

In the context of formal education we are, perhaps more so than in other social settings, acutely aware of a power differential between actors. At the most basic level, we observe that teachers typically know more than students about the issues they are teaching and they also assess students on these issues. Then again, looking at this from a different perspective, one might suggest that power does not only rest with teachers. Rising tuition fees, increased global competition for students, and greater external pressures with respect to the public accountability of teaching – the last also combined with the expectation that universities prepare students for 'employability' – have bestowed students with considerably greater power than in the past. Moreover, students who feel treated unfairly by their teachers, one might argue, can make their concerns known in end-of-course evaluations, or by filing a formal complaint with someone even more powerful, such as the head of department.

Both teacher and student are thus armed with potent devices that can induce harm to the other. However, this form of 'touché' does not make the relationship equal. Teachers can easily cause considerable damage to students through statements, perhaps more often thoughtless rather than deliberate, which make students feel unworthy of attending university or embarrass them in front of their peers. As well, teachers who constantly praise the contributions of one student but dismiss those of another, or are not even aware of the presence of another, can undermine the student's self-worth and self-confidence. Being dependent on the teacher's assessment of their work, or the thesis supervisor's support, is also a most vulnerable position for students to be in. In higher education there is then clearly an issue of power that needs to be recognised; and although both parties, students and teachers, have and can exercise power in a variety of ways, it is on balance still a hierarchical relationship.

Power is a contested concept that has been conceptualised and shown to operate in different ways (e.g. Foucault, 1980; Giroux, 2010; Habermas, 1983), a point we will return to in our discussion of critical reflection in Chapters 6 and 8. For our purposes in the present chapter it is instructive to draw on the traditional leadership literature, where power is typically defined as the ability of one person to influence the behaviour or attitude of another. In this literature one often encounters reference to two main sources of power, personal power and position power (e.g. French & Raven, 1959), whereby the former is further sub-divided into expertise power and referent power. Position power is associated with the teacher's authority to cast judgement on the student's performance. Expertise power is associated with the teacher's greater knowledge of the subject. Referent power refers to the ability to influence how others respond to us based on their perception and assessment of how we relate to them. Although one can take issue with how power is conceptualised in this literature, namely as something a person *has* or *possesses*, the three forms of power do have some relevance to our discussion of reciprocity.

The teacher's expertise in the subject is obviously a key resource for student learning. Teachers share their expertise power when they situate the subject in the students' experience and invite students to become directly involved in the construction of knowledge (see Baxter Magolda, 1999). In order to bring the subject alive for students, Palmer (1998) argues, it is equally important that teachers convey that they are personally invested in their subject, are genuinely aware of the students they are working with, and honestly care about their students' learning. But power is also shared, for example, when teachers disclose to students the difficulties they themselves went through when they initially tried to make sense of the material, the frustrations and joys this involved, the questions and issues they are still grappling with, and why these questions and issues continue to be of particular relevance. By disclosing parts of themselves in this way teachers shift power over to students. When teachers show personal investment in both the subject and the students, they share not only 'expertise power' but also reveal part of their own humanity. Students in turn are encouraged to explore whether the subject holds personal meaning also for them. Moreover, students are 'empowered' in a sense that their difficulties in connecting with the subject are honoured and their own initial sense-making is encouraged and validated. Teachers who affect their students in this way can be thought of as exercising 'referent power'.

While the teacher's role is to increase the students' expertise power, referent power works in a more reciprocal way. Students who feel that they are listened to by the teacher, that their ideas and contributions matter, and that they are recognised as legitimate members of the learning and knowledge community, are more likely to convey to the teacher that he or she is in a safe place also. In such an environment teachers will be more inclined to continue to learn and grow through their interactions with students. We might then say that as teachers provide opportunities for students to become authentic, they, in turn, will benefit from the opportunity to further grow into their own authenticity. This is one sense in which teachers become more authentic *through* their teaching. In developing this claim I also draw on Peter Jarvis's observation that:

> Authentic action is to be found when individuals freely act in such a way that they try to foster the growth and development of each other's being.... Instructors who merely expound their knowledge in an authoritative manner are in no position to learn from their students.
>
> (Jarvis cited in Cranton, 2001, p. 84)

To sum up this last section, I argue that the difference in power between teachers and students must not be denied. However, teachers who genuinely care about fostering the development of students will seek to minimise their control over students by virtue of them having greater position and expertise power. Instead they will seek to enhance the students' expertise power by sharing their knowledge and will also seek to create an environment in which students feel validated and ready to take risks as they engage in knowledge construction and re-construction. Taking risks will involve the students trying to find their own meaning and voice in relation to the subjects they are studying. As Freire (1970) observed: 'The teacher cannot think for her students, nor can she impose her thought on them' (pp. 63–64). Only if students are both allowed and encouraged to think for themselves, or as Barnett (2007) put it, become 'disencumbered' from other voices (p. 45), is teaching different from indoctrination. When the students feel they can take risks in this way, they also extend this same invitation to the teacher. The student and teacher then come to share referent power. It is in this way, I suggest, that Buber's I–Thou relationship also has some relevance for us in the context of higher education teaching.

Authenticity *through* teaching: students coming into their authenticity

Moving towards greater authenticity, I argued earlier, is associated with a willingness to avoid complacency and compliance and engage in contestation (Kreber, 2010a). This is also the case when students grow into their own authenticity. Approached from an *existential* perspective, we might say that students come into their authenticity as they grow into themselves, learn for themselves, become 'disencumbered' from other voices (Barnett, 2007) and become authors of their own lives (Baxter Magolda, 1999, 2009). Students grow into an awareness of their own unique possibilities and strive towards these. Coming into their authenticity may then involve students in developing a disposition to learn for themselves (Entwistle, 2009; Entwistle & McCune, 2009). Additionally, it may involve them in grasping a subject they are learning in a new, and importantly, their *own* way (Kreber, 2009), possibly as a result of engagement in authentic conversations with peers and teachers around significant or unresolved issues in relation to the subject or discipline (Palmer, 1998). This latter sense of authenticity, we have seen earlier, focuses on the meaningfulness of that which is being learned, the relevance that students attribute to this learning and the ways in which students are able to make connections between what they are learning and their personal lives. Students coming into their authenticity then often means that they develop greater knowledge of a particular subject; but importantly, they do not just come to know more but come to know in a different way than they did before. This qualitative change in knowing is often accompanied by a shift in their identity and a greater sense of personal commitment. Similarly, Baxter Magolda (2009) argues, in her extension of Perry's (1970) work on the intellectual and ethical development of college students, that self-authorship involves not only that students develop intellectually but also personally and socially or relationally. The three dimensions of development are interdependent and hinge on one another. Intellectual maturity involves 'evaluating relevant evidence, problem-solving in context, and making wise decisions based on complex analysis' (Baxter Magolda, 2009, p. 144). Personal maturity includes 'understanding one's own history, confidence, the ability to act both autonomously and collaboratively, and integrity' (p. 144). Social maturity is defined by 'respect for one's own and others' identities and cultures to enable productive collaboration to integrate multiple perspectives' (p. 144). Intellectual development requires both personal and interpersonal growth. Viewed from an existential perspective, students growing into their authenticity can be conceived of as achieving their full potential of being.

   Building on this, but now looking through a *critical* lens, students growing into their authenticity become aware of their real possibilities through critical reflection and critical *self*-reflection – identifying assumptions and envisioning alternatives to their present ways of understanding themselves and the academic and social issues they encounter, and acting on this new understanding (Brookfield, 1987). This includes becoming aware of how the beliefs and expectations they hold about what is possible for them have limited their choices up to now. A student might realise, for example, that the image he has constructed of himself as someone who is not capable of postgraduate studies had been shaped by him being the first in his family to attend university. Student authenticity, from a critical lens, is associated with students experiencing a process of *subjective reframing* stimulated by critical *self*-reflection on assumptions, or transformative learning (Mezirow, 1998). At the heart of transformative learning is a process of becoming aware of how assumptions or presuppositions we uncritically assimilated at an earlier age have powerful consequences for how we think and act (see

Chapters 5 and 6). Subjective reframing can be observed in the mature working-class student Rita in the play and film *Educating Rita*. With the help of her tutor, who is intrigued by Rita's passion for English Literature, Rita initially experiences *objective reframing* as she learns how to interpret texts according to the conventions of literary criticism. According to Mezirow (1998), we objectively reframe things when we 'critically examine the assumptions of established definitions, theories, and practices to better understand the paradigms and canon that their writings represent' (p. 192). Such analysis certainly constitutes important learning at university level. However, the more profound learning occurs for Rita when she is told by her tutor that, although she now has read most of the great texts, uses proper language, follows established academic conventions and writes just 'like them', her own spirit had disappeared from her work. Dismayed and hurt, Rita begins to question why higher education is really important to her and in this process of *subjective reframing* eventually discovers her own voice and envisages new possibilities for herself.

Finally, viewed from a *communitarian* perspective, students coming into their authenticity understand themselves as members of a wider social community, if not as citizens of the world (Nussbaum, 1997) towards which they feel a commitment and responsibility. As we saw earlier, Baxter Magolda (1999, 2009) argues that an important purpose of higher education is to promote the student's self-authorship, which she conceives of in terms of intellectual, personal and relational maturity. Relational maturity involves 'understanding of and commitment to one's own interests in interaction with understanding and commitment to the interests of others' (Baxter Magolda, 2009, p. 144). Self-authorship, or authenticity, then entails the ability to recognise others' points of view. Self-authorship, or authenticity, demands that we are affected by others without being determined by these others. But self-authorship also requires acting ethically, to have an *understanding and commitment to the interests of others*. To feel such a commitment towards the interests of others means to recognise others' need for authenticity. Similar considerations to what has been argued in this section on 'Authenticity *through* teaching', led Bonnett and Cuypers (2003) to conclude that:

> Properly conceived, student authenticity must remain a central concern of education because of its internal relationship with personal significance in learning, moral education, interpersonal understanding, and education for democratic citizenship. It is also, of course, integral to what it is to be a full human being – constituting as it does much of what is meant by human integrity and dignity.
>
> (Bonnett and Cuypers, 2003, p. 339)

The main points of this discussion are summarised in Table 2.1. As stated earlier, although the three perspectives on authenticity are distinct, they are not unrelated. Achieving one's full potential of being involves questioning one's

Table 2.1 Authenticity *in* and *through* teaching

	Authenticity *in teaching:* authentic engagement in (the scholarship of) teaching	Authenticity *through teaching:* students coming into their authenticity
Creating a better world *in* higher education	*Existential perspective* • avoiding complacency • willingness to challenge oneself.	*Existential perspective* • students are offered opportunities to grow into their authenticity, to achieve their full potential of being.
	Critical perspective • avoiding uncritical compliance with practices one does not agree with	*Critical perspective* • students become aware of their real possibilities through critical self-reflection (subjective reframing).
	May also lead to: • inviting students into 'authentic conversations' about the subject (giving students access to the 'community of truth')	May also lead to: • students become 'disencumbered' from other voices; they learn to grasp a subject in a new or, importantly, their *own* way, experience a shift in identity (self-authorship).
	Communitarian perspective • placing individual reflective pursuits within a wider horizon of shared ideals in higher education teaching • authentic motivation: doing what is in the important interest of students (i.e. the human capabilities approach).	*Communitarian perspective* • as students grow into their own authenticity, they come to appreciate the importance of recognising and supporting the authenticity of their peers.
Creating a better world *through* higher education	*Critical and Communitarian perspective* • fostering in students the dispositions and qualities which motivate them to make a contribution to a reduction of the problems and inequalities facing our societies.	*Critical and Communitarian perspective* • as students grow into their own authenticity, they understand themselves as members of a wider social community, if not as citizens of the world towards which they feel a commitment and responsibility • they come to appreciate the importance of recognising and supporting the authenticity of others and, as a result, develop 'a care' for our common world.

Authenticity *in* and *through* teaching

Academics who engage in teaching authentically (authenticity *in* teaching) provide opportunities for students to become authentic (i.e. fostering the *students'* authenticity *through teaching*).

As teachers provide opportunities for students to become authentic (i.e. fostering the *students'* authenticity *through* teaching), they share their referent power and become more authentic (Buber's I–Thou) (i.e. teachers develop their *own* authenticity *through* teaching).

choices and recognising that one's own flourishing hinges on the flourishing of others. The latter is central to critical theory and communitarianism and is also essential to Heidegger's notion of authentic being (i.e. although for Heidegger authenticity involves breaking away from 'the they', in a sense of breaking away from unexamined ways of being, 'the they' is also the social world we are part of that provides orientation and guidance on how to live together).

This chapter would not be complete if it did not provide at least some pointers with regards to how we might promote the authenticity of students. The capabilities approach to higher education pedagogies provides us with a meaningful framework to guide us in our (scholarship of) university teaching, but by itself it does not offer us concrete suggestions for how authenticity could be encouraged. In the following section, I will provide just a few practical suggestions in relation to each of the three perspectives on authenticity that are discussed in this chapter.

Fostering student authenticity

The notion that seems most fundamental to promoting student authenticity understood from an *existential perspective* is that of 'care'. Following Friedrich Nietzsche's distinction between *pity* and *compassion* in how we relate to others, Heidegger distinguishes between 'leaping in' and 'leaping ahead' (Zimmerman, 1986, pp. 94–95). When we *leap in* for someone, we take over responsibility for the person and thereby diminish the other's authenticity. In contrast, when we *leap ahead* of the other we let her take responsibility herself (or in Heidegger's language, we let her 'take over her own possibilities') and act in ways that instil confidence. By *leaping ahead* we authentically care and foster the other person's authenticity. Zimmerman (1986), discussing Heidegger, explains that 'to care for something *in*authentically means to manipulate it for selfish purposes. To care for something authentically means to let it manifest itself in its own way' (p. 44). Heidegger's 'leaping ahead' is what Noddings (2003a) means by true caring: 'To care for another person, in the most significant sense, is to help him grow and actualise himself' (Milton Mayeroff, cited in Noddings, 1983, p. 9). Certain acts of caring do not qualify as true caring if they diminish the person's independence or development. True caring is based on empathy, affection and genuine regard. Importantly, however, true caring is not always a matter of meeting the students' expressed needs. Think, for example, of the teacher who always leaves the student alone who does not participate in group discussions. While the teacher's empathy with the student's feeling of uneasiness about speaking up in a group is clearly a desirable quality in a teacher, it is also the case that the capacity to develop an argument and subject it to the scrutiny of others is a skill that ultimately adds profound value to the student's quality of life, and the contributions he or she can make in any relationship with others, including that to larger society. Nussbaum (1997) emphasises the importance of developing in students the capacity to construct arguments that they feel prepared to defend in public. Specifically she argues that:

...failure to think critically produces a democracy in which people talk at one another but never have genuine dialogue. In such an atmosphere bad arguments pass for good arguments, and prejudice can all too easily masquerade as reason. To unmask prejudice and to secure justice, we need argument, an essential tool for civic freedom.

(Nussbaum, 1997, p. 19)

Of course, thinking critically and speaking up in class discussions are not necessarily related. The student who is silent during class may be thinking more critically about the issues being debated than the one who is the most vocal. For introverts, especially, it is often a particular challenge to participate in large group discussions. This is the case not because they have fewer opinions or arguments than extroverts. Jung (1971) observed that introverts are innately predisposed to focus their mental energies inwardly rather than outwardly. Focusing mental energies outwardly, typical of extroverts, finds natural expression in the sharing of thoughts and engaging with others in large groups. We should also acknowledge that classrooms can be rather inhospitable places, as when the same students always get overlooked, only certain views receive approval, and only certain ways of expressing one's views count. Brookfield's (2005) comment that discussion can be experienced as 'a competitive ordeal, the occasion for a Darwinian-style survival of the loquaciously fittest' (p. 118) sums up perfectly what many of us have experienced ourselves as participants in group discussions. At the same time we also recognise the potential pedagogical value of this mode of teaching. Teachers surely play a key role in how discussions are conducted. A caring teacher is aware of the many inequalities and power relations that can characterise discussion groups (Brookfield, 2001a, 2005) and at least tries to make them more democratic. But, additionally, true caring on the part of the teacher will be expressed by also encouraging and supporting the introverted, and perhaps the unconfident or simply shy student, to participate in class discussions, while remaining empathetic to the enormous challenge, sense of anxiety and personal vulnerability this involves. Helping students distinguish between their felt and real needs (Brookfield, 1986) is then an essential aspect of authentic caring.

From a critical perspective, the educator's care is expressed by helping the student to distinguish between 'felt' and 'real' needs by calling into question personal assumptions that tend to limit the student's experience. The notion that seems most fundamental to promoting student authenticity understood from a *critical perspective* is therefore that of 'challenging what is taken for granted' or 'encouraging critical reflection on assumptions'. Suggestions made in the literature on how to foster critical reflection include, for example, discussions, debates, the skilful employment of critical incidents, autobiographies, role play, repertory grids, concept maps, collaborative inquiry groups, free writing and journaling, metaphor analysis, and creative/expressive activities such as collages, drawings or sculpture. Common to all approaches is the intent to offer contexts in which participants are encouraged to identify the core presuppositions underlying their interpretations of particular situations, subject these to critical scrutiny, and explore alternatives. Inspired by Foucault, Brookfield (2000) furthermore suggests that critical reflection is promoted 'by turning logic on its head, reversing images, looking at situations sideways, and making imaginative leaps', as by means of these practices 'we realize that things are the way they are for a reason' (p. 130) but could be otherwise. Barnett (1990) had something similar in mind when he argued:

> A genuine higher learning is subversive in the sense of subverting the student's taken-for-granted world, ... A genuine higher education is unsettling; it is not meant to be a cosy experience. It is disturbing because, ultimately, the student comes to see that things could always be other than they are.
>
> (Barnett, 1990, p. 155)

A caring teacher will encourage students to challenge themselves, to move out of their comfort zone, to come into themselves, and thus to achieve their full potential for their being.

The notion that seems most fundamental to promoting student authenticity understood from a *communitarian perspective* is that of 'narrative imagination'. One way to foster students' willingness to contribute to social justice and invest themselves in the significant questions facing our humanity is by promoting their 'narrative imagination' (Arendt, 2003; Greene, 1995; Nussbaum, 1997, 2010). As noted in the Introduction, 'narrative imagination' refers to the capacity or disposition to consider a situation from the perspective of someone different from oneself, a process Arendt called 'visiting'. Literature and film bring us in direct contact with the particularities of others' lives or circumstances, which, in turn, make us aware of the distinctively human qualities we share with them. Through such pedagogies – we might refer to them as 'pedagogies of compassion – we realise that the fate of others is also a possibility for ourselves, and it is for this reason that these others deserve our compassion. Poetry, music and meditation (see below), furthermore, can promote a state of being within ourselves that makes us more open to the situation of others. While it is perhaps less difficult to appreciate the application of these ideas for humanities subjects, a particular challenge is how to further the imagination in science or social science programmes. In addressing this question Nussbaum (2010) optimistically suggests that:

> When practiced at their best, moreover, these other disciplines [she means science and social science] are infused by what we might call the spirit of the humanities: by searching critical thought, daring imagination, empathetic understanding of human experiences of many different kinds, and understanding of the complexity of the world we live in.
>
> (Nussbaum, 2010, p. 7)

Infusing higher education with 'the spirit of the humanities' (Nussbaum, 2010) remains a profound challenge but also an imperative for higher education.

Arguing from the perspective of 'pedagogies of contemplation' rather than 'pedagogies of compassion', Kahane (2009) suggests that in order for students to be able to open up to the suffering of others it is critical that they confront their own inner fears and do not hide from them. He proposes that contemplative pedagogies, such as free writing or meditation, 'can help students to understand the habits of thought, judgement, and reaction that keep them trapped in the cocoon of their own privilege' (p. 59). By encouraging students to confront the reasons for their dissociation from those who suffer by means of connecting more deeply with their own humanity, he also promotes their authenticity. Interestingly, Kahane (2009) also makes clear that his efforts aimed at promoting the students' sensitisation towards the plight of others, is directly linked to his own authenticity as a teacher:

> As I learn to bring contemplation more fully into my own life, and my own life into my teaching, I gain a sense of what it means to be authentic in my role as a teacher, and to hold this seat with the authority of someone who is not hiding from himself.
>
> (Kahane, 2009, p. 59)

Writing within the context of what they call 'radical' adult education, Brookfield and Holst (2011) recently called for an aesthetic dimension of learning to inform education. Specifically, they argued that 'art offers us a chance of breaking with the familiar, of inducing in us an awareness of other ways of being in the world' (p. 146). While art generally has the potential to make us see and appreciate situations from different vantage points, which in and of itself fosters the imagination, Brookfield and Holst were particularly interested in music, photography, film, fiction, poetry, theatre, sculpture, or painting that intentionally incorporated political or social themes with the explicit intent to provoke a response. They summarise the various roles that such intentionally subversive art might play in education as: 'sounding warnings, building solidarity, claiming empowerment, presenting alternative epistemologies and ontologies, affirming pride, and teaching history' (p. 152). Focusing on more traditional forms of art, Maxine Greene (1995) highlighted the potential of art to open up different possibilities, to make us question the taken for granted and to learn to look at things as if they could be otherwise. The imagination, Greene writes, allows for empathy, for feeling connected to others, and for any renewals, or new beginnings, of the world. Since art has the potential to raise awareness, to critique and bring people together for a common cause, it seems particularly suited for encouraging authenticity.

Given that studies in the United Kingdom and the United States demonstrated that the experience of higher education has positive effects on civic engagement (Egerton, 2002) and is also associated with greater tolerance towards difference, as well as more liberal political values and attitudes (Pascarella & Terenzini, 2005), one could conclude that these attitudes, including the capabilities discussed earlier (e.g. opportunities for practical reason, emotional integrity, respect, imagination, etc.), develop naturally for students studying on any course. Such a conclusion, however, should strike any reasonable person as rather naive. In our efforts to promote student authenticity we will need to make more intentional decisions with regards to curriculum and pedagogies. Some of the ideas discussed above may be useful for this purpose. There is also a developing literature on pedagogies and curricula suitable for the twenty-first century, which is clearly relevant to promoting authenticity (e.g. Barnett, 2007; Barnett & Coates, 2004; Baxter Magolda, 1999; Cortese, 2003; McLean, 2006; Nixon, 2012; Walker, 2004, 2006).

Concluding comments

In this chapter I have addressed the four broad claims made in the Introduction. In addressing these claims I developed a set of interrelated arguments that can be summarised as follows. First, authenticity *in* (the scholarship of) teaching requires that we orient ourselves according to a 'horizon of significance', which refers to the shared ideals, purposes and values that underpin our practice as academic teachers. Second, the horizon of significance, by which we orient ourselves must not be limited to doing what needs to be done to satisfy external demands; nor must it be limited to doing what is of value to us personally. Instead it also ought to include doing what is in the important interests of students. Clearly, questions concerning what shall constitute the horizons of significance, which ought to guide us, need to be reflected upon and critiqued, and horizons occasionally revised. Third, it is in the important interests of students that they grow into their own authenticity. Fourth, the human capabilities approach offers a meaningful framework, or horizon of significance, by which to decide how to serve the important interests of students. The capabilities approach to higher education pedagogies promises to promote students' flourishing, or authenticity, in two ways: a) students are offered the opportunity to grow into their own authenticity; and b) by applying the capabilities they have been afforded through higher education to the world outside of academia, students may advance capability formation, and hence authenticity, in others. By engaging in (the scholarship of) teaching authentically, teachers work towards developing greater social justice and equality *in* and *through* higher education. I also offered some concrete suggestions for how teachers might foster students' authenticity.

Thus far I have employed the clumsy linguistic representation '(the scholarship of) teaching', thereby using the terms 'teaching' and 'the scholarship *of* teaching' as if they were interchangeable. As briefly noted in the Introduction, it is more common these days to argue that 'teaching' and 'the scholarship *of* teaching' stand for two different activities. In the following chapter, therefore, it will be imperative to say more about how others have construed the notion of a 'scholarship *of* teaching', how the position developed in this book relates to these conceptions, and how the very idea of *scholarship* itself has changed over time.

Chapter 3

Placing the scholarship of teaching within a broader notion of academic professionalism

In the previous chapter I used the terms 'teaching' and 'scholarship *of* teaching' more or less interchangeably. While I hinted at the reasons for this in the Introduction, it is necessary to say a little more at this stage about the relationship between university teaching and scholarship. I begin this chapter with a brief discussion of how the meaning of scholarship is shaped by historical context. I then take a closer look at the Carnegie report *Scholarship reconsidered* (Boyer, 1990), which identified the 'scholarship of teaching' as a distinct domain of scholarship, alongside the scholarship of integration, the scholarship of application (later relabelled as the scholarship of engagement) and the scholarship of teaching (later relabelled as the scholarship of teaching and learning). I observe that, although the report put scholarship at the centre of academic practice and stressed the inseparability of core academic functions, it failed to provide a sound articulation of what scholarship itself involved and, by extension, could not offer a strong rationale for the inseparability of core academic activities. Following what I perceive was the original intent with the model, I suggest that scholarship is a distinct form of engagement that academics demonstrate in relation to their practice, regardless of the particular academic function pursued. I conclude that it does indeed make sense to refer to this distinct form of engagement with teaching as the 'scholarship of teaching' but argue that this engagement is best understood as a form of academic professionalism. This professionalism is characterised by informed, focused and critical reflections on the policies, practices, processes and purposes of university teaching and learning, with the goal of arriving at shared ideals, or 'horizons of significance', according to which academic teachers develop their identities and orient their practices.

Scholarship or *forms of* scholarship?

'The meaning of a word is its use in the language', Wittgenstein (1953, p. 43) once famously noted. To make sense of the notion of a 'scholarship of teaching', it is instructive to explore how the terms 'scholarship', 'scholarly' and 'scholarship of teaching' have been employed in relevant publications and how their meaning has shifted over time. The term 'scholar' (derived from the Latin word *scholaris*) typically refers to student or pupil. The medieval word 'scholastic' is at times still used as a synonym for 'scholarly', 'intellectual' or 'academic'. Scholasticism was a particular method of inquiry based on dialectical reasoning characteristic of the medieval universities, which focused on the accommodation between Christian doctrine and rational investigation (see on-line Oxford Dictionary, Oxford Companion to French Literature). The on-line Merriam Webster Dictionary claims that the modern word 'scholarship' was first used in 1536. Of course, the fields of inquiry pursued within the university have changed drastically since its medieval origins, and scholasticism as a school of inquiry had waned by the end of the medieval period. New disciplines were added over the centuries and became further specialised into numerous sub-disciplines. More recent times have witnessed the evolution of many inter- and multi-disciplinary fields, leading to the blurring of disciplinary boundaries. Given this diversity in intellectual pursuits, the term 'scholarship' today has evidently a much broader meaning and no longer refers to a particular field of inquiry.

According to the on-line American Heritage Dictionary the term scholarship refers to 'the methods, discipline, and attainments of a scholar or scholars' and to 'knowledge resulting from study and research in a particular field'. Similarly the Collins English Dictionary associates scholarship with 'academic achievement; erudition; and learning' and the Cambridge Dictionary classifies scholarship as 'serious, detailed study'. What is interesting about these definitions is that they point to two dimensions of scholarship: the Cambridge Dictionary highlights the process of inquiry (e.g. 'serious detailed study') while the others emphasise both the process of inquiry *and* the product that follows from it (i.e. it refers to learning *and* the resulting knowledge). Regardless of whether one adopts the definition of scholarship as a *process* or as a *product* of inquiry, or both, one might plausibly say that universities have always been engaged in 'scholarship'; however, the meaning of 'scholarship' has shifted over the years in response to the changing economic, political and social contexts in which universities operate (e.g. Boyer, 1990; Dirks, 1998; McCarthy, 2008; Nicholls, 2005).

Traditionally scholarship referred to the extension and interpretation of existing knowledge, and this was achieved not just through individual study but also through the process of teaching. By the second half of the twentieth century, however, 'scholarship' had basically come to mean the advancement of disciplinary knowledge through 'research', this being typically disseminated through specialised peer-reviewed journals. This was initially particularly obvious in the United States, which, much earlier than British universities, had been influenced by the German research university model of the Humboldtian tradition that had evolved in the nineteenth century (although Boyer, 1990, mentions that the word 'research' was first used in England in the 1870s and introduced to American higher education only in 1906). In North America, this shift to an emphasis on research activity occurred simultaneously with the massive expansion of higher education observable in the gradual shift from an elite to a mass system of higher education following the Second World War. By the late twentieth century, universities were not only expected to carry out ground-breaking research that would strengthen the nation's economy and competitiveness in a global market, but they also were counted on to accommodate a much larger and more diverse student population. In 1990, the Carnegie Foundation for the Advancement of Teaching in the United States published a report which declared that the time had arrived to 'give the familiar and honorable term "scholarship" a broader, more capacious meaning, one that brings legitimacy to the full scope of academic work' (Boyer, 1990, p. 16). Within the American higher education context, this led to the proposal for a more inclusive model of scholarship which would give authority to all aspects of academic work that contribute to knowledge acquisition.

The motivation behind the report *Scholarship reconsidered* (Boyer, 1990) was to address the commonly perceived imbalance in the university reward system, which was seen to recognise research but do little more than pay lip service to the other aspects of academic work. Equating the notion of *scholarship* exclusively with basic research, Boyer (1990) argued, was too restrictive and ignored the wider meaning the term had enjoyed historically. He pointed out that the tendency to associate scholarship exclusively with the advancement of discipline-specific knowledge and to consider the other domains of academic work as being of secondary status (because, allegedly, they only grow out of this research but, by themselves, are not scholarly activities) was a recent phenomenon. Originally, so Boyer reminded his readers, scholarship had meant to interpret and disseminate knowledge, and later, particularly with the founding of the land-grant colleges in the nineteenth century in the United States, it had come to mean also the creation of useful knowledge that addresses community concerns. He also observed that, at a time when the boundaries of knowledge have been shifting, scholarship should be seen to include the search for connections between what is known to build not only a deeper but also broader interdisciplinary knowledge base. '*Reconsidering*' the meaning of scholarship, therefore, involved, on the one hand, looking back and reclaiming older conceptualisations, such as sharing knowledge and applying knowledge, *and*, on the other hand, looking forward and developing new ones, such as discovering and integrating knowledge. Boyer (1990) expressed this more inclusive conception of scholarship in this way:

> Surely, scholarship means engaging in original research. But the work of the scholar also means stepping back from one's investigation, looking for connections, building bridges between theory and practice, and communicating one's knowledge effectively to students. Specifically, we conclude that the work of the professoriate might be thought of as having four separate, yet overlapping, functions. These are: the scholarship of discovery; the scholarship of integration; the scholarship of application; and the scholarship of teaching.
>
> (Boyer, 1990, p. 16)

What is intriguing about the above statement is that the term 'scholarship' is employed in two different ways. On the one hand, the statement suggests that scholarship *includes* discovery, application (later called engagement), integration and teaching; on the other hand, it says that there are *four distinct categories* of scholarship. Boyer was aware that the separation of intellectual functions was potentially problematic and so he commented towards the end of the report:

> We acknowledge that these four categories – the scholarship of discovery, integration, application and teaching – divide intellectual functions that are tied inseparably to each other. Still, there is value, we believe, in analysing the various kinds of academic work, while also acknowledging that they dynamically interact, forming an interdependent whole.
>
> (Boyer, 1990, pp. 24–25)

The idea behind the report was to put scholarship at the centre of academic work, as depicted in Figure 3.1, whereby research, or the scholarship of discovery, was just one of several core domains.

Although emphasising that the four categories formed an interdependent whole, Boyer, in the eyes of many, had introduced four different *forms* of scholarship. Among the many questions that *Scholarship reconsidered* had left underexplored, the most important one arguably was whether there is an *essence* to the notion of scholarship that informs all four academic functions, and thereby renders scholarship the *unifying or core construct* underlying all four domains of academic work, or whether scholarship is different in relation to each function. And if the

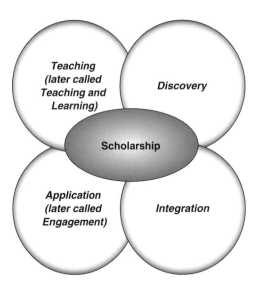

Figure 3.1 The Boyer model (adapted from Herteis (2006), reproduced here with permission of the author).

former, what are the quintessential characteristics of scholarship that would carry across these functions and tie them together? Suggesting that the four functions of scholarship were distinct but also *overlapping* did not go far enough towards answering this question, as it remained unclear just *what* the overlapping aspects were and also *how* the four functions were necessarily dependent on one another.

In the decade following the publication of *Scholarship reconsidered*, others, including Boyer's colleagues from the Carnegie Foundation, engaged in the important task of identifying what might be fundamental features of scholarship that cut across domains (e.g. Andresen, 2000; Glassick *et al.*, 1997). Within the US context, Glassick *et al.* (1997) proposed a single set of standards by which academic work in each domain could be judged as 'scholarship' (for details see Chapter 4). Whilst this served to facilitate the assessment (and, by implication, reward) of academics engaged in any of these separate domains of academic work, it is questionable whether these standards offered any clearer sense of how the four functions inform one another. It is important to realise, therefore, that in North America interest in the scholarship of teaching was propelled largely by the observed imbalance in the academic reward structure for individual academics, whose contributions to teaching were widely perceived as being undervalued, whereas in the United Kingdom the debate centred on the relationship between teaching and research (Healey, 2000).

The notion of 'a scholarship of teaching' remains contested in the United Kingdom despite the fact that more frequent uptake of the term can be observed. The London Scholarship of Teaching and Learning (SoTL) conference, for example, has witnessed a steady increase in numbers of participants since 2001, the date of its inception, when it brought together only a dozen delegates. A decade later the London SoTL conference attracted well over one hundred delegates (Fanghanel, 2011b). The phrase 'scholarship of teaching' now also appears more frequently in university-wide conversations about teaching, and occasionally in university mission statement-type documents. Examples include the Teaching and Learning Strategies of the College of Sciences and Engineering at the University of Edinburgh (2011) and the University of Ulster (2008). However, it is doubtful that this gradual increase in usage challenges Nicholls's (2005) observation that only few academics know what the term means.

Two distinct stances in response to the Boyer model can be identified among UK academics, and these can be categorised into two camps. In the first camp are those colleagues who find in Boyer's framework a welcome counter-argument against the separate government funding schemes for university teaching and research (e.g. Elton, 1992; Healey, 2000). Scholarship, defined by Elton (1992) as the interpretation of what is known, is highlighted by this group as being fundamental to both teaching and research and as the glue that holds these functions together. In the second camp are colleagues who see in Boyer's classification a rationale for developing 'teaching-only' posts. These posts are heavily contested. Those challenging the implementation of these new positions argue that they threaten the unity of academic functions and could further exacerbate an already existing tiered system of academic workers, with externally funded research-active staff making up the top tier and the others the bottom tier. Proponents of these new positions (at some universities) counter that their institution's reward system allows for progression to the highest academic rank based on contributions to teaching. Obviously, these are both complex and contentious matters and there is no commonality across UK universities in the extent to which such posts are encouraged, what is expected of colleagues holding such posts (for example, are they just expected to teach more or do research on teaching?), let alone how their career progression is organised. The purpose of raising these controversies at this stage is to show how Boyer's model offered arguments for either camp; and the reason for this can be traced back to the conflicting message in *Scholarship reconsidered*, where scholarship was defined as that which unifies the various academic functions *and* that which is particular to each function.

In search of a rationale for the inseparability of academic functions

Within the UK context, an alternative framework to Boyer's four-faceted model of scholarship was proposed by Nixon (2008). Like Boyer, Nixon claims that the core academic activities are inseparable, but he does so more consistently and offers an explicit rationale for this claim. In his book *Towards the virtuous university*, Nixon (2008) offered an intriguing theoretical argument for how the three essential academic activities, which he summarises as *teaching, research & scholarship* and *collegiality*, are underpinned by the same core virtues (he selected truthfulness, respect, authenticity and magnanimity). Together, these three academic activities are seen to make up *academic practice*. The term *academic practice*, more so than academic work perhaps, draws attention to the fact that the three activities together form the essence of the cooperative activity that defines the academic community. Replacing the traditional notion of administration with *collegiality* emphasises the human or ethical dimension of working with others. Nixon's argument is that for the virtues to thrive, and for academic practice itself to flourish, they need to be exercised and mutually reinforced through engagement in all three broad areas of practice simultaneously. Figure 3.2 offers a visual illustration of the idea of academic practice being underpinned by virtue.

In making this argument, Nixon (2008) draws on MacIntyre's (2007) notion of narrative unity, implying that the virtues that guide academic practitioners in one domain of academic practice carry over into the other domains they are engaged in. However, take one activity or domain away, for example *research & scholarship*, and the goods to be gained from the practice are no longer the same. This is so because the virtues themselves, which help us attain the internal goods associated with academic practice, can no longer be fully developed. While one can be virtuous in each domain, that is in terms of *teaching*, in terms of *research & scholarship* and in terms of *collegiality*, the virtues are fully exercised only

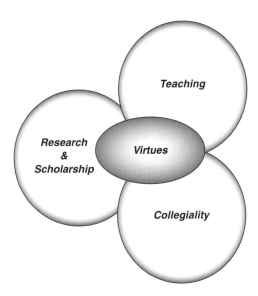

Figure 3.2 The Nixon model. Academic practice underpinned by the virtues of truthfulness, respect, authenticity and magnanimity.

through engagement in academic practice as a whole. This, anyway, is how I understand Nixon's argument against the increasing fragmentation of academic work as evidenced by the stratification of the higher education system into teaching-oriented versus research-oriented institutions, short-term contracts, 'teaching-only' or research posts, and so forth.

What is interesting about the models proposed by Boyer and Nixon is that both emphasise the inseparability of core academic functions but do so on different grounds. Nixon bases his argument on virtues, while Boyer based it on the notion of scholarship. However, in Chapter 4 I will argue that this conclusion is perhaps premature since scholarship itself can be seen as being underpinned by certain virtues. Therefore, the real difference between the two models, which I would like to highlight at this stage, is that Boyer did not offer a substantive rationale for the inseparability of academic functions. By emphasising the different domains of scholarship, the essential point that the four functions were inseparable was neglected in later interpretations. In this book I would like to reconnect with the idea that scholarship itself is a unifying construct for core academic activities: it is at the heart of teaching, engagement with the larger community, discovery of new knowledge and the integration of what is known. At the same time the various intellectual/academic functions themselves are all interrelated (see Figure 3.1). Below I shall argue that the literature on the 'scholarship of teaching' published in the wake of the Carnegie report has emphasised linkages between the 'scholarship of teaching' and the 'scholarship of discovery', but has paid comparatively little attention to the linkages between the scholarship of teaching and the other two academic functions.

In recent years a sizable literature has been developing on the relationships between teaching and research (for a comprehensive and recent bibliography on the topic based on over 550 references, see Healey, 2011). The emphasis in this literature is on how we can build stronger synergies between research in the discipline, teaching and learning. Healey (2005), for example, proposed that such synergies could be strengthened through a university curriculum built around research-*led*, research-*oriented*, research-*based* and research-*tutored* teaching, and Brew (2006) pointed to as many as six ways in which institutions could try closing the divide between teaching and research. This literature has helped us to think about the relationships between teaching, learning and research more seriously and creatively; but these linkages are not the ones I have in mind here. Instead, what I mean when I observe that the literature on the 'scholarship of teaching' emphasises its connection with the 'scholarship of discovery' is that the term 'scholarship of teaching' is increasingly interpreted as research *on* teaching and learning (or pedagogical research). We might also say that the 'scholarship of discovery' is increasingly *applied to* teaching. If this observation is correct, it stands in direct contrast to a recommendation offered by Cross and Steadman (1996). These authors had argued that the 'scholarship of teaching' is enhanced by drawing on all three of the remaining domains of scholarship, not just 'the scholarship of discovery'. To be sure, the 'scholarship of teaching' may, occasionally, take on the form of the 'scholarship of discovery', or research on teaching (and learning). But the point I would like to stress here is that the scholarship of teaching is clearly strengthened also by its linkages to the 'scholarship of engagement' and 'the scholarship of integration'. The 'scholarship of engagement', which refers to academic work that is aimed at meeting community needs, strongly overlaps with the 'scholarship of teaching', in that questions around what our students learn, who they become, and how they choose to engage with the world once they graduate, matter fundamentally to the well-being of our local communities and wider society. The 'scholarship of integration', which refers to interdisciplinary work, overlaps with the 'scholarship of teaching' any time that we seek to gain new insight into university teaching by integrating knowledge from various academic fields, not just psychologically based theories of learning and of instructional design but, for example, educational philosophy, ethics, sociology, anthropology, history or aesthetics. The scholarship of teaching then is not adequately understood as research on teaching (or the scholarship of discovery applied to teaching). Nor, however, is it practiced entirely independently of the scholarship of discovery, the scholarship of engagement and the scholarship of integration.

A difficult question is now pressing on this discussion: Does accepting the above view – that is, the idea that the various academic activities are interrelated, necessarily inform one another and are constitutive elements of an integrated notion of *academic practice* – not pre-empt the scholarship of teaching from being conceivable as a practice by reason of its own nature? In other words, does it make sense to refer to the scholarship of teaching as a distinct *practice* as I shall argue in the next chapter? Below I offer three brief responses that build on one another.

The logic of considering the scholarship of teaching a distinct 'practice'

My first response is that there is a difference between exploring the scholarship of teaching as a practice in order to facilitate a deeper understanding of it and in suggesting that it exists in isolation from other academic activities. My intent is to do the former not the latter. The perspective I take in this book is that the scholarship of teaching is supported by it being firmly nested within a broader sense of *academic practice*, that is, a work environment characterised by all four domains of scholarship (Boyer, 1990) and three academic functions (Nixon, 2008). Nonetheless, there is value in exploring more deeply what the scholarship of teaching itself is and, importantly, what it *could be*, particularly at a time when it has been interpreted in perhaps not so helpful ways (an issue I shall return to in Chapter 7). In this sense I am following Boyer's footsteps, arguing at one and the same time that although the various functions are dynamically interrelated it makes sense to analyse them individually. In order to be able to do this, however, it will be imperative in the next chapter to be specific about what the core elements of a practice, and of scholarship, are and what form these might take in relation to teaching.

My second response is that the features that define a practice, in a MacIntyrean sense, apply just as well to the scholarship of teaching as they do to academic work as a whole (a point I will discuss more fully in the next chapter). Another way of putting this is to turn Nixon's (2008) argument on its head, at least for the moment. In keeping with MacIntyre's (2007) notion of narrative unity, one might observe that the attributes or dispositions necessary for academic practice can in fact be classed as virtues *because* they are necessary for each individual activity but carry over in a consistent way to the other activities that are also essential to the academic's life; say from the activity of teaching to the activity of research & scholarship to the activity of collegiality. Interpreted in this way, the activities of teaching, research & scholarship and collegiality might each be considered *practices* in their own right. MacIntyre (2007) suggests that this is so because *practices*, unlike other activities, rely for the attainment of their internal goods on the exercise of certain virtues. He further argues that their internal goods have value to (all) those engaged in the practice. Both observations would seem to support the argument that the scholarship of teaching can be considered a practice in and of itself. Suggesting that the scholarship of teaching can be conceived of as a practice based on the above criteria does not challenge Nixon's (2008) main point, however. It is entirely reconcilable with the notion that the internal goods to be gained from the work done by academics in universities, by which Nixon essentially means their contributions to the good society, are best achieved through an integrated notion of academic practice.

My third and perhaps most relevant response is by way of a question, namely whether the *scholarship of* teaching is the same as *teaching*, or whether it is something else. If the activity of the *scholarship of* teaching could be shown to be different from the activity of teaching, this might further support the claim that the scholarship of teaching is a distinct practice. A better way of addressing this issue might be to ask how the activity of the *scholarship of* teaching is positioned relative to the activities of teaching, (pedagogical) research and educational development. The short answer is that it is related to all three yet different from each one; however, it is necessary to say a little more here.

'Scholarship of teaching' and 'teaching'

How one interprets the term 'scholarship of teaching' is likely to vary with the extent to which one has intentionally thought about the meaning of scholarship or is familiar with any of the formal conceptions that have been proposed. To explore this claim empirically, I once asked colleagues, whose expertise was in the area of university teaching and learning, how they understood the notion of the 'scholarship of teaching' and then compared their conceptions to those of colleagues whose expertise lay in a different academic field. Results showed that both the expert panel (including eight Americans, one Australian and two Canadians) and mainstream academic staff (including 100 American and Canadian colleagues) associated the 'scholarship of teaching' with inquiry and critical reflection; however, while experts emphasised peer review and scholarly standards, regular academic staff thought of the 'scholarship of teaching' principally as good teaching (Kreber, 2002a, 2003). A survey of 42 American sociologists attending a conference on the scholarship of teaching showed that 10 respondents (roughly 25 per cent) identified peer review and a focus on student learning as essential to such scholarship and another 15 (roughly 35 per cent) stated that links to previous literature and scholarship were important (Atkinson, 2001). Healey's (2003) survey with 77 academics in the United Kingdom demonstrated that over 90 per cent of them agreed that the 'scholarship of teaching' involved studying, reflecting on, and communicating about teaching and learning, and was closely associated with the context of one's discipline. Nicholls (2005), on the other hand, reported that UK academics tended to associate scholarship mainly with research (in the discipline) rather than with teaching, and thus 'were very unsure as to the meaning of the term "scholarship of teaching" or "scholarship in teaching"' (p. 70). Given this variation in how academics conceptualise the idea of 'a scholarship of teaching', it is interesting to look more closely at how Boyer himself saw the relationship between 'teaching' and the 'scholarship of teaching'.

Discussing what he meant by the 'scholarship of teaching', Boyer (1990) emphasised that academic teachers must be able to build bridges between their own understanding of the subject and that of students and must 'continuously examine' (p. 24) their pedagogical procedures. Citing Palmer (1998), he also associated the 'scholarship of teaching' with inspirational teaching and creativity, suggesting that teaching, at its best, would not only transmit but importantly *extend* and *transform* knowledge. He further underscored that 'great teachers create a common ground for intellectual commitment. They stimulate active, not passive, learning and encourage students to be critical creative thinkers, with the capacity to go on learning once their college days are over' (Boyer, 1990, p. 24). In this section of *Scholarship reconsidered*, it is difficult to see a clear distinction between (*good*) teaching and the *scholarship of* teaching. What we learn is that those who teach well also examine their practices and that there is a necessary link between teaching well and continuous examination.

A year prior to the publication of *Scholarship reconsidered*, Rice (1989) had distinguished three elements of a 'scholarship of teaching': synoptic capacity, pedagogical content knowledge and knowledge about learning. Synoptic capacity referred to 'the ability to draw the strands of a field together in a way that provides both coherence and meaning, to place what is known in context and open the way for connection to be made between the knower and the known' (p. 15). The notion of pedagogical content knowledge was originally introduced by Shulman (1987), who defined it as knowing 'the ways of representing and formulating the subject that make it comprehensible to others' (p. 9). The precise ways by which academic teachers might develop these elements of a 'scholarship of teaching' were not clearly spelled out by either Boyer or Rice, although it had been emphasised that acquiring knowledge about teaching and learning and *examining one's practices* would be the key element to such scholarship. When Shulman (1999) was President of the Carnegie Foundation for the Advancement of Teaching in the United States, he stressed the importance of inquiry into pedagogical processes arguing that:

> We can hardly be a moral community with mission statements that talk about the central place of teaching and learning if we are not also places that investigate those processes and place them at the centre of the scholarship in which we properly take such pride.
>
> (Shulman, 1999, electronic source)

There was little doubt then that the 'scholarship of teaching' involved examining and investigating teaching and learning.

A diversity of opinions exists on the meaning of good teaching, scholarly teaching, and the 'scholarship of teaching' (e.g. Allen & Field, 2005; Healey, 2003; Hutchings & Shulman, 1999; McKinney, 2007; Richlin, 2001; Shulman, 2000). Typically though, good teaching, scholarly teaching, and the 'scholarship of teaching' are understood as levels in a hierarchy, with the 'scholarship of teaching' encompassing the other two but going beyond these. In a widely cited essay published in the US *Change* magazine, Hutchings and Shulman (1999) proposed:

all faculty have an obligation to teach well, to engage students, and to foster important forms of student learning – not that this is easily done. Such teaching is a good fully sufficient unto itself. When it entails, as well, certain practices of classroom assessment and evidence gathering, when it is informed not only by the latest ideas in the field but by current ideas about teaching the field, when it invites peer collaboration and review, *then* that teaching might rightly be called scholarly, or reflective, or informed. But in addition to all of this, yet *another* good is needed, one called a scholarship of teaching, which in another essay, we have described as having the three additional central features of being public ('community property'), open to critique and evaluation, and in a form that others can build on.

(Hutchings & Shulman, 1999, electronic source)

This distinction between 'good teaching', 'scholarly teaching' and the 'scholarship of teaching' can be very useful, particularly if we want to ensure that we have a common language in which to talk sensibly about our different forms of engagement with teaching. Nonetheless, there is value in exploring these terms a little further, as upon closer scrutiny it may not be possible to separate good teaching and the scholarship of teaching quite as neatly as the above statement suggests. We might find instead that the scholarship is embedded in (good) teaching as much as in the research we do.

To make this argument more explicit, let us take the following premise as a start for this discussion: Teaching at university level should always be underpinned by scholarship, or a scholarly disposition; if it is not, it could simply be called bad teaching (Elton, 1992). This scholarly disposition, we might argue, is demonstrated in two ways: university teachers are able to offer interpretations of the latest research findings in their discipline *and* they take a critically reflective and informed stance in relation to the policies, practices, processes and purposes of university teaching. In other words, both their research in the discipline and their teaching is underpinned by being curious, being reflective, and a desire to continue deepening their knowledge base. Hutchings and Shulman also think that this form of engagement with teaching is important, and call it 'scholarly, reflective or informed teaching'. 'The scholarship of teaching', they suggest, includes 'being public, open to critique and evaluation, and in a form that others can build on'. Typically this statement is interpreted as publishing one's work in conventional ways. However, a different reading of this statement is open to us. Making our work public need not involve sharing results from empirical investigations at conferences, through journals or on designated websites, although such activity is clearly worthwhile. Making public may, or ought to, include a form of public engagement characterised by fostering kinds of public dialogue within our communities that are aimed at making a difference in teaching and learning. As I shall argue in Chapter 8, others can build on this public dialogue as they participate in it. It is in this sense that we might recognise this dialogue, in and of itself, as valuable community property.

There is also some ambiguity in Hutchings and Shulman's statement that good teaching engages students and fosters important forms of learning. Here we certainly need to ask what, for us, counts as *important* forms of learning! In the Introduction I argued that teaching, just like scholarship, authenticity and practice, means different things to different people. For one academic teaching refers to imparting the knowledge of a particular subject, while for another it refers to 'sculpting lives' (Beidler, 1987) and yet another understands it as 'reconstructing society' (Pratt, 1992), to mention just three possibilities. If Hutchings and Shulman mean that good teaching also promotes the students' intellectual, personal and ethical development, helps them achieve the full potential of their being, and as such supports them in their striving towards authenticity, then I agree with their notion of 'good teaching'. Given that university teaching should always be aimed at offering an *education* or the opportunity for authenticity (see also Brook, 2009), teaching cannot just be about initiating students into a discipline or providing them with a way into certain subjects that they would find it difficult to study on their own. University teaching is always also about cultivating students' minds, more broadly, fostering their imagination and helping them find their way in life. Good teaching is clearly, as has been argued by others, an intellectual and not just a technical activity. However, given the above considerations, it needs to be recognised that it is also a moral activity. Good teaching involves that one be engaged in purposeful, focused and critical reflections. Reflection extends not only to one's subject and the technical aspects of teaching it but also, and importantly, to questions concerning what university education is for and whether the educational opportunities we presently provide for individuals are fair. This means that good teaching is informed by critical inquiry and reflectivity, which, in turn, are associated with what it means to be a *scholar*. Not all university teaching is 'good' in the way just described; but when it is, it is characterised by those processes that are distinctive to scholarship.

Scholarship of teaching and pedagogical research

The literature on the scholarship of teaching reveals subtle differences in how the relationship between the scholarship of teaching and pedagogical research has been conceptualised. According to one particularly popular conception, the 'scholarship of teaching' is seen as equivalent to *teacher-led* pedagogical research (e.g. Richlin, 2001). This position argues that, to the extent that academics engage in pedagogical *research* within the particular contexts of their own teaching and disseminate their results, they *do* the scholarship of teaching. A second perspective understands the 'scholarship of teaching' to be represented by the codified knowledge about teaching and learning that is publicly available through books, articles, websites and so forth. Those who produce or develop this publicly available knowledge may or may not be teachers themselves. According to this second perspective, existing pedagogical research *is* the scholarship of teaching. When academics draw on this public work in order to inform

their teaching practice, they are seen to take a *scholarly approach* to their teaching (e.g. Menges & Weimer, 1996). According to a third perspective, academics are seen to practise the 'scholarship of teaching', as they base their teaching on evidence brought about by pedagogical research; but unlike in the second perspective, the scholarship of teaching refers to what teachers do with the published research, not the published research itself (e.g. Perry & Smart, 2007). According to this third perspective, academics practise the 'scholarship of teaching', as they are *guided by* existing research. So while both the first and third perspectives refer to the 'scholarship of teaching' mainly as a process, that is, as something that academics do, the second perspective understands the scholarship of teaching mainly as a product, that is, the results of pedagogical research. Clearly, all this is to say that what is referred to as 'scholarly teaching' according to the second perspective, is called the 'scholarship of teaching' according to the third. A more important observation, and one that leaves such variations in terminology aside, can be made, however. We can observe that the second and the third perspectives espouse a view of *research on teaching as a basis for teaching practice,* while the first perspective is more strongly linked to a view of *teaching practice as a basis for research* (see Stenhouse, 1983). This is a point I will return to in Chapter 7.

I prefer to think of the 'scholarship of teaching' as inquiry carried out by the person doing the teaching. *As I am engaged in the scholarship of teaching I examine my own teaching and that of my community.* Also, in my view, inquiries into one's own teaching activities should be informed not only by one's personal reflections but also by what is or can be known about teaching and learning, the latter including the perspectives of others (particularly students), empirical studies and different theoretical constructs and frameworks. 'Teacher-led research on teaching (and learning)', therefore, I see as one possible form of expression that engagement in the scholarship of teaching might take, and public research findings on teaching as one available source of knowledge. It is in this sense that the scholarship of teaching may draw on the 'scholarship of discovery'. But crucially, in my mind, all academics who teach have a professional responsibility to approach their teaching with the same level of curiosity, knowledge and care as they adopt in relation to the other aspects of their academic work.

Although a decade ago I distinguished a scholarly approach to teaching (which I had referred to as teaching expertise) from the scholarship of teaching, arguing that scholars of teaching make their work public whereas the experts do not (Kreber, 2002b), I no longer find this distinction to be particularly helpful. Today I still consider going public essential to the scholarship of teaching, but I am doubtful that the traditional ways of making one's work public, by themselves, necessarily lead to the kind of dialogue and exchange that is required for the improvement of university teaching and learning, and for creating a fairer world *in* and *through* higher education. What going public *could* involve is explored in greater detail in Chapter 8.

Scholarship of teaching and educational development

Engagement in the scholarship of teaching is seen to further the educational development of academics and institutions (see also Hutchings, Huber & Ciccone, 2011). However, unlike formal educational development programmes (e.g. workshops or accredited courses), the scholarship of teaching is tied to the specific contexts that teachers find themselves in and thus is centred on those questions that they perceive to be of real relevance. The scholarship of teaching, therefore, is *self-* rather than *other-*directed and, ideally, is transformative (see also Atkinson, 2001; Cranton, 2011; Huber & Hutchings, 2005; Hutchings, 2000; Kreber, 2005a). It is contrasted with educational development programmes that tend to reduce teaching to a set of predictable processes and behaviours and thus promote 'surface learning' about teaching (Rowland, 2001).

To sum up

In answer to the question of how the *scholarship of* teaching is positioned relative to university teaching, (pedagogical) research and educational development, we can now say: (1) the scholarship of teaching is indeed different from university teaching that does *not* take a critically reflective, inquiring and informed stance in relation to the practices, processes and policies, as well as the social and political purposes, of university teaching; (2) it is different from pedagogical inquiry/research that is *not* linked in some way to the contexts of one's own teaching; and (3) it is a special form of educational development that encourages self-direction and is guided by a transformational agenda. In this book the scholarship of teaching is understood as a critically reflective, self-reflective and inquiring approach that one takes not only towards one's subject but also towards the technical and, importantly, the moral aspects of one's teaching. The above account of what the scholarship of teaching *is* is inextricably linked to my perspective on what the scholarship of teaching is *for*. I see the purpose of this work as serving the important interests of students and thus enabling students to come into their authenticity. Authentic engagement in the scholarship of teaching involves teachers becoming more authentic and working towards developing greater social justice and equality *in* and *through* higher education. In short, the purpose of (the scholarship of) university teaching is to create a better world in which to learn, teach and live.

A number of authors have offered perspectives on the scholarship of teaching that resonate well with the standpoint taken in this book. The view advanced here is compatible with Huber and Hutchings's (2005) 'big tent' notion of the scholarship of teaching, which encompasses reflections on local practice and large-scale pedagogical research projects. It also chimes with their conviction that 'Educators need to engage in pedagogical inquiry so as to meet the challenges of educating students for personal, professional and civic life in the twenty-first century' (p. x). The perspective taken in this book is informed also by

Weimer's (2006) observation that 'the wisdom of practice' (by which she means our shared experience-based knowledge about teaching) and pedagogical research are two equally important aspects of the scholarship of teaching. As noted, the vision of a scholarship of teaching I have developed so far builds on Cross and Steadman's (1996) argument that the scholarship of teaching draws on all four of Boyer's domains of scholarship (i.e. teaching, discovery, integration and engagement).

In the final section of this chapter I would like to address the discipline-specificity that is highlighted in much of the literature on the scholarship of teaching. I propose that the scholarship of teaching ought to be pursued not exclusively from a disciplinary perspective but from a sense of academic professionalism that transcends disciplinary boundaries.

The scholarship of teaching as academic professionalism

The connections between subject matter knowledge and knowledge of pedagogy, epitomised in the notion of pedagogical content knowledge (Shulman, 1987), led to the scholarship of teaching being closely associated with the disciplines (e.g. Healey, 2000; Huber & Morreale, 2002). Boyer (1990) had sensibly argued that 'those who teach must, above all, be well informed, and steeped in the knowledge of their fields' (p. 23) and 'build bridges between their understanding and the student's learning' (p. 23). As we saw in Chapter 2, Palmer (1998), too, suggested that good teachers succeed in bringing students into 'the circle of practice' in their disciplines, 'into its version of the community of truth' (p. 122) so that they can practice the discipline's core ideas, concepts and ways of functioning. Similarly, Entwistle (2009) refers to the inner logic of the subject and its corresponding pedagogy. While part of the scholarship of teaching then necessarily must be discipline-specific, some authors have observed that a purely disciplinary perspective could be a potential limitation to the academics' critical engagement with teaching and learning (e.g. Nicholls, 2005; Weimer, 1997). This is a point I would like to explore a little further, particularly in relation to academic community and identity.

Shulman (1998) contended that the scholarship of teaching should be 'susceptible to critical review by the *teacher's professional peers* and amenable to productive employment in future work by members *of that same community*' (p. 6; emphasis added). In another publication he stressed that 'Each of us in higher education is a member of at least two professions: that of our discipline, interdiscipline or professional field (e.g. history, women's studies, accounting) as well as our profession as educator' (Shulman, 2000, p. 49). While this distinction is useful, it remains ambiguous whether Shulman means that the teachers' professional peers are those educators who share the same discipline or whether they include *all* academic educators, regardless of discipline. In a later article on the signature pedagogies of the professions, Shulman (2005) more clearly advocates the view that signature pedagogies should be shared across professions (e.g. Medicine, Law or Engineering), as each profession tends to emphasise the intellectual, practical and moral dimensions of practice to varying degrees, thereby potentially failing to address certain important characteristics of professional performance. He even goes as far as arguing that 'the liberal arts and sciences can profit from careful consideration of the pedagogies of the professions' (p. 58). Here then we get a clearer sense that, according to Shulman (2005), pedagogical practices distinctive to particular disciplines (here the professions specifically) should be shared across disciplinary boundaries; we might also say with other members of our 'profession as educator' (Shulman, 2000, p. 49).

Disciplinary affiliation has been shown to continue to play a central role in academics' sense of identity (e.g. Henkel, 2005; Kreber, 2010b). Nonetheless, Brookfield (1990) very explicitly encouraged university teachers to look beyond their own disciplines and see themselves also as members of a community of teachers engaged in a common purpose. This, he maintained, is an essential aspect of the academic's professional identity. Specifically he argued that:

> If college teachers define themselves only as content or skill experts within some narrowly restricted domain, they effectively cut themselves off from the broader identity as change agents involved in helping students shape the world they inhabit. What is needed to counter this tendency towards isolated separatism is an underlying rationale for college teaching. This rationale, although it would acknowledge the importance of specialist curricula and expertise, would go beyond these to unite college teachers who work in very divergent contexts in the pursuit of shared purposes.
>
> (Brookfield, 1990, pp. 17–18)

The common rationale for teaching that Brookfield encourages academics to identify with resonates well with the notion of a 'horizon of significance' that I introduced in the previous chapters. Academics authentically engaged in the scholarship of teaching, I proposed, define and orient themselves by a 'horizon of significance', or common rationale, in relation to what their work as teachers is for. This rationale, although it would need to be open for debate and deliberation, ought to include acting in the important interests of students, which, by extension, involves helping students grow into their own authenticity. This, in turn, will be to the benefit of both students and teachers and for the good of society.

Drawing on Brookfield, I now further argue that the scholarship of teaching is enriched by being pursued from a sense of teacher professionalism that transcends disciplinary boundaries. Hutchings et al. (2011) recently made a similar point when they recommended that we 'Connect the scholarship of teaching and learning to larger, shared agendas for student learning and success' (p. 118), which could include themes such as 'undergraduate research, the relationship of affective and cognitive development, and liberal learning' (p. 118). I will frame my argument around Hoyle's (1975) classic distinction between two models of 'teacher professionality', *restricted* and *extended*, which I propose are particularly helpful in advancing our understanding of what engagement in the scholarship of teaching might entail.

Evans (2002) defined Hoyle's two models of 'professionality' as 'an ideologi-cally-, attitudinally-, intellectually-, and epistemologically-based stance on the part of an individual, in relation to the practice of the profession to which s/he belongs, and which influences her/his professional practice' (pp. 6–7) and later interpreted the two models as the ends of a continuum (Evans, 2008). At the one end, there is the 'restricted' professional, characterised by teachers relying princi-pally on experience and intuition, and focusing on daily classroom practicalities. At the other end of the continuum, there is the 'extended' professional, charac-terised by teachers who value the theory underpinning practice, take a more intel-lectual and rationally based approach and hold a broader vision of education.

While in one sense present conceptions of the scholarship of teaching have encouraged engagement with teaching that reflects the extended professionality pole of the continuum, it seems to me that in another sense this has not been achieved. Indeed, I would argue that present conceptions of the scholarship of teaching have also encouraged a rather 'restricted' form of professionality. How could this be? I suggest that an extended sense of professionality in the scholar-ship of teaching is distinguished by two important features: a broader sense of what counts as relevant theory and a broader vision of university education.

Relevant theory in the scholarship of teaching

Although several commentators highlight the importance of theory in the scholarship of teaching (e.g. Roxa, Olsson & Martensson, 2008; Trigwell, Martin, Benjamin & Prosser, 2000), current discourse on the scholarship of teaching is characterised by heated arguments over 'which theories are relevant' and 'what is the role and nature of theory' in this work (Huber & Hutchings, 2008; Hutchings, 2007; Hutchings *et al.*, 2011). As was observed in the Introduc-tion, there is also a view that many investigations remain under-theorised (e.g. Boshier, 2009; McLean, 2006). Studies can be viewed as 'under-theorised' or 'under-intellectualised', for example, when data are collected without a sound con-ceptual framework to guide their interpretation. Although it is possible to carry out investigations with the explicit goal to build theory, studies that would live up to the gold standard of 'grounded theory' are still rare in this field. To be clear, theory-informed (and occasionally theory-inspiring) examinations of classroom processes and activities within one's own disciplinary context can make an important contri-bution to our understanding of teaching and learning. However, such studies would make an even stronger contribution to the scholarship of teaching, and would be conceptually richer, if the theories they were informed by came from more than one disciplinary tradition.

Many studies presented at the scholarship of teaching conferences I have attended over the years aim to investigate the relationship between instructional strategy and students' cognitive processing of the material taught. Implicitly or explicitly, these investigations draw on psychological theories of student learning and development that, so far, have arguably had the strongest influence on the scholarship of teaching. This may not be surprising, as understanding how students learn is considered an essential, by some the most fundamental, aspect of becoming a good teacher. And clearly, studies exploring how students learn the subject matter that is distinctive to our disciplines, how they, for example, work through 'bottleneck concepts' or 'troublesome knowledge' in these disciplines, undoubtedly represent vital forms of engagement in the scholarship of teaching; and some of the theories these studies are based on (e.g. Meyer & Land, 2005; Perkins, 2005) are important sources of knowledge informing this scholarship. However, studying the cognitive challenges students experience in the learning of subject matter without also paying attention to the disparate identities and resulting diversity in the challenges and motives experienced by different students, and the unequal opportunities students have to achieve their potential through higher education, may not go far enough if the scholarship of teaching is to really make a difference in the world. It is for this reason that engagement in the scholarship of teaching involves listening not only to psychology but also, for example, to philosophy and sociology. The scholarship of teaching is significantly enhanced, and becomes intellectually richer, by the sharing of disciplinary (and theoretical) perspectives (e.g. Huber & Morreale, 2002; Huber & Hutchings, 2008) and also by developing, as Brookfield (1990) and McLean (2006) remind us, a common rationale for university teaching. It is in this sense that the scholarship of teaching is strengthened when it draws on the 'scholarship of integration'.

A broader vision of university education

The second and related distinguishing feature of an extended sense of professionality is critical engagement with issues beyond one's own classroom practice and disciplinary community (see Gale, 2009). Such issues include policies affecting higher education, their underlying values and their implications for society. Scholars of teaching, thus construed, are still concerned with exploring and improving learning within their own classrooms and disciplines, but at the same time they recognise the importance of exploring and deliberating the purposes of university education in our times, of what preparing students for meaningful participation in society means, and what this demands of their own role as academic teachers.

Regardless of whether we teach biochemistry, mathematical computing, environmental engineering, political history, health sciences, philosophy, informatics, dentistry, medicine, law, sports science, languages, business, architecture or film studies, as scholars of teaching we recognise that the larger social purposes of university teaching also matter (see Brookfield, 1990). To be clear, I am not arguing against the importance of students acquiring academic knowledge of the disciplines, and not against academics exploring how best to assist students in their learning of this subject matter. My intent is rather to argue for a broader conception of the scholarship of teaching, one according to which questions of how students construct knowledge in a particular subject or discipline are examined within the larger context of furthering our own and our students' authenticity. We would assume that students' ability and willingness to engage critically with issues affecting our world is supported by their study of academic disciplines. Nonetheless, the linkages between the students' *academic learning* in the disciplines and the *ways of being* that we hope they will develop through participation in higher education can be drawn more explicitly. Likewise concerned with these same linkages, Gale (2009) speaks of a 'Level-Three' form of engagement in the scholarship of teaching that asks 'questions about student learning that speak to and influence issues of significance to our society, addressing our values writ large, what we need to understand as members of a local, national, global community' (p. 7). Similarly, Leibowitz (2010) advocates a *critically engaged* scholarship of teaching that demonstrates awareness of the socio-political contexts in which we teach. It is in this sense that the scholarship of teaching is strengthened by drawing on the 'scholarship of engagement'.

Humanities disciplines would seem best placed to teach the capabilities I discussed in the previous chapter (e.g. Nussbaum, 1997; Walker, 2009) but, in line with the authors mentioned above, I argue for a broader vision of the scholarship of teaching, one that applies across disciplines, and where endeavours aimed at improving learning and creating a better world within which to *learn* and *teach*, are nested within the larger concern for creating a better *world*. Many years ago Entwistle (1988) distinguished between a narrow and a broad view that teachers may hold about the purposes of education: 'The narrow view accepts the existing role of education in reproducing society as it is now, while the broad view may envisage education as a way of changing society' (p. 226). The scholarship of teaching, I want to argue, is most appropriately located within this broader perspective. Moving towards such an ideal is certainly difficult but not impossible. We saw in the previous chapter that Nussbaum (2010) addressed the challenge by proposing that all disciplines, when 'practiced at their best' are 'infused by what we might call the spirit of the humanities: by searching critical thought, daring imagination, empathetic understanding of human experiences of many different kinds, and understanding of the complexity of the world we live in' (p. 7).

The scholarship of teaching needs to be linked to ethical considerations, specifically questions of what we think we are committed to in higher education teaching, what we consider its purpose to be, and whether the opportunities we presently provide for individuals to benefit from education are fair. Defining ourselves around such commitments and purposes would be part of developing a new sense of professionalism as academics (e.g. Brookfield, 1990; Nixon, Marks, Rowland & Walker, 2001), and hence an integral aspect of the scholarship in which we are engaged.

Conclusion

In this book I take the perspective that the scholarship of teaching is enacted when we engage in purposeful and critical reflections on our own teaching. This includes being able to offer plausible interpretations of theories and the latest research in our fields. However, as well as this reflection on the content of our teaching, the scholarship of teaching pertains also to being reflective in relation to the procedural or technical but, most importantly, the *moral* aspects of teaching. The latter comprises reflections on how students learn and develop (specifically their ways of meaning-making), our classroom practices, our educational ideals, the social purposes of higher education, and the policy contexts in which we teach and our students learn. Catalysts for reflection include our experience of working with students but also relevant theories and findings from investigations into significant questions related to teaching. Finally, the scholarship of teaching involves going public with the insights gained from these reflections, thereby encouraging further critical deliberation and active engagement in the enhancement of teaching. In Chapters 5 and 6 I turn to the various reflective processes that underpin the scholarship of teaching when conceived of as a transformative learning process. First, however, it is necessary to explore in the following chapter whether the vision of the scholarship of teaching developed here finds some justification when placed within a wider theoretical framework. Alasdair MacIntyre's notion of a 'practice' offers a rich foundation for such an analysis.

Chapter 4

Exploring the role of virtues and internal goods in the scholarship of teaching

In this chapter I examine whether, and under what conditions, our engagement in the scholarship of teaching is an activity that fulfils the criteria of a 'practice', in the particular sense in which Alasdair MacIntyre construed the term. My purpose here is twofold: first, to explore what the scholarship of teaching would look like if it satisfied MacIntyre's criteria of a 'practice' and second, to delve into the question of whether something of true import or significance is at risk if the scholarship of teaching were not, or ceased to be, a practice thus construed.

At the outset of such an inquiry, one might ask whether this could possibly matter in any profound way; after all, although once described as an 'elusive' (Kreber, 1999, p. 323) and 'amorphous' term (Menges & Weimer, 1996, p. xii), over the past quarter-century the scholarship of teaching has gained much clearer contours. We clearly have come a long way since colleagues at the Carnegie Foundation first introduced the notion of 'a scholarship of teaching' (Boyer, 1990; Rice, 1989). On many university campuses we now witness more conversations, perhaps even more thoughtful conversations, about teaching, and some of the pedagogical studies and/or innovations shared at conferences or through journals have enriched our understanding of teaching and student learning. Nonetheless, there remains a lack of an overall conceptual or theoretical framework that could offer guidance for this work. Such a framework would take account of the definitions, interpretations and traditions that have evolved but importantly, as is its role, it would raise questions about the value or desirability of present forms of engagement with (the scholarship of) teaching. As indicated in the Introduction, theoretical and particularly philosophical notions, such as that of a *practice*, carry the potential to help us think about the scholarship of teaching in novel and perhaps deeper ways, thereby opening up new possibilities and pathways for engaging with this work.

My way into this discussion is to spell out what MacIntyre means by a *practice*, particularly the relationship between virtues and values that his definition implies. I then explore whether the scholarship of teaching meets the five individual criteria of a practice that MacIntyre identified. The chapter will connect with the main ideas we have encountered in this book so far, specifically those of authenticity, capabilities, inquiry and reflectivity, with the goal of proposing a larger theoretical framework for the scholarship of teaching within which to locate the various definitions, interpretations and traditions that have been developed and, more importantly, the activities that characterise our present engagement in this domain of academic work.

The notion of a 'practice'

In his by now classic text '*After virtue*', MacIntyre (2007) states that:

> by a practice I am going to mean any coherent and complex *form of socially established cooperative human activity* through which *goods internal* to that form of activity are realised in the course of trying to achieve those *standards of excellence* which are appropriate to, and partially definitive of, that form of activity, with the result that *human powers to achieve excellence*, and *human conceptions of the ends and goods involved*, are systematically extended.
>
> (MacIntyre, 2007, p. 187, emphasis added)

MacIntyre's definition can seem rather opaque; however, it is not quite as impenetrable as an initial read suggests. Practices, according to MacIntyre, are inherently social activities; that is, they take place within a community (see also the more familiar notion of 'communities of practice' introduced by Etienne Wenger, 1998). They are also defined by particular rules, traditions, virtues and standards for doing things. Moreover, involvement in the practice helps us to realise certain goods and leads us to conceptualise these goods in a particular way. Goods can be conceived of as the benefits that ensue from our participation in the activity. We might also say that goods refer to what we value. Being a member of a choir, for example, offers access to the goods of enhancing or perfecting one's singing, of enjoying creating musical effects with others, of supporting the choir in a performance, and so forth. The reason why an individual might decide to join a choir, or maintain membership even during difficult times, is that he or she values these benefits.

MacIntyre (2007) argues that goods internal to the activity in which we are engaged become available to us as we exercise certain 'virtues'. Although the notion of virtue has informed an extensive body of literature in the philosophy of education (see for example, Carr, 1991; Haldane, 1999; McLaughlin & Halstead, 1999; Steutel, 1997) higher education practitioners do not customarily think of their work in terms of 'virtues'. There might be two main reasons for this. The first is that the very term 'virtue' strikes many of us as rather antiquated and evokes questionable images of asceticism, puritanism and absolute self-sacrifice. The second is our tendency to attribute success in our professional lives to the level of skill, finesse or knowledge applied, and occasionally to good fortune, rather than to our dispositions or character. It is for this reason too that Parker Palmer's (1998) work on the identity and integrity of the teacher continues to present a strong challenge to dominant discourses on higher education pedagogy. Arguing against the prominent place of technique and skill in many books and workshops on learning to teach in higher education, Palmer suggests that what really matters is the integrity and identity of the person doing the teaching. Underlying his argument is the idea that how teachers engage with their professional role – that is, how they engage with both their subject and the students they work with – is the key to a meaningful professional life and a successful teaching–learning transaction. Following Palmer, I propose that *how we engage* with our professional practice is usefully explored through the notion of virtue.

How might we understand the notion of 'virtues'? Would not a great deal of confusion be avoided if we simply ditched the word and referred to them as values instead, a term that we may find much more accessible? The brief answer is that at times virtues and values are indeed used interchangeably but they are, strictly speaking, not the same. Virtues and values stand in a particular relationship to one another, and understanding this relationship is fundamental for understanding practices. The next section explores this relationship further.

Value versus virtue

Asked to state their *values* individuals might readily generate diverse lists, including items such as happiness, wealth, fame, collegiality, spirituality, altruism, intimacy, friendship, health, physical fitness, autonomy, kindness, wisdom, knowledge, freedom, trust or power. We do not necessarily hold all our values consciously; nonetheless, characteristic of values is that they guide the choices we make in our professional and private lives (Harland & Pickering, 2011; Inlow, 1972). Values refer to things that have worth to us; in brief, the stuff we find important, desirable, precious or 'valuable' in our lives. Virtues are of a different order.

In her book *The fragility of goodness*, Nussbaum (1986) showed that *virtues* direct us to the proper things in life, that is, to those things that are in accord with our humanity. Virtues, she suggests, guide us in what it means to be human. Virtues, therefore, are necessary for the good life, or the life of human flourishing and well-being, which the ancient Greeks referred to as *eudaimonia*. MacIntyre (2007) defined a virtue as 'an acquired human quality the possession and exercise of which tends to enable us to achieve those goods which are internal to "practices"' (p. 191). Drawing on both Nussbaum and MacIntyre, we can conclude that virtues represent guides for living, the human powers, inner dispositions or personal resources we need in order to achieve excellence. The important link between virtues and values centres on the fact that what we *ought to* value, in order to live the good life, is guided by virtues. Thus virtues lead us to value some things but not others. Before we can explore what all this might mean for engagement in the scholarship of teaching, this relationship between virtues and values needs to be unpacked further. In order to do this, it seems necessary to ask first of all: 'What are these virtues, which, allegedly, are of such fundamental consequence to how well we live our lives and engage with our activities'?

MacIntyre (2007) has an answer for us. He claims that 'we have to accept as necessary components of any practice with internal goods and standards of excellence the virtues of justice, courage, and truthfulness' (p. 191). The virtues underlying practices are of necessity interdependent. For example, being accurate or honest (truthfulness) and being fair, just or caring (justice) will at times necessarily imply a willingness to take risks (courage). Given that individuals involved in a practice are all guided by the same virtues, the relationship between individuals involved in a practice is also defined by these same virtues.

In furthering our understanding of the relationship between values and virtues, we must now explore more specifically what Macintyre means by goods that are *internal goods* to a practice.

Internal goods

Macintyre has a number of things to say here. First, he suggests that internal goods are not universal but unique to the particular practice in which we are engaged. The internal goods to be gained through the practice of research, for example, are different from the internal goods that can be acquired through the practice of theatre or journalism, or perhaps more obviously, through the contrasting practices of law, architecture, musical composition or navigating the sea. There may certainly be some overlap in the goods to be gained; however, the point is that internal goods are not defined a priori and then subsequently imported into a practice but that they originate from the particular experiences that are definitive of engagement in the practice.

Every practice has both internal and external goods. While the external goods alone could also be pursued through other activities, the internal goods can be gained only through involvement in the particular practice. In reference to an earlier example, we might say that joining a choir may be motivated by meeting and interacting with people, countering boredom or doing something other than work. To the extent that all these outcomes could be attained by joining a tennis club, signing up for a course, becoming a member of a reading group, booking a group holiday or going to the pub, they are external goods. Motivations such as perfecting one's singing, enjoying creating musical effects with others, or supporting the choir in a performance, on the other hand, are internal goods since they can be attained only by being a member of a choir.

Another claim MacIntyre makes is that the internal goods can be identified and appreciated only by those directly involved in the practice (for a discussion of why this is a more controversial claim see, for example, Hager, 2011). In order to understand the internal goods associated with being a member of a choir, I have to be part of the community involved in this practice; without such direct involvement I might have some sense of the goods involved but cannot fully identify and appreciate them. Similarly, Nicholls (2005) once suggested that an understanding of scholarship can be derived only from those engaged in academic practice and not from the outside – from policy writers, for example. Importantly, Macintyre further argues that it is only by exercising the virtues of justice, courage and truthfulness that we can both sustain the standards of excellence that have historically developed within a practice and gain access to the internal goods of the practice. In short, without virtue the internal goods will be concealed from us.

According to MacIntyre, external goods are not just external to the activity but they are also objects of competition; thus there are always winners and losers. The examples of external goods he cites include money, power and status. These external goods are always someone's personal or private property. Internal goods, by contrast, although experienced or enjoyed by the individual involved in the practice, benefit the entire community and thus are community property. An example might help in further clarifying this point. A performing musician who perfects her skill at guitar playing and introduces an entirely novel way of working the strings and interpreting a tune may eventually be externally rewarded by the audience's signs of appreciation after a concert, by being invited to publish another CD, or by a favourable write-up in the local newspaper the following day. These goods, which very roughly relate to power, money and fame, respectively, can be considered external in a sense that, although they follow directly from the practice, they could, strictly speaking, also be attained in other ways. For MacIntyre external goods have negative connotations but they are pernicious only if the internal goods are lost along the way. So if, in order to get ahead in the world of musical fame, our musician cheats (for example, by stealing the creative work of another or by deceiving the audience by blending sounds from various sources rather than generating them on her own guitar), she might, at least temporarily, still achieve the same external goods; but she would have missed out on some internal goods or values, which, as we have seen earlier, become available only by exercising particular virtues.

In summary, MacIntyre claims that any activity that qualifies as a practice is guided by the *virtues* of justice, courage and truthfulness. Being guided by these virtues offers access to certain internal goods that can be attained only through participation in the particular practice. We might also say that the virtues lead us to value the proper things about the activity in which we are engaged. These internal goods, or those experiences that we learn *to value* through participating in the practice, are distinct to each practice. Practices are therefore guided by a certain ethic. What we *ought to value* about the practice, that is, the internal goods of the practice, becomes accessible to us by being 'virtuous'. MacIntyre draws directly on Aristotle in the idea that virtues need to be exercised to become more fully developed. Aristotle held that we exercise the virtues by doing 'virtuous acts', similar to how we exercise our muscles by going to the gym. By being involved in practices, we exercise and thus develop the virtues. While the virtues of justice, courage and truthfulness apply to any practice, the specific goods or values reveal themselves to us only in the context of the particular practice in which we are engaged. Having established what MacIntyre means by a practice we are now ready to turn to the question of whether our engagement in the scholarship of teaching satisfies the criteria of a practice.

The scholarship of teaching

As noted previously, I view the scholarship of teaching as a particular form of engagement with teaching that is characterised by curiosity, reflectivity, a deep knowledge base and the motivation to do good work. Hence, I described the 'scholarship of teaching' as teaching that is *underpinned* by scholarship, where 'scholarship' is expressed in two ways: being able to offer interpretations of the latest research findings in one's discipline *and* taking a critically reflective and informed stance in relation to the practices, processes, policies and aims, and purposes of university teaching. In this section I will explore whether this particular conceptualisation of the scholarship of teaching finds some justification, and possibly gains additional purchase, when examined through the lens of MacIntyre's notion of a practice. I should emphasise that my intent is to discuss whether the activity of *scholarship* (in the context of university teaching) might qualify as a practice. I am not concerned here with the question of whether the activity of *teaching* (including school teaching) might qualify as a practice; for interesting discussions of this issue, readers may find inspiration in the work of Noddings (2003b), Carr (2003) and McLaughlin (2003).

What would the scholarship of teaching look like if it were a practice?

For it to qualify as a practice the scholarship of teaching would have to fulfil five criteria. First, it would be recognisable as a socially established activity that is practised cooperatively, which is to say within a community. Second, engagement in the scholarship of teaching would lead us to recognise internal goods, not just external goods. Third, these goods would be realised as we seek to achieve certain standards of excellence. Fourth, the scholarship of teaching would be guided by certain virtues, among them truthfulness, courage and justice, which in turn would help us recognise the internal goods associated with the activity. Last, while engaged in the scholarship of teaching we would be involved in a transformative process of subjective reframing, leading us to reconceptualise, and eventually achieve, the internal goods to be gained from such scholarship. I shall now consider each of these in turn.

A socially established activity that is practised within a community

Several commentators have referred to the scholarship of teaching as a growing movement of international scope (Asmar, 2004; Bender, 2005; Hughes, 2006; Hutchings, 2004; Kreber, 2005a; McKinney, 2002). Movements, by definition, are cooperative activities. The founding of the International Society for the Scholarship of Teaching and Learning (IS-SOTL) and several journals with similar titles are further indicators that the scholarship of teaching has established itself as a social cooperative human activity. The important work of the Carnegie Foundation since the 1990s also helped the scholarship of teaching to become better coordinated, cooperative and visible. But how might we define the community that is engaged in this activity?

Hutchings and Shulman (1999), as we saw in the previous chapter, argued that the scholarship of teaching is not for everyone and distinguished it from good teaching and scholarly teaching. While all three groups – 'good teachers', 'scholarly teachers' and 'scholars of teaching' – are seen to make important contributions to teaching, scholars of teaching are seen to represent an exclusive or special group. This community of scholars of teaching perhaps includes colleagues who attend conferences on the scholarship of teaching (for example, the IS-SOTL conference), participate in scholarship of teaching initiatives organised by the Carnegie Foundation and similar groups, or contribute to relevant journals.

Adopting the alternative notion of the scholarship of teaching I developed in the previous chapters we might argue that the community involved in the scholarship of teaching includes all academics involved in university teaching. According to the position I am defending, the scholarship of teaching, then, is also not a recent phenomenon but, in principle, one that has been practised since the founding of the early universities. This, I concede, is an idealised view as it cannot be assumed that teaching, even at university level, is always underpinned by scholarship: university teachers, today as in the past, are not always willing and/or able to offer plausible interpretations of the latest research findings in their discipline *and* they do not necessarily take a critically reflective and informed stance in relation to the practices, processes, policies and purposes of university teaching. However, one might be justified in saying that being a scholar, or academic teacher, *ought to* imply a disposition to meet both of these criteria. This is what Hutchings and Shulman (1999) mean when they say that all academics have an *obligation* to teach well.

According to the view that has developed over the past 25 years the community involved in the 'scholarship of teaching' is made up of those individuals who participate in what we now understand to be 'typical' scholarship of teaching initiatives (e.g. presenting work at scholarship of teaching conferences, publishing in scholarship of teaching journals, etc.); however, the alternative view I outlined assumes that all academics whose engagement with teaching is based on a scholarly, inquiry-oriented or reflective disposition are engaged in the scholarship of teaching and, hence, are members of this community. There is then no perfect consensus on who comprises the community of practice in relation to the scholarship of teaching. How broadly or narrowly we define this community depends on how (broadly or narrowly) we interpret the notion of inquiry. Despite this lack of perfect consensus we can nonetheless conclude that the scholarship of teaching is practiced within 'a community'. It therefore fulfills the first of MacIntyre's five criteria of a practice. Whether it also meets the second criterion is the question that concerns us next.

Internal goods and external goods

Goods, as we saw earlier, can be interpreted as the things that we value; and what we value can be understood as our reasons, or underlying purposes, for engaging in a particular activity. Engagement in the scholarship of teaching can bring about both external and internal goods. We might think of the external goods, or values, as the fame, publications, promotion, grants, or awards that could follow from involvement in this work. External goods belong only to me. The more grants I get, the less grant money there is for others. The more articles I publish in prestigious journals, the less journal space there is for others. The more awards I secure, the fewer there are for others. The more famous I become, by definition, the less clout there is for others (since if we were all famous none of us would be). Internal goods are of an entirely different nature. They refer to the enjoyment, achievement or satisfaction we experience by:

- inquiring into significant questions relating to teaching and learning;
- deepening our understanding of these issues;
- growing into ourselves and becoming critically aware of the inner motives that guide us in this work;
- doing what is in the important interests of students, thereby contributing to the betterment of teaching and learning, and, by extension, the world we live in.

In Chapter 2 we saw that according to Grimmet and Neufeld (1994) there are three possible motivations that might drive the actions of teachers: doing what is externally rewarded; doing what is personally rewarding, and doing what is 'good'. The differences between these three motivations are significant to professional practice and can be identified also in reference to the external and internal goods just described. The academy externally rewards us for the publications, grants, or awards we receive as individuals (and the academy itself, in turn, is rewarded for this performance through state funding, as in the UK-wide Research Excellence Framework, for example). Fame or prestige is also certain for those who secure many grants, although with a few exceptions funding allocated to teaching and learning is typically minuscule compared with that in other fields. In the UK context, exceptions include: (1) the £315 million that were distributed by the Higher Education Funding Council for England for the establishment of 74 Centres for Excellence in Teaching and Learning (CETLs) over five years from 2005/06 to 2009/10 (each CETL received a capital sum ranging from £0.8 million to £2.35 million, plus £200,000–£500,000 per annum for five years) (Smith, 2006); (2) the higher education strand of the Teaching and Learning Research Programme (TLRP) of the Economic and Social Research Council (ESRC) (higher education teaching and learning projects were supported through substantial funds from 2000 to 2008); and (3) the National Teaching Fellowship Scheme supported by the Higher Education Funding Councils of England, Wales and Northern Ireland (I include this here because a national Teaching Fellowship is a most prestigious award even though successful applicants receive only £10,000). However, at a time when state funding for higher education research is being cut back, yet having led externally funded projects is increasingly expected of junior academics seeking promotion, securing grants of even small monetary value has become an imperative for survival in the academy. A recent call by the Higher Education Academy in the United Kingdom for small grants of up to £7,000 for teaching and learning research projects, attracted well over 700 applications, of which in the end only about 50 (roughly 7 per cent) could be supported. Survival within the academy, based on publications, grants and awards, we might observe, is surely an important but nonetheless external good associated with this work.

The second motivation identified by Grimmet and Neufeld (1994), doing what is personally rewarding, is reflected in the enjoyment, satisfaction, achievement or pleasure we experience by inquiring into significant questions relating to teaching and learning; by deepening our understanding of these issues, by growing into ourselves and becoming critically aware of the inner motives that guide us in this work. The third motivation, doing what is 'good', is reflected in doing what is necessary and in the important interests of students. Serving the important interests of students, as we saw in Chapter 2, involves helping students grow into their own authenticity. Of course, all three motivations can be present simultaneously, and the third may very well be identical with the second; a problem arises only if doing what is externally *rewarded* and doing what is personally *rewarding* takes pre-eminence over doing what is *good*.

Internal goods are still the outcome of a competition to excel, or here to do 'good work', but their achievement enriches the entire community involved in the practice. While the external goods can also be gained in other ways, the internal goods can be gained only through the scholarship of teaching, and, to be clear, only if the scholarship of teaching is engaged in as 'a practice'. If the internal goods are not pursued, the scholarship of teaching ceases to be 'a practice'. So, for example, I might achieve fame by publishing articles, obtaining grants or winning awards for my engagement with teaching, but, in principle, I could do so without extending my disposition toward those virtues that help me recognise, let alone achieve, the internal goods or values that can be gained from the activity.

As a small detour, I add that publications (for example, journal articles) are an interesting case of an external good, as they are both an individual's property (it has my name on it) and are at the same time in the public domain. There is within the academic community a strong belief that the reason we make our work publicly available through books, journals and presentations at conferences is to enrich the community so that others can build on this work (e.g. Huber & Hutchings, 2005; Merton, 1973; Shulman, 2000). In as far as publications are community property, or as Arendt (1958) would have said, 'public goods', they also qualify as internal goods. To the extent that it is our goal to advance the knowledge base of teaching and learning, the claim that publications are community property certainly holds. However, if engagement in the activity of the scholarship of teaching is not just about enhancing the knowledge base of teaching and learning but about effecting changes in practice, that is, about developing authenticity in teaching and helping students grow into their own authenticity, then conventional publications may not be the most important form of community property. Several years ago Huber and Hutchings (2005) coined the notion of the 'teaching commons', by which they mean a public and conceptual space where insights about teaching are shared by colleagues from all disciplines with whom we share membership in the academic profession. This is an important idea but this common space needs to go beyond publications as conventionally conceived if the internal goods associated with the scholarship of teaching are to be achieved. The premise that for it to count as scholarly (or as 'scholarship') our work needs to be publishable in conventional ways can also be examined in reference to another, much more contested, notion that features strongly in MacIntyre's thinking about the nature of practices: this is the notion of a tradition. Nussbaum (2012) heavily criticised what she interprets as MacIntyre's seemingly blind faith in the authority of self-evident first principles bestowed upon us through tradition, arguing that 'we should not ... sink for comfort into the embrace of an authority, whether religious or secular, that will give us order at the price of reason' (p. 67). Without wishing to 'overtheorise' this point I would like to argue, based firmly on the work of Nussbaum, that if we rely on reason rather than on tradition to guide us in our thinking about what shall constitute meaningful forms of expression or demonstration of the scholarship of teaching, we perhaps come to realise that traditional ways of publishing our work tend to hold us back rather than help us move forward in improving university teaching and learning and making a difference in this world. If the scholarship of teaching, as I argue in this book, is indeed about creating better teaching, better learning and ultimately a fairer, more compassionate and sustainable world, rather than about expanding our codified knowledge base about teaching and learning, then traditional peer review and publication do not get us very far. I shall return to this point in Chapter 8.

To sum up this section we might conclude that engagement in the scholarship of teaching brings with it not just external but, importantly, also internal goods and thus meets MacIntyre's second criterion of a practice. We now need to explore whether the internal goods we have identified in this section are realisable through the process of trying to achieve those standards of excellence that are appropriate to the form of activity that we call the 'scholarship of teaching'.

Standards of excellence

A practice is always defined by certain traditions and norms, and thus by accepted standards of excellence. Different standards of excellence have been proposed for the scholarship of teaching. I will make brief reference to five. According to

Diamond (1993) the traditional criteria used to evaluate scholarship include that the work requires a high level of discipline-specific expertise, breaks new ground or is innovative, is replicable or can be elaborated, can be documented, can be peer-reviewed, and is of significance or impact. Glassick *et al.* (1997) argued that the work of the scholar should demonstrate clear goals, adequate preparation, appropriate methodology, effective presentation, significant results and reflective critique. Andresen (2000) identified what he considered to be the four quintessential features of scholarship. He proposed that scholarship requires deep knowledge, an inquiry-orientation and critical reflectivity, as well as peer review and going public. Although not speaking of 'scholarship' *per se* but about the distinctive nature of learning in the context of higher education, Barnett (1992) once proposed that: 'Contained within the idea of higher education are the notions of critical dialogue, of self-reflection, of conversations, and of continuing redefinition. They do justice to the idea of higher education . . . .' (p. 29). Given that scholarship is at the heart of learning in higher education, I suggest that these same notions do justice to scholarship as well. Commenting specifically on the scholarship of teaching, Shulman (2000) suggested that such scholarship implies that our work as teachers becomes public, peer-reviewed, critiqued and exchanged with members of our professional communities. While each of these five standards have value, I will limit the subsequent discussion to the standards proposed by Andresen (2000) and Barnett (1992), as I consider their reference to reflectivity particularly relevant to the task at hand.

We might then ask whether our striving towards the standards of excellence associated with the scholarship of teaching, namely our motivation to *develop a deep knowledge base, adopt an inquiry-orientation, engage in critical reflectivity* and *seek out peer review* and *make public*, helps us recognise, and desire, the internal goods, values or real purposes underlying the scholarship of teaching. These internal goods, I proposed earlier, are to experience enjoyment, satisfaction and achievement by carrying out the inquiry (including deepening our understanding of these issues, growing into ourselves and becoming critically aware of the inner motives that guide us in this work), and doing what is in the important interests of students. Serving the important interests of students involves helping students grow into their authenticity and, in doing so, working towards greater justice and equality *in* and *through* higher education. External goods, such as traditional forms of publications, grants and awards may ensue from this activity, but external goods would never be the sole or principal reason for engaging in this work. Let us now look at each of these standards of excellence more closely.

The *knowledge base* with regards to university teaching, as was argued earlier, refers to both knowing about the discipline, including the latest developments within it, *and* knowing about the practices, processes, policies and purposes of university teaching. This, of course, is a rather crude way of looking at the knowledge base of teaching. In the following chapter we will encounter a more differentiated view as different types and domains of knowledge relevant to university teaching are discussed. For our purposes in this present chapter, however, the crude distinction between the content of what we teach and the process of teaching gets us far enough. Adopting an *inquiry-orientation* means that we do not unquestioningly take our knowledge for granted but remain open and prepared to re-examine it. We take an informed, critical and inquiry-oriented approach to our teaching, as we engage in *reflectivity* in relation to what we think we know or understand about the discipline and, importantly, the practices, process, policies and purposes associated with university teaching and learning. This form of reflective engagement with university teaching, I suggest, may lead us to identify and realise the internal goods associated with the scholarship of teaching. The final criteria proposed by Andresen (2000), *peer review* and *going public*, or as Barnett (1992) put it, critical dialogue and conversation with others, are those processes that inform and *strengthen* our reflectivity. Without peer review and going public our reflectivity would remain largely inward-looking and we would be less aware of the assumptions we customarily take for granted. We need peer review and a process of making public so as to challenge our thinking and revise our assumptions and practices accordingly. We might then be justified in saying that by seeking to attain the standards of excellence associated with the scholarship of teaching, that is, by developing a deep knowledge base, adopting an inquiry-orientation, engaging in critical reflectivity and seeking out peer review, and going public (Andresen, 2000), we move towards recognising and realising the internal goods that are associated with the scholarship of teaching. If this argument appears somewhat contrived it is because trying to fulfil certain standards of excellence is always only a *necessary* but never a *sufficient* criterion to be met by those engaged in a practice. MacIntyre (2007) also claims that *practices*, as compared to other kinds of activity, are guided by certain virtues. Whether the scholarship of teaching meets this fourth criterion we need to examine next.

An activity guided by certain virtues

The on-line Merriam-Webster Dictionary suggests that scholarship refers not only to the 'activity and attainments of a scholar' but also to 'the character and qualities of a scholar'. Likewise, the Oxford Dictionary defines scholarship in terms of activity and attainment (specifically as 'learning at a high level' and 'academic study or achievement') but offers as an example of usage the puzzling sentence: '*the intellectual dishonesty has nothing to do with lack of scholarship*'. We clearly perceive a tension between the Merriam-Webster definition, which emphasises the character and qualities of the scholar, and the Oxford Dictionary example of usage. In this section my purpose shall be to argue that the notion of character, inner disposition, or *virtue* is critical to engagement in scholarship. Intellectual honesty, I will show, has everything to do with the scholarship and, moreover, it is not the only virtue that guides us in the practice of the scholarship of teaching.

In exploring the relationship between virtue and the scholarship of teaching, four questions are of particular interest:

1 What would the scholarship of teaching look like if it were guided by the virtues of truthfulness, courage and justice?
2 Does the scholarship of teaching also involve other virtues, in addition to these three?
3 What is the relationship between standards of excellence and virtues?
4 How might virtues guide us in what we value?

Others have applied a virtues framework to higher education (Barnett, 2007; Macfarlane, 2004; Nixon, 2008) suggesting compatible, although not identical, sets of virtues. I propose in this section that the virtues associated with the scholarship of teaching also include, as well as the moral virtues identified by MacIntyre, phronesis and authenticity. However, in order to defend the claim that phronesis and authenticity are critical to our engagement in the scholarship of teaching, it is important to first explore the role that truthfulness, courage and justice play in this practice.

Truthfulness is a multifaceted concept. It may simply refer to 'not cheating', 'being honest' and 'being sincere' but, as we have seen in Chapter 2, it can also have a more complex meaning. 'Being truthful' may also mean 'being honest with oneself', as in becoming aware, through critical self-reflection, of how one's assumptions have been distorted and thereby developing a more valid perspective on issues. *Courage* refers to a disposition to do what one believes the situation requires while being aware of the risks involved. Finally, fairness or *justice* involves not only playing by the rules but also making sure that those who are disadvantaged are supported in asserting their claims to recognition. In Chapter 2 we discussed this latter virtuous disposition as 'compassion'. The virtues of truthfulness, courage and justice are thus interrelated. Being truthful, and being fair or just, both require courage and compassion. Together, these virtues support authenticity. The virtues of courage and truthfulness are both associated with the existential and critical perspectives on authenticity, since confronting the truth about oneself requires these virtues. The virtue of justice is most closely associated with the communitarian perspective on authenticity, as justice implies that we look out for one another. But how do we develop these virtues? According to MacIntyre (2007), virtues are developed through experience. Referring directly to Aristotle, we might also say that we become virtuously disposed as we engage in virtuous acts. As we saw earlier, we exercise the virtues through such acts. However, to make sense of this claim in the context of the scholarship of teaching we need to dig a little deeper.

The scholarship of teaching, I argued, is a particular form of engagement with teaching, characterised by a scholarly, reflective or inquiring approach we take to matters of university teaching and learning. In the previous section I identified the standards of excellence associated with this work and suggested that through the process of striving towards these standards we come to recognise and possibly attain the internal goods that can be gained through engagement in the scholarship of teaching. The virtues are the underlying dispositions that are both *needed for*, and *are further developed as a result of*, trying to achieve the standards of excellence associated with this work. In other words, unless we at least try to be truthful, courageous and just, the standards cannot be fully achieved. For example, developing a knowledge base in university teaching would be impossible for us without being *truthful*, that is, accurate, sincere, honest and also 'true to ourselves'. We build and extend our knowledge base as we adopt an inquiry-orientation. But true inquiry would be inconceivable without a willingness to take risks or be *courageous*. Moreover, an inquiry-orientation is supported by critical reflectivity. This implies stepping back and considering whether conclusions we have reached are accurate and/or desirable and whether alternatives are possible. Reflectivity, therefore, is likewise inconceivable without *truthfulness* and *courage* but it also requires *justice* or *fairness*. Being *just or fair* means that everything is open for examination, not only those questions that are easy to inquire into, are straightforward to document or publish, or leave undisrupted how things are ordinarily done.

As we have seen earlier, peer review and going public are based on inquiry and critical reflectivity, and these again require *courage* and *truthfulness*. Going public is not just a matter of submitting a paper to a journal or presenting at a conference; it involves stating one's conclusions freely and publicly and thus is an invitation to others to question the claims to validity underlying one's arguments. As such, peer review and going public also require *justice*. The achievement of these standards of excellence is underpinned by the virtue of justice if the space in which questions are raised is as inclusive as possible or, we might say, representative of many different voices. Conferences on teaching and learning represent only one of many spaces where such dialogue could take place.

Attaining the standards of excellence associated with the activity of the scholarship of teaching, therefore, requires the virtues of truthfulness, courage and justice. Given this important role that virtues assume in relation to practices, MacIntyre (2007) concludes that a practice is 'clearly never just a set of practical skills even when directed at some unified purpose' (p. 193). The scholarship of teaching, too, is never just a matter of knowing a lot about different research methods to be applied to education and/or knowing about how to carry out a sound, rigorous and reliable empirical investigation into teaching and learning; it involves, at a minimum, also a disposition to ask or confront the right questions or issues, an ability to choose the most appropriate approach to address the identified question or issue, and a willingness to honestly and accurately interpret and act on one's observations or insights. Engagement in the scholarship of teaching, therefore, also implies openness to change.

Virtues guide us in what we *ought to* value; thus they lead us to value certain things over others. But why should this be the case? How could the virtues guide us in identifying the goods associated with the scholarship of teaching? When our striving towards the standards of excellence in the scholarship of teaching is guided by truthfulness, courage and justice, the internal goods come into reach for us. Engaged in this striving we may realise that what is of value to us is not first and foremost a matter of doing what is externally rewarded (that is, to publish, get an award or develop a name for ourselves – we might also call these the 'external goods'); nor is what we value mainly a matter of doing what we ourselves find personally rewarding (for example, enjoying the inquiry or getting a release from aspects of our work that we might enjoy less). Rather, what is of value to us, we may come to realise, involves also doing what is in the important interests of students, which includes promoting the students' authenticity. This purpose I called, in drawing on Charles Taylor (1991), the 'horizon of significance', a wider horizon of shared ideals in relation to which we define our professional identity as scholars of teaching.

Guided by the virtues of truthfulness, courage and justice, the scholarship of teaching can also be conceived of as an 'authentic practice'. Pushing ourselves forward and avoiding complacency, and being prepared to challenge practices and broader policies affecting higher education we do not agree with, are actions and dispositions associated with authenticity viewed from the *existential* and *critical* perspectives. These dispositions require principally the virtues of truthfulness and courage. Argued from a *communitarian* perspective (but adding a layer of critical reflectivity) authenticity also involves being willing to openly deliberate questions about what it is that we ought to value in our engagement in the scholarship of teaching so as to arrive at a horizon of shared purposes in higher education teaching. In Chapter 2 we linked this horizon of shared purposes to the capabilities approach to higher education pedagogies (Walker, 2006), as this is an approach to university pedagogy that emphasises the possibility of authenticity for each student. This 'horizon of significance' by which we orient and define ourselves as scholars of teaching then requires principally the virtue of justice.

As an 'authentic practice', however, the scholarship of teaching also requires the development of *phronesis*. According to Aristotle, phronesis refers to practical judgement. Dunne (1993) highlights, as well as the experiential grounding of phronesis:

> [the] immediacy of its involvement in concrete situations, and the responsiveness and resourcefulness in these situations that come to it only from the character and dispositions of the person, formed in the course of his life-history, and not from any knowledge that can be made available in treatises or manuals.
>
> (Dunne, 1993, p. 228)

The strong association of phronesis with character suggests that it is perhaps not exclusively an intellectual virtue, as suggested by Aristotle in the Nicomachean ethics, but, at least partially, also a moral virtue. It is through phronesis, we might say, that we come to realise and appreciate what is important in the scholarship of teaching and what actions are required in particular situations that are in line with its ends and values. Phronesis thus underlies the recognition and achievement of the internal goods associated with the scholarship of teaching. Phronesis does not develop independently of the virtues of courage, truthfulness and justice but is supported and made possible by these virtues. The virtue of phronesis will concern us again later on in this book (especially in Chapters 5 and 7). The point I wish to highlight for now is that the scholarship of teaching is guided not only by the virtues of truthfulness, courage and justice, although these are essential, but also by the overarching virtues of phronesis and authenticity. This point becomes clearer by exploring whether, and if so how, the scholarship of teaching fulfils MacIntyre's final criterion of a practice, which is the transformative function that engagement in a practice entails.

Developing 'human powers of excellence' – a transformative process

The final criterion Macintyre discusses is the transformative function associated with engagement in a practice. Drawing a direct link between authenticity and phronesis, Gallagher (1992) emphasises the transformative character of developing phronesis, arguing that the person involved in responding to the contingency and unpredictability of his or her environment is constantly 'drawn out of himself towards his own possibility and is remade by his experience' (p. 189). The person who develops phronesis does not just acquire new knowledge but is also changed as a result of this process. Likewise, we might say, the person entering into the practice of the scholarship of teaching, and who through involvement in this practice develops the virtue of phronesis (and the virtues of truthfulness, courage and justice), is implicated in a self-transformative process. Participation in the practice of the scholarship of teaching is then not just a matter of gaining more knowledge about teaching and learning, or of meeting certain standards of excellence, but a matter of extending and transforming ourselves through this process. Here we are reminded also of Barnett's (1992) observation that learning in higher education, which I suggested earlier is underpinned by scholarship, involves 'self-reflection' and 'continuing redefinition' (p. 29). Being involved in the practice of the scholarship of teaching, therefore, is essentially a process of becoming, a process of moving towards greater authenticity. Table 4.1 summarises the key points that have been made in this discussion so far.

Conclusion: what would be lost if the scholarship of teaching were not a practice?

Crudely put, if the scholarship of teaching were not a practice it would have no internal goods. Standards of excellence might exist but their attainment would not be guided by virtue. Virtue would then also not guide the relationships amongst those involved in the activity. Reflection, inquiry and peer review may all be visible in the activity, but because the activity is void of the virtues of truthfulness, courage, justice, phronesis and authenticity, many important questions would likely never be asked and consequently many significant issues in relation to teaching and student learning would get ignored. Ultimately, engagement in

Table 4.1 The scholarship of teaching as a *practice*

- A socially established activity that is practised cooperatively:
  - a community of scholars (of teaching).
- Leads us to recognise *internal goods*, or values, *not just external goods*:
  - *internal goods*: the enjoyment, achievement or satisfaction we experience by inquiring into significant questions relating to teaching and learning; by deepening our understanding of these issues, by growing into ourselves and becoming critically aware of the inner motives that guide us in this work, by doing what is in the important interests of students, and by contributing to the betterment of teaching and learning, and, by extension, to a fairer, more compassionate and sustainable world.
  - *external goods*: fame, publications, promotion, grants, or awards.
- Internal goods are realised as we seek to achieve certain *standards of excellence*:
  - deep knowledge
  - an inquiry-orientation
  - critical reflectivity
  - peer review and going public
  - critical dialogue
  - conversations.
- An activity that is guided by certain 'human powers of excellence' or *virtues*, which in turn help us recognise the internal goods, or values, associated with the activity:
  - truthfulness, courage, *justice*
  - *phronesis, authenticity*.
- Developing 'human powers of excellence' or virtues – a transformative process:

  As we strive towards
  - deep knowledge
  - an inquiry-orientation
  - critical reflectivity
  - peer review and going public
  - critical dialogue
  - conversations

  we exercise and further develop
  - truthfulness
  - courage
  - justice
  - *phronesis*
  - *authenticity*

  which may lead us to appreciate
  - the enjoyment, achievement or satisfaction we experience by inquiring into significant questions relating to teaching and learning; by deepening our understanding of these issues, by growing into ourselves and becoming critically aware of the inner motives that guide us in this work, by doing what is in the important interests of students, and by contributing to the betterment of teaching and learning, and, by extension, a fairer, more compassionate and sustainable world.

the scholarship of teaching would not be a self-transformative process and we would not become virtuously disposed toward greater authenticity. Given that we would not grow in authenticity we would also be unlikely to be in a position to encourage the authenticity of students. I therefore suggest that only if engaged in as a *practice* underpinned by virtue is the scholarship of teaching a truly worthwhile activity.

The point of this theoretical analysis was to show that, although we now have clearer definitions of the scholarship of teaching, such definitions, or standards, by themselves, do not guarantee that the work that is carried out serves the important interests of students. We might, for example, have clear goals, adequate preparation, appropriate methodology, effective presentation, significant results and so-called reflective critique (Glassick *et al.*, 1997), or as Shulman (2000) put it peer review, critique and exchange with members of our professional communities, but without virtue, these standards remain weak (I return to this point in the next chapter). Just as I can win a game of chess by cheating, I can meet the minimum standard of excellence associated with the scholarship of teaching by 'cheating' or, put differently, without being virtuous. Publishing journal articles on teaching and learning for example, which for some is the hallmark of peer review and going public, may or may not be guided by the virtues of truthfulness, courage and justice. My engagement in so-called 'reflective critique', too, may in reality never move beyond simply identifying and confirming my preconceptions and long-held convictions. Real critique or reflectivity naturally involves calling these convictions into question, but this, as we saw earlier, requires virtue.

While I disagree with MacIntyre's over-reliance on the notion of tradition, I propose, nevertheless, that his notion of a *practice*, with its emphasis on virtue, standards of excellence and internal goods, offers a much needed theoretical context for the scholarship of teaching against which to assess the various definitions or conceptualisations of this work that have evolved over the past twenty-some years and, more importantly, the activities by which we seek to support the learning and development of students. I furthermore suggest that it is through critical reflectivity that the internal goods associated with the scholarship of teaching become recognisable and attainable. What reflection, and particularly critical reflection, in the scholarship of teaching involves is explored in the next two chapters.

Chapter 5

Questioning knowledge claims

The core construct in this chapter is the notion of critical reflection, which at times I will also refer to as critical reflectivity. Critical reflection is fundamental to scholarship (e.g. Andresen, 2000). It is intrinsic to inquiry, essential for developing a deep knowledge base and vital for meaningful peer review and going public. As was argued in Chapters 1 and 2, critical reflection is also fundamental to moving towards greater authenticity. For each of the three broad perspectives on authenticity discussed in this book, the existential, the critical and the communitarian, reflection holds a central role: it inspires a person's separation from 'the they' ('das man') so as to achieve his or her full potential of being; it brings about a person's realisation of how assumptions he or she has taken for granted are shaped by social historical context; and it lies behind a person's recognition that his or her own flourishing is reciprocally linked to enabling the flourishing, or authenticity, of others, thereby aiming to work towards shared ideals by which to define one's own identity. Critical reflection, therefore, is pivotal to both scholarship and authenticity.

As noted in the Introduction, critical reflectivity in relation to teaching relates to two distinct domains. With regards to the first domain, reflective teachers continuously examine what they think they know or understand about their discipline or the subjects they teach. Being reflective in this 'subject or content domain' includes asking questions such as: What do these latest research findings in my field mean? How do the arguments the authors make in this recent text challenge how we used to understand or explain particular phenomena? How has my discipline evolved over time, what factors have contributed to this development, and where are we headed? Being reflective in this way would likely enhance teaching at any level of education but in *higher* education such reflectivity is an imperative. However, reflecting on the subject or content of our courses is not all that adopting an inquiry-orientation towards one's teaching involves. Inquiring teachers demonstrate critical reflectivity also in relation to a second domain of teaching. This second or 'process domain' relates to the various practices, policies, processes, aims and purposes associated with university teaching and learning. It is this second domain of reflectivity, and the various questions it gives rise to, that is the focus of this chapter.

In this and the next chapter I explore how this 'process-oriented' form of reflective engagement is implicated in justifying the knowledge claims academics make about university teaching. I further intend to show how academics' engagement in critical reflection is fundamental to identifying and realising the goods that are internal to the scholarship of teaching. The internal goods, or values, associated with the scholarship of teaching involve the enjoyment, achievement or satisfaction we experience as we: inquire into significant questions relating to teaching and learning; deepen our understanding of these issues; grow into ourselves and become critically aware of the inner motives that guide us in this work; do what is in the important interests of students; and contribute to the betterment of teaching and learning, and, ultimately, a fairer and more compassionate world (see Table 4.1). For the goods internal to the scholarship of teaching to become available to us we need to engage in the scholarship of teaching as a *practice*, which means in ways that are guided by the virtues of justice, courage, truthfulness, phronesis and authenticity. Through our engagement in the scholarship of teaching in this way, we also further cultivate these same virtues.

Essentially, I demonstrate in this and the following chapter how academics' engagement in critical reflection and critical *self*-reflection furthers their own authenticity as teachers and how their reflections are linked to promoting the authenticity of students. In developing these arguments I first explore the meaning of critical reflection. I then place the notion of critical reflection within a larger theory of adult learning and development. Following this I turn to a model of the scholarship of teaching that is partially based on this theory. This model distinguishes different types and domains of teacher knowledge, different functions of reflection, and different forms of learning. Eventually I will show that the scholarship of teaching is associated with instrumental, communicative and emancipatory learning processes, as well as objective and subjective reframing, and show how these are linked to authenticity.

What do we mean by *critical* reflection?

Critical reflection is a contested concept and different authors writing from different philosophical positions interpret the notion differently. As I have argued elsewhere (Kreber, 2012), according to one particular position critical reflection is conceived of as being closely related to reflective thinking (e.g. Dewey, 1991), critical thinking (e.g. Norris & Ennis, 1989; Siegel, 1988), and the concept of reflective practice (e.g. Schön, 1983); however, proponents of this position would emphasise that an essential element that distinguishes critical reflection from these other constructs is critical reflection's solid foundation in critical theory (e.g. Freire, 1970; Gramsci, 1971; Habermas, 1971, 1983), and variations of it enriched by postmodern ideas (Brookfield, 1995, 2005; Tierney, 1993; Tierney & Rhoads, 1993). It is this critical theory tradition that connects reflection explicitly with social and political purposes and ideology critique, and hence makes it *critical*. Critical reflection, thus conceived, is inextricably linked to power, and just how power itself is to be construed has been an issue of considerable debate (e.g. Ashenden & Owen, 1999; Kelly, 1994), a point I revisit in Chapters 6 and 8.

In this present chapter I explore the meaning of critical reflection in the context of Jack Mezirow's (1981, 1991, 2000) Transformation Theory. Although Mezirow's Transformation Theory is strongly informed by the critical theory tradition, in particular the work of Brazilian educator and social activist Paulo Freire (1970) and the German cultural critic and social philosopher Jürgen Habermas (1971, 1983), it also incorporates several other intellectual positions including pragmatist constructivism, psychoanalysis and psychotherapy and, to an extent, analytical philosophy or logic. Given the 'conceptual eclecticism' inherent in Mezirow's Transformation Theory, it makes sense to say just a little more about how he draws on these other traditions.

Much of the literature on reflection is inspired by the legacy of John Dewey, a leading proponent of American pragmatism, and Mezirow, too, found insight in Dewey's work. In *How we think*, Dewey (1991, originally published in 1910) defined reflective thinking as 'active, persistent and careful consideration of any belief or supposed form of knowledge in the light of the grounds that support it, and the further conclusions to which it tends' (p. 6). He emphasised that reflective thinking was called for in contexts characterised by genuine uncertainty about how to best solve a problem and understood it to be characterised by a willingness to endure a condition of mental disturbance, to suspend immediate judgement and to carry out further systematic inquiry. Dewey employed the term *critical* inquiry to describe the scientific method used during the problem-solving process. His notion of critical inquiry was basically a process of testing the validity of our assumptions through experimentation. He also highlighted the important function critical inquiry serves in freeing people from dogmatism and tradition, commenting:

> Certain men and classes of men come to be accepted guardians or transmitters– instructors of established doctrines. . . . inquiry and doubt are silenced by citation of ancient laws . . . . *This attitude of mind generates dislike of change, and the resulting aversion to novelty is fatal to progress.* What will not fit into the established canons will be outlawed.
>
> (Dewey, 1991, p. 149, emphasis added)

Mezirow (1991) comments that he extended Dewey's (1991) work in two ways. First, he demonstrated that the process of validity testing of knowledge claims (assumptions) is not limited to the '*instrumental*' domain of learning but takes place also within a '*communicative*' domain of learning, although within the latter the nature of validity testing takes on a different form. Briefly put, in the instrumental domain of learning the established method of inquiry employed to test the validity of beliefs is the scientific method or experimentation. In the communicative domain of learning the established method is interpretation with the goal of reaching mutual agreement within a horizon of understanding that has traditionally evolved within a community.

Mezirow's second extension of Dewey's work on reflective thinking was inspired by both critical theory and psychotherapy. Mezirow claims that, although Dewey recognised that reflective thinking inevitably involved consideration of validity claims, he did not clearly distinguish the function of reflection that is directed at critically assessing the validity of assumptions related to how we define and solve a problem from the function of reflection that is directed at critiquing core presuppositions. Moreover, Mezirow proposed that his own notion of reflection, which is the vital element in his theory of transformative learning, stresses, as well as the willingness to suspend immediate judgement in how we define and solve problems, 'how habits of expectations (meaning perspectives) affect reflective thought – as in problem posing – or how reflective thought might affect them – as in consciousness raising or psychotherapy' (Mezirow, 1991, pp. 101–102). Underlying Mezirow's point here is the important distinction between 'objective reframing' and 'subjective reframing' already encountered in Chapter 2. I shall return to this distinction shortly. For now I would like to hold on to the point that Mezirow's notion of critical reflection is explicitly associated with what he, following Habermas (1971), calls the '*emancipatory*' domain of learning. I shall say more about the differences between instrumental, communicative and emancipatory learning later in this chapter.

As already intimated, although strongly informed by critical theory, critical theory does not pervade Mezirow's work consistently and this is the case for two main reasons. First, like Dewey, Mezirow is concerned with how we define, describe, and solve a problem through the testing of validity claims (and not only with questioning core presuppositions). The second reason is that when discussing the questioning of premises or core presuppositions (or paradigmatic assumptions) he fluctuates in the extent to which he emphasises that critical reflection is essentially about identifying how structural relations of power distort experiences. Influenced by the psychoanalytical tradition (e.g. Gould, 1978), research on the development of dialectical thinking in adulthood (e.g. Basseches, 1984; Riegel, 1973), as well as constructivist psychology (Kelly, 1955), Mezirow does not always point to the linkages between the personal and the social that is so fundamental to critical theory (e.g. Freire, 1970; Fromm, 1941). Ideology critique, therefore, is not the only, and perhaps not even the principal, concern of his transformation theory.

We can thus differentiate two overlapping senses of critical reflection. The first links critical reflection to the testing of validity claims and the questioning of core presuppositions but focuses on the individual and his or her *personal* transformation. The second includes the testing of validity claims and the questioning of core presuppositions but is concerned principally with identifying structural forms of power, thereby revealing the relationships between the personal and the social. I will address these two perspectives separately. In this present chapter, I show how Mezirow's distinction between different *functions* of reflection and *types of learning* is useful for understanding what critical engagement in the scholarship of teaching looks like, while in the next chapter I will show how the notion of critical reflection in the scholarship of teaching is much enhanced when it also considers structural relations of power and ideology critique. Since there is considerable overlap between these two takes on critical reflection, it follows that we will encounter Mezirow's work in both chapters.

The different functions of reflection in Mezirow's transformative learning theory

Mezirow (1991) defines reflection as 'the process of critically assessing the content, process and premise(s) of our efforts to interpret and give meaning to an experience' (p. 104). Critical reflection may lead to transformative learning, and transformative learning, according to Mezirow, cannot occur without (critical) reflection. The terminology of content, process and premise reflection is not necessarily intuitive. What Mezirow means by these terms is wholly unrelated to the difference between the two basic domains of reflectivity in teaching I identified earlier: the content of our teaching (reflecting on our subject matter) and the process of teaching (examining the various practices, policies, aims and purposes associated with university teaching and learning). In this chapter we are concerned solely with the second (process-oriented) domain of reflectivity in teaching and it is argued that Mezirow's three discrete functions of reflection – on content, process and premise – can be usefully applied to this second domain. How then does Mezirow understand the difference between content, process and premise reflection?

Mezirow (1991) argued that: 'We may reflect on the *content* or description of the problem . . . , the *process* or method of our problem-solving, or the *premise(s)* upon which the problem is predicated' (p. 117, emphasis in original). Premise reflection 'involves becoming aware of *why* we perceive, think, feel or act as we do and of the reasons for and consequences of our possible habits of hasty judgements, conceptual inadequacy . . . ' (p. 108, emphasis in original). Premise reflection he continues 'may cause us to become critical of epistemic, social and psychological presuppositions' (Mezirow, 1991, p. 108). Premise reflection is thus of a higher order to either content or process reflection and calls into question core presuppositions or paradigmatic assumptions.

Having distinguished these three functions of reflection, Mezirow (1991) is in a position to distinguish two types of transformative learning. The first pertains to the transformation of what he calls 'meaning schemes' through content and process reflection. The second pertains to the transformation of what he calls 'meaning perspectives' through premise reflection. In making this distinction Mezirow is influenced by George Kelly's (1955) notion of a personal construct and a personal construct system. A personal construct is a meaning (or interpretation) scheme, such as the one colleagues and I elicited from participants in our study on conceptions of authenticity reported in Chapter 1. A personal construct system is a hierarchically structured network of personal constructs.

Meaning *schemes*, Mezirow (2000) says, are 'sets of immediate specific expectations, beliefs, feelings, attitudes, and judgments ...' (p. 18), more recently called 'points of view' (p. 18). Such a meaning scheme (or point of view) might be that I do not expect a student who entered higher education via alternative access routes to do well in my courses. Through content reflection I could first make this specific expectation or belief explicit to myself (as I might not consciously hold it) and through process reflection I could test its validity. Process reflection might involve observing how well the student is actually doing in my course, paying attention to things such as class participation, marks on assignments, and attendance. If he or she turns out to do well I should be prepared and motivated to revise my assumptions. Using Mezirow's language we would say that I then revise my meaning scheme (which is 'alternative access students do not do as well as other students').

Meaning *perspectives*, Mezirow says, are 'broad, generalized, orienting predispositions' (Mezirow, 2000, p. 17), more recently called 'habits of mind' (p. 17). Meaning perspectives (or habits of mind) refer to the larger frames of reference by which we interpret the world around us, which are supported by core presuppositions or premises that we take for granted. Our meaning schemes (specific expectations, beliefs or judgements) derive from, or are nested within, these larger meaning perspectives (just as a personal construct is nested within a construct system). For example, my meaning perspective may rest on the core presupposition, premise or fundamental construct that previous academic merit is the only really fair criterion for access to higher education (hence my expectation that a student who entered via alternative access routes would not do well in my courses). Through dialogue with friends interested in higher education issues, colleagues, students in my graduate higher education courses or by reading John Rawls's *A theory of justice*, I might one day be provoked to suddenly question what up to this point I considered to be an obvious truth – the only fair criterion for entry to higher education is previous attainment or academic merit! Up to this point it has never entered my mind to question this assumption, it was obviously true. Then I suddenly encounter the argument that, given the strong correlations between income, class, geographical location of the school and school achievement, systemic inequality in our society is actually perpetuated by higher education access policies that are based on previous success in high school. It is the first time that I actually think about the implication of my previous assumptions, which culminates in the perpetuation of systemic social inequality. Having become aware of these implications, I may revise my previous presupposition, which, according to Mezirow's theory, eventually leads to a transformation of my meaning perspective.

Transformative learning, therefore, involves content, process and premise reflection but reflection on premises (or core presuppositions) is central to empowerment and emancipation as it may lead to a more profound transformative experience. Had I engaged only in content and process reflection, and through a process of validity testing found my expectations to be invalid, I still would have experienced a transformation of a meaning scheme ('alternative access students do not do as well as other students'), but my meaning perspective would have remained unchallenged. Thus Mezirow (1991) argues that the most profound learning in adulthood happens when meaning perspectives become transformed through reflection on our core presuppositions.

Mezirow also distinguishes between two different kinds of premises or core presuppositions, a point that was left underexplored in his core text (Mezirow, 1991) but one that he addressed in later writing. In this more recent work, Mezirow (1998, 2000) distinguishes explicitly between objective and subjective reframing, the first referring to Critical Reflection on Assumptions (CRA) and the second to Critical *Self*-Reflection on Assumptions (CSRA). We encountered this distinction between the two forms of premise reflection in Chapter 2 when we referred to the learning experienced by the mature university student Rita. Objective reframing includes reflecting on assumptions underlying what is communicated to us ('narrative CRA', Mezirow, 1998) or in task-oriented problem-solving ('action CRA', Mezirow, 1998, inspired by action science as popularised by Argyris, Putnam & MacLain Smith, 1985). For example, we question the presuppositions underlying a news report we read in the paper or hear on the news, as in the case of narrative CRA, or we decide that the problem we were working on needs to be reframed, as in the case of action CRA.

A university teacher might experience objective reframing, for example, when the findings from a scientific study she carried out to better understand why students choose not to attend her lectures lead her to challenge widely held views within the department of the phenomenon of poor lecture attendance. The problem then needs to be redefined in light of this change in premises of why students do not attend lectures. In contrast, subjective reframing refers to questioning why I am prone to construing a problem in a certain way (that is according to my own habits of expectations). It pertains to critical reflection on one's *own* psychological and cultural assumptions, or premises, that undergird one's meaning perspectives, filter one's perceptions and hence limit one's experiences. To offer just three examples, a university teacher experiences subjective reframing when she becomes aware of how her need for authority in the classroom has been shaped by fear of being found out as an 'impostor'. Another university teacher experiences subjective reframing when after moving institutions he comes to realise how his previous conceptions of what constitutes good teaching were shaped by the norms and values espoused by his former department. Again another university teacher experiences subjective reframing when she recognises, questions and eventually overcomes her homophobia as a result of working with an openly gay research assistant during the summer months, over the course of which she gets to know him as a person. Such critical reflection on one's own core presuppositions or premises, Mezirow (1991) argued, can lead to 'emancipation from . . . forces that limit our options and our rational control over our lives but have been taken for granted or seen as beyond control' (p. 87).

How is all this theory on critical reflection relevant to the scholarship of teaching? As noted in the Introduction, I understand our engagement in the scholarship of teaching as an ongoing *transformative learning process*. This process is intimately bound up with us becoming more authentic and furthering the authenticity of students, thereby working not only towards a better world in which to *learn* and *teach* but, ultimately, towards a better *world*. Engaging in the scholarship of teaching, therefore, involves adopting a critically reflective and inquiring approach towards teaching, including reflecting on the practices, wider goals, social purposes and present policies of higher education (Atkinson, 2001; Cranton, 2011; Kreber, 2005a) and importantly, our *own* assumptions, viewpoints or perspectives on these. Mezirow (1991) argues that 'distorted assumptions', meaning those that we have uncritically assimilated and would find wanting if subjected to critical reflection, lead people 'to view reality in a way that arbitrarily limits what is included, impedes differentiation, lacks permeability or openness to other ways of seeing, or does not facilitate an integration of experience' (p. 118).

Such distorted assumptions were involved in all the examples cited earlier. Part of engaging in the scholarship of university teaching is for us to become aware of such distortions, test the validity of our assumptions and consider the question of why we adopted these assumptions to begin with. This reflective process leads us to construct a deeper understanding of issues as well as of ourselves and promotes a move towards greater authenticity (see also Cranton & Carusetta, 2004). Mezirow's distinction between three different functions of reflection (on content, process and premises), and between three types of learning (instrumental, communicative and emancipatory), is particularly helpful in developing this argument and for demonstrating what such reflective engagement in the scholarship of teaching might look like in practice. Both objective and subjective reframing are involved in this process, but the latter is essential to authenticity. It is the concrete application of transformative learning theory to our engagement in the scholarship of teaching I wish to turn to next.

A model of the scholarship of teaching based on critical reflectivity

The concept of reflection has received considerable attention within the field of teacher education (e.g. Calderhead, 1989; Hatton & Smith, 1995; Zeichner, 1986) and numerous studies on reflection have been carried out within higher education contexts (for reviews of some of this literature see for example Kane, Sandretto & Heath, 2002 or Kahn *et al.*, 2006). Most of these studies share with this book the assumption that teachers' engagement in reflection has a desirable impact on their practice and, by extension, the learning experiences of students. However, the notion of reflection underpinning them is typically not explicitly rooted within any larger theory of learning and development. Indeed, a distinctive feature of the scholarship of teaching model I discuss below is that by being firmly embedded in Mezirow's (1991, 2000) theory of transformative learning, the model explains how being reflective is linked to professional development in teaching (see also Cranton, 1996). It thereby makes explicit what other models of reflection (and models or definitions of the scholarship of teaching) often leave implicit. The model is furthermore proposed as a generic framework applicable to varied disciplinary contexts, in that the thematic questions that are raised in content, process and premise reflection can be tailored specifically to those issues that are considered relevant within particular disciplinary contexts. Huber and Morreale's (2002) observation that there are disciplinary styles in the scholarship of teaching characterised by distinct questions and methodological approaches seems relevant here. At the same time, the model encourages academics to reflect on the overarching aims and purposes of university teaching with the goal of developing a common rationale, thereby not staying constrained by disciplinary traditions and identities.

In previous work, colleagues and I applied some of the core elements of Mezirow's theory of transformative learning to the scholarship of teaching (Kreber, 1999, 2005b, 2006a,b; Kreber & Castleden, 2009; Kreber & Cranton, 2000). We showed how the three different functions of reflection and forms of learning inform academics' knowledge about teaching in three different domains. We also distinguished between two different types of teacher knowledge: what teachers know as a result of personal (or collective) teaching experience *and* what they know as a result of theory or research, or both. Below I discuss the model of the scholarship of university teaching that we developed, drawing on some of the teacher knowledge literature that seems especially relevant to the arguments presented. I start with the two types of teacher knowledge that are involved in the scholarship of teaching, arguing that each is furthered through critical reflectivity.

Types and domains of teacher knowledge

Fenstermacher (1994) usefully distinguishes between formal and practical teacher knowledge. Formal teacher knowledge refers to knowledge about teaching that is produced by educational researchers and, usually, is supposed to hold true across contexts. Practical teacher knowledge is the knowledge held by teachers and is local or contextually bound. Crucially, Fenstermacher argues that for something to count as *knowledge*, with regards to either formal or practical knowledge, it must be justified by the person making the claim to know. 'Such justification', he maintains, 'requires some notion of standards that the claims must meet before they can properly be regarded as knowledge' (Fenstermacher, 1994, p. 36). He then goes on to suggest two ways of justifying knowledge claims. The first is the *use of evidence*, a procedure typical for the formal knowledge domain but one which may extend also to the justification of knowledge claims in the practical knowledge domain in teaching. Take the claim that heavy reading assignments and testing discourage students from taking a deep approach to their learning. Fenstermacher argues that the evidence offered in the justification of this knowledge claim could be the perceived student performance under both conditions, students being exposed to lighter reading loads and fewer tests and students being exposed to heavy reading loads and a high number of tests.

The second form of justification of knowledge claims, and the one distinctive to the practical knowledge domain, in Fenstermacher's argument, is the development of good or grounded reasons. This form of justification Fenstermacher refers to as *practical reasoning*. Practical reasoning, which refers to reasoning within particular social contexts, he argues has both epistemic merit and addresses the moral dimension of teaching. In other words, practical reasoning may not only reveal the grounds for why a particular action was the most sensible approach to take but also that a particular action was the fair or the 'right' thing to do under the circumstances. Practical reasoning, therefore, extends to questions of value and ethics, a point I will return to later in this chapter and again in Chapter 7.

The scholarship of university teaching crosses over the domains of formal and practical teacher knowledge. Although most pedagogical inquiries academics pursue serve to inform either their own practice or that of their immediate or local community, some take this work one step further so as to inform an even wider audience (Ashwin & Trigwell, 2004). Ashwin and Trigwell refer to this third level of pedagogic investigation as *research*, while the work that informs one's local community (second level) they refer to as *scholarship*, and the work that principally informs oneself (first level) they refer to as a *scholarly reflective approach* to practice. In keeping with Fenstermacher (1994), we might call the knowledge generated through pedagogic research formal teacher knowledge. Formal knowledge refers to the codified knowledge that is available in the public domain. Such knowledge may be generated through either empirical–analytical or interpretive–hermeneutic methods. The knowledge that primarily informs oneself and/or one's local communities fits more comfortably with the notion of practical teacher knowledge.

Fenstermacher's (1994) main purpose was to show that 'practical knowledge' (p. 50), that is, the context-specific knowledge (about teaching) held by teachers, 'is a legitimate epistemological category, so long as we attach to it demands for justification or warrant in the same way such demands are attached to formal knowledge' (p. 50). Hence, practical knowledge is not inferior to formal knowledge so long as its claims are justified. In this book I discuss the scholarship of teaching as the pedagogical inquiries academic teachers themselves carry out within their own local contexts. While such inquiry shares features with the school-based teacher research movement (e.g. Cochran-Smith & Lytle, 1993; Stenhouse, 1983), I take a broader view on this. Practitioner-led inquiry to me principally means that academics take a critically reflective, inquiring and informed stance in relation to the policies, practices and processes, as well as the aims and purposes of university teaching and learning. On occasion, this inquiry will take on the form of teacher-led *research* that results in formal codified knowledge; however, many significant inquiries teachers pursue do not take on the form of fully fledged research projects. What is significant is that our inquiries lead us to think about our local practice in a new light, evoke within our communities alternative views of doing things, and thus raise the likelihood of us providing educational experiences that offer students the opportunity to grow into their authenticity. The process of students coming into their authenticity is facilitated by students learning simultaneously about the subject matter and themselves, as well as the world around them and how they can contribute to a re-making of this world.

In reference to Fenstermacher (1994), I suggest that academics' critically reflective learning about teaching (i.e. their engagement in the scholarship of teaching) contributes to, and is informed by, the two different types of knowledge he identified. Practical knowledge is located in academics' personal experience of teaching and is verified through either practical reasoning *or* the use of evidence. Weimer (2006) referred to this type of knowledge as 'the wisdom of practice' and in previous work I referred to this as 'experience-based knowledge' (e.g. Kreber, 2006a,b). Formal knowledge is associated with codified knowledge or theories about university teaching and is verified through the use of 'evidence' (I will return to the notion of 'evidence' in Chapter 7). Academics encounter this knowledge by reading the relevant literature, by attending research conferences, or by talking to a colleague who happens to know the literature well or is a researcher of teaching.

In earlier work I referred to formal knowledge as 'theory-based/research-based' knowledge. The reason I choose the somewhat clumsy expression 'theory-based/research-based' knowledge is that, although we can reasonably expect theories to be the outcome of in-depth investigations, these investigations are not necessarily of the empirical kind. In the humanities theories are often not empirically testable in the way they are in the sciences. Theories in the humanities are largely based on conceptual analysis or 'ideas' rather than 'research' in the traditional sense, where ideas (or rather 'hypotheses') require empirical substantiation in order to be deemed valid. As noted in Chapters 2 and 3, theories of higher education pedagogy that are grounded in philosophical inquiry, for example, the capabilities approach to higher education (e.g. Walker, 2006) or the concept of authentic being (e.g. Barnett, 2004a,b; 2007), can inform teaching and learning in higher education just as usefully as can empirical research findings in the field of psychology.

The scholarship of teaching model also distinguishes three different domains of teacher knowledge. It is these I wish to turn to next.

The different domains of teacher knowledge

When we think of the kinds of knowledge teachers should be concerned with, what typically springs to mind for most of us is the need to have good understanding of the subjects we teach. However, while obviously necessary, such content knowledge does not constitute a sufficient knowledge base for university teaching. It is also important to have a clear sense of:

A   appropriate or meaningful *aims, purposes and goals of education*, both with respect to specific students, courses and programmes and with respect to higher education more generally (originally, we had called this domain 'curricular knowledge', Kreber & Cranton, 2000);

B   forms of *learning and student development* that underlie the realisation of these aims, purposes and goals (originally, we had called this domain 'pedagogical knowledge', Kreber & Cranton, 2000);

C   *curricula and pedagogies* (i.e. teaching and assessment strategies) that are suitable for promoting students' learning and development in the direction of these aims, purposes and goals (originally, we had called this domain 'instructional knowledge', Kreber & Cranton, 2000).

These three domains are inextricably linked. What counts as worthwhile knowledge about learning and student development, and about appropriate curricula and pedagogies, depends crucially on the aims, purposes and goals we associate with the courses we teach, and the larger programmes these are part of. Without any sense of what higher education is for, what purpose it should serve in society, for whom, and in what ways we hope students will be affected by the experience of participating in higher education, our teaching would remain void of any substantive meaning. Engagement in the scholarship of teaching involves asking important questions such as: What role does higher education play in society? What qualities or dispositions should students have an opportunity to develop during their university years? Who should have a chance to participate (and succeed)? What do we mean by success?

Constructing knowledge in each of these three broad domains is essentially a process of inquiry that involves testing the validity claims associated with defining, describing and solving problems/issues we encounter in our practice and questioning underlying core presuppositions (i.e. it is a matter of engaging in content, process and premise reflection). Such inquiries are always informed by experience-based knowledge and they extend this knowledge. Often they are also informed by theory-based/research-based knowledge and at times they even extend theory-based/research-based knowledge. In previous studies I offered several examples of different inquiries that academics might pursue, dividing these into theory-based/research-based and experienced-based activities (Kreber, 2005b; Kreber & Castleden, 2009; Kreber & Cranton, 2000).

The point I would like to emphasise here is that it is the depth of the reflective processes underlying these inquiries that matters most to our professional learning and development, not the level of how formally we engage in these reflective processes. What matters is whether we engage in only content reflection, in process reflection or also in premise reflection. Carrying out a formal study on teaching and learning and publishing the results in a reputable journal does not necessarily mean that I will have a more profound professional growth experience than I would by engaging in informal inquiries. Engagement in informal inquires might involve regularly discussing teaching and learning with interested colleagues, reading good books or articles about teaching, being a mentor to a colleague, trying out new approaches in my teaching, leading a curriculum change initiative in my department, employing classroom assessment techniques as suggested by Cross and Steadman (1996), or carefully listening to students in order to get a sense of how they are doing, how they think and how they make sense of their world. Engagement in formal inquiry, only because it resembles 'research', makes me neither any more pedagogically skilled nor any more ethically aware as a teacher than less formal inquiry. Nor are my students necessarily any better supported in their learning and development if I become a researcher of teaching!

Of course, some formal inquiries that are presented at scholarship of teaching conferences, or published in journals, strike us as being exceptionally valuable. Often these inquiries challenge entrenched practices or assumptions, including our own. What moves us about this work is the nature of the problem (question) that was identified, the depth in which the authors/presenters engaged with this 'problem', and the extent to which they were able to use the insights they gained from their inquiry to inform their practice and, hence, support the learning and development of their students. As listeners or readers we discern that what is reported matters profoundly to the people who carried out the inquiry. We feel that the project was not just an academic exercise but instead was motivated by attaining the internal good of acting in the important interests of students. Underlying these studies is a willingness to reflect critically on teaching. These inquiries, therefore, often start out informally by teachers asking difficult or uncomfortable questions and then become more formal, in that data are collected and then analysed in more systematic and sophisticated ways. In these cases what is learned from the formal inquiry goes beyond what was possible through informal inquiry. Formal inquiries of this kind are being carried out at many campuses. If done well, and if communicated well, such formal inquiries not only inform a larger audience but serve to motivate and inspire others to become engaged in similar types of projects. But not all teacher-led research is like this.

How often do we read or listen to studies that leave us in a state of 'numbness'? There were clear goals, the methodology matched the research questions, analyses were carried out properly and presented clearly, and concluding comments followed logically from the reported findings. There was even an impressive up to date literature review! And still, these studies fail to inspire us. We cannot help but wonder about the significance of the results and the level of reflective critique involved (Glassick et al., 1997) and, crucially, the importance or weight of the problem that was addressed. Even more troubling is that these same inquiries often do not appear to have much inspired the people who carried them out. As listeners or readers we get a sense that this work is not really connected to their inner motives for teaching, and as a consequence, these stories do not touch us.

But if the problem that was addressed does not matter to them on a deeper personal level, what motivated these colleagues to devote a great deal of their time and effort to this work? The reason cannot be that these colleagues do not care about their teaching. Surely they would not do this time-consuming work if they did not care. I rather suspect that conceptions of the scholarship of teaching emphasising that this work, in order to be respected, should resemble 'research' encourages forms of engagement that make us, at times, lose sight of its internal goods. This can lead to an emphasis on proper procedure (on appropriate research technique) at the expense of considering the actual purposes of engaging in the activity. The widely held belief that the scholarship of teaching, in order to count within the academy, needs to be 'like research' is in fact a powerful ideology, and I shall return to this point in Chapter 8.

At this stage I would like to summarise the two main arguments of this present discussion. First, it is the depth of engagement in the critically reflective processes underlying the inquiry that makes the scholarship of teaching a profound activity, not how formally we engage in these reflective processes. Informal inquiry based on critical engagement in premise reflection is likely to involve a more profound professional learning and development experience than formal inquiry that remains at the level of content and/or process reflection. Formal inquiry into teaching and learning, or teacher-led research, *can* contribute greatly to creating a better world in which to learn, teach and live but this hinges on a willingness to engage in a questioning of presuppositions or premises. Then again, informal inquiries often can contribute as much. Second, as we engage in critically reflective inquiry both experienced-based knowledge and theory-based/research-based knowledge are involved. In the next section I discuss what the questioning of knowledge claims through content, process and premise reflection might look like.

Questioning knowledge claims through three functions of reflection

Content, process and premise reflection all have a distinct function. Through content reflection we consider the assumptions underlying how we define and describe a problem. Through process reflection we consider how we address or solve the problem. Through premise reflection we question underlying core presuppositions. Figure 5.1 offers a visual illustration of how these three reflective functions relate to each of the three knowledge domains discussed earlier.

Over the years I have interpreted Mezirow's three different functions of reflection in slightly different ways (Kreber, 2006b; Kreber & Castleden, 2009; Kreber & Cranton, 2000). While I find Mezirow's statement that 'We may reflect on the *content* or description of the problem . . . , the *process* or method of our problem-solving, or the *premise(s)* upon which the problem is predicated' (p. 117, emphasis in original) clear enough, his elaboration of what content and process reflection, in particular, involve is rather more ambiguous. In content reflection, Mezirow (1991) argues 'we assess what we have defined as our options in order to make the most appropriate next move' (p. 107), while in process reflection we focus 'on *how* we perform these functions of perceiving, thinking, feeling or acting and an assessment of our efficacy of performing them' (p. 108, emphasis

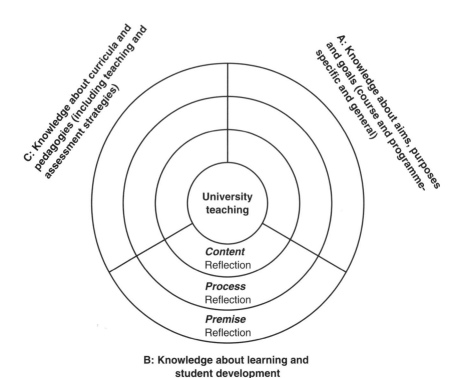

Figure 5.1 The scholarship of teaching model (adapted from Kreber & Cranton, 2000).

in original). The fact that his definitions allow for more than one interpretation, however, can also be viewed positively, as it leads to a richer tapestry of reflective questions that can be posed. I offer the questions below as one possible interpretation of Mezirow's three reflective functions in the specific context of learning about teaching.

Mezirow (1981, 1991, 1998) has developed several taxonomies over the years with the goal of clarifying different aspects of his theory, of which the classification into content, process and premise reflection is only one example. These taxonomies can at times seem overly complex, rigid and stifling. Do people really think like that when they are engaged in their day-to-day professional activities or personal lives? (E.g. 'Let's see, it's approaching five o'clock and I'm on track with my content reflection but I still have to fit in my half hour of process reflection today, and I plan to catch up with my premise reflection tomorrow afternoon . . .'). Since such a view is clearly absurd, I should make clear what the questions below are not. These questions are not meant as recipes, prescriptions or a workout regimen of what to do in order to become an authentic teacher ('Practice them twice a day and you will be pleased with the results at the end of the year!'). Instead they are principally analytical and heuristic tools that can guide us in our deliberations as teachers. Each of the questions is to be understood as a broad theme under which much more detailed questions pertaining to the same theme could, and should, be asked by teachers working in particular contexts (and with particular students). The value of the scholarship of teaching model is that it brings different aspects of our practice, and our personal views on these aspects, into focus and encourages us to examine them. In particular, it shows the important distinction between reflection on content and process and reflection on premises. Below I address each of the three reflective functions separately with reference to each of the three knowledge domains identified earlier (A, B and C).

In *content reflection* we describe and define the problem or issue we are concerned with. To me this means asking questions under the following themes:

A   What are the aims, purposes and goals of my (our) teaching, in relation to this particular class or course or programme and in relation to higher education more generally?

B   What do I (we) expect or demand of students in terms of the learning that they need to master? What are the challenges for different students? What are their present ways of knowing and being, and what knowing and being do we find desirable?

C   What curricula and pedagogies are needed to support students in their learning and development?

In *process reflection* we focus on how, and how well, we are doing. To me this means asking questions about how well we are doing with regards to supporting students and employing certain curricula and pedagogies. However, it also includes asking questions about the value and quality of the issues we identified in content reflection. Questions could be asked under the following themes:

A   How do I (we) know that these are good aims, goals and purposes? How meaningful are these aims, goals and purposes?

B   How do I (we) know that these ways of knowing and being are important? How well do I (we) support students in developing these ways of knowing and being? Who is doing well, who is not doing well?

C   How do I (we) know that these curricula and pedagogies (and specific teaching and assessment strategies) we decided on are good ones? How good am I (are we) at implementing them?

Premise reflection, finally, is about questioning core presuppositions. To me this means asking questions that address the following themes:

A   Why did I (we) decide on these aims, goals and purposes? Are they equally
      relevant for all learners? What might be other possibilities/alternatives?
B   Why do I (we) believe these ways of knowing and being are important? Are
      they equally relevant for all learners? Do all learners have an equal chance to
      develop them? Why do I (we) expect learners to behave in these particular
      ways? What might be other possibilities/alternatives?
C   Why did I (we) decide on these curricula and pedagogies? What considera-
      tions were driving these decisions? How inclusive are these curricula and
      pedagogies? Are they appropriate for all students? What might be other
      possibilities/alternatives?

Pat Hutchings (2000) introduced a taxonomy of questions scholars of
teaching might ask, distinguishing between 'what is?', 'what works?', and 'what's
possible/what could be?' questions. These seem to be broadly compatible with
the questions posed by content, process and premise reflection. Together with
Lee Shulman, she also suggested that academics ask questions such as: 'What are
our students really learning? What do they understand deeply? What kinds of
human beings are they becoming – intellectually, morally, in terms of civic
responsibility? How does our teaching affect that learning, and how might it do
so more effectively?' (Hutchings & Shulman, 1999, electronic version). These
questions resonate particularly well with the position taken in this book. I am
suggesting, though, that as we are trying to answer these questions we also be
guided by the different functions and domains of reflection discussed above. This
implies that as scholars of teaching we cast a critical eye also on our *own* assumptions, rather than explore teaching and learning as if these existed as 'objective
entities' unaffected by interpretation, or personal and social construction. Essentially, engaging in content, process and particularly premise reflection means to
question the assumptions, beliefs and values we take for granted, which is a key
element in transformative learning.

So far I have argued that it is through critical reflection on content, process and
premises that we examine the validity of our claims to knowledge. Knowingly or
unknowingly, what we identify as meaningful educational aims, goals and purposes of education, significant student learning and development, and appropriate curricula and pedagogies is all based on the knowledge claims we make.
Should reflection call the validity of these claims into question, the potential for
revising our assumptions arises. If assumptions or core presuppositions are
revised, transformative learning has occurred. In the case of revised premises, the
transformative experience is more profound, as such a change leads to a reconstruction of our frame of reference or, in Mezirow's language, a transformation
in our 'meaning perspective' (Mezirow, 1991) or 'habits of mind' (Mezirow,
2000). In the case of specific assumptions, beliefs or values being challenged and
changed as a result of content and process reflection, we experience a shift in particular 'meaning schemes' (Mezirow, 1991) or 'points of view' (Mezirow, 2000),
while our overall frame of reference, supported by unchallenged presuppositions,

remains intact. Content, process and premise reflection are not sequential stages, which is to say that premise reflection does not hinge on being preceded by content or process reflection.

We have seen that reflectivity, and transformative learning, in the scholarship of teaching may occur at the level of content and process reflection *and/or* at the level of questioning premises. What we have not yet explored are the forms of learning that these three reflective processes involve, and how engagement in these forms of learning is linked to cultivating the virtues of truthfulness, courage, justice, phronesis and authenticity. It is these important linkages I turn to next.

Reflection, forms of learning and the development of the virtues

In content reflection we consider how we define and describe a problem or issue, thereby making our assumptions explicit. By asking questions such as 'What are the aims, purposes and goals of my/our teaching, in relation to these students, this particular class or course, this programme, and higher education generally?' or 'What do we expect/demand of students in relation to the learning that they need to master?', we define problems in a particular way. Process reflection builds on this but turns to problem-solving. Here we might ask 'How do we know that these are good aims, goals and purposes?' or 'How well do we support students in developing these ways of knowing and being?' In order to be able to answer these questions we need to engage in two very different kinds of 'problem-solving': instrumental learning and communicative learning (Mezirow, 1991; Habermas, 1971). In the case of premise reflection we challenge core presuppositions. We might ask 'Why did we decide on these aims, goals or purposes?' 'Why do we expect students to behave in these particular ways?' 'Why does the department encourage these particular ways of assessment?' When the premises that are revised through reflection are our own, we are involved in *subjective reframing*; when the premises we question have been communicated to us by others we are involved in *objective reframing*. Reframing is associated with emancipatory learning. Instrumental, communicative and emancipatory learning are guided by different intentions. Below I discuss the distinct nature of each of these three kinds of learning.

In instrumental learning our objective is to control our environment and thus to manipulate and predict the outcomes of events. Instrumental learning is based on a technical interest, characterised by means–end reasoning. An assumption, belief or assertion is verified by subjecting it to the empirical–analytical method. The key question we ask in instrumental learning is 'What are the most effective means by which to achieve particular ends?'. Aristotle referred to activities that are based on this type of thinking as *poiesis* (or production). Production pertains to the activity of making or bringing about a specified end. The cognitive power underlying production is a form of technical expertise or 'techne', which Aristotle identified as an intellectual virtue. The activity of making or producing is concerned with technical judgements. The question 'How well do we support students in developing these ways of knowing and being?', for example, fits into this category. Instrumental learning is associated principally with content and process reflection. We can refer to this activity as '*objective framing*'.

Communicative learning is the learning principally associated with the activity Aristotle called *praxis*. Praxis refers to acting, relating and communicating with others. Unlike production, praxis has no end outside itself – the end of praxis is simply to relate or act well. Communicative learning, too, is associated with content and process reflection. Key questions are not 'Is this effective?' or 'Does it work?' as in instrumental learning, but 'What do we mean?' and 'Which means and ends are worth pursuing?'. Communicative learning, therefore, is implicated in making moral judgements. An assertion or belief is deemed valid if agreement or consensus on it can be reached within a community, which itself is governed by certain socially constructed traditions and cultural views. We might say that communicative learning is associated with '*inter-subjective framing*'. The cognitive power needed for praxis is practical judgement or 'phronesis', which Aristotle identified as another intellectual virtue. The question 'How do we know that these are good aims, goals and purposes?' fits into this category. Communicative learning is associated with an interest in furthering mutual understanding based on agreed upon norms. This practical interest is informed by existing norms and traditions but does not concern itself with the question of how these norms and traditions have come about. When Habermas argues that '...in grasping the genesis of the tradition from which it proceeds and on which it turns back, reflection shakes the dogmatism of life-practices' (Habermas, cited in Dunne, 1993, p. 183), he points to the emancipatory and critical potential of reflection. In his earlier work, he saw emancipatory learning as a third domain, alongside to the instrumental and the communicative.

Following Habermas's (1971) early work, Mezirow (1981) distinguishes three forms of learning. Differentiating between communicative and emancipatory learning, he argues that important aspects of adult learning do not occur on the basis of inter-subjective understanding within a given social context defined by certain norms and traditions but involve a critical analysis of how these norms and conditions, and our ways of thinking and feeling, have come to be. It is this critical analysis that underlies emancipatory learning. Such a critical analysis moves beyond pure validity testing to a deeper level of transformation. The key question posed by emancipatory learning is 'How have these norms, these feelings, these values, these traditions and so forth developed and how do they influence our thinking and practice?' The nature of knowledge that results from this form of reflection is empowerment or emancipation and the cognitive power that brings it about is a 'critically inspired phronesis' (Flyvbjerg, 2001; Kreber, 2010c). Such critically inspired phronesis can also be associated with the virtue of authenticity. The activity itself is one of personal or *subjective reframing*. Underlying emancipatory learning is reflection on personal premises (Mezirow, 1990). Questions such as 'Why do we believe in these aims, goals and purposes?' 'Why do we believe these ways of knowing and being are important for students to develop? 'Why did we make these decisions about curricula and pedagogies?' 'What considerations were driving these decisions?' 'Where did these come from?' 'Why do we assume that these curricula and pedagogies are equally relevant for all learners?' 'What are other possibilities/alternatives?' clearly fit into this category. While this distinction between instrumental, communicative and emancipatory learning seems fairly straightforward, Habermas changed his views by the early 1980s and Mezirow incorporated these changes into his own theory. The implications of this I briefly outline below.

By the early 1980s, Habermas (1983) no longer conceives of critique as a third interest that is separate from the technical and the practical as he did in his earlier work (Habermas, 1971). Instead he envisages critical reflection to become an inherent part of people's lifeworld where important decisions about how to live together as a society are reached. Through a practice characterised by 'communicative action', validity claims are now tested on the basis of different discourses (for example, the theoretical, practical and aesthetic), which correspond to the three knowledge domains he had identified in his earlier work. This entailed a fusion not only of the practical domain with critical discourse but a fusion of the instrumental domain with critical discourse. It is for this reason that Mezirow (1998, 2000) eventually decides to place the notion of objective and subjective *reframing* (i.e. critique) within both the instrumental and communicative domains. In other words, both the instrumental and communicative domains now offer the potential for emancipatory learning.

As an example of emancipatory learning within the instrumental domain, Brookfield (2000) evokes the image of a person involved in trying to understand how the scientific method was socially and politically created and how it came to hold its present powerful status in our minds. Earlier in this chapter I offered the example of a teacher who, based on a scientific study she carried out, challenged views that were widely held within her department. There are, however, two key differences between these two examples: first, for Brookfield, critique (or emancipatory learning) is always of necessity subjective reframing (or *self*-reflection), as this is how he understands the very notion of ideology critique (a point I will return to in the following chapter). In my example, the teacher challenges assumptions that had been communicated by others in her department; hence the issue is one of objective reframing. Second, the question Brookfield poses can actually not be addressed through instrumental learning but only through communicative learning. In my example, the teacher carried out a scientific study, by definition an example of instrumental learning. Why should this be relevant? I suggest that four conclusions follow from this.

First, critically reflective inquiry into matters of teaching and learning may take place exclusively on the basis of content and process reflection within either the instrumental or communicative domain of learning. Second, in the case of premise reflection, or questioning of core presuppositions, such inquiry takes place on a deeper level and is associated with emancipatory learning. Third, premise reflection within the instrumental domain may occasionally occur by drawing on instrumental learning approaches (as in my own example above) although communicative approaches would be more likely (as in Brookfield's example). Fourth, the questioning of premises or core presuppositions can be a matter of either subjective or objective reframing. Table 5.1 summarises these observations.

Lewis Elton (2000b) once argued that the scholarship of teaching is not so much about *doing things better* but rather about *doing better things*. I suggest that content, but especially process, reflection in instrumental learning leads us to do

Table 5.1 The relationships between different kinds of reflection, kinds of learning and the virtues

What kind of reflective activity are we engaged in?	What kind of learning is involved?	What is the nature of the knowledge?
Making (*poiesis*)	**Instrumental**	**Expertise**
Principally content and process reflection	What are the most effective means to achieve particular ends?	Technical judgements Virtues: • 'techne'
'Objective Framing'	*Doing things better*	• 'truthfulness' (here 'objective truth/ accuracy').
Acting, relating and communicating (praxis)	**Communicative**	**Practical knowledge/ wisdom**
Content and process reflection	Which means and ends are worth pursuing?	Moral judgements Virtues: • 'phronesis'
'Inter-subjective Understanding/Framing'	*Doing better things/doing the right things*	• 'justice' • 'truthfulness' (here 'honesty').
Reframing *Premise reflection* *'Subjective **Reframing**' and 'Objective **Reframing**'*	**Emancipatory** (*extends to both the Communicative and Instrumental domains*) How have norms and knowledge of what is considered true or right developed and how do they influence our practice and/or our consciousness? *Doing the right things better*	**Empowerment** Emancipatory moral judgements Virtues: • 'critically inspired phronesis' • 'courage' • 'justice' • 'truthfulness' (here 'authenticity').

things better, while process and premise reflection in communicative learning lead us to do better things, or we might say *the 'right' things*. Clearly, though, engagement in the scholarship of teaching should be about 'doing the right things better', which ultimately means that we will need to be engaged also in premise reflection and all three forms of learning.

Table 5.1 also associates the different forms of learning with the virtues we encountered in Chapter 4. The virtue of 'truthfulness' is linked to all three forms of learning; however, it carries a different meaning in each. In instrumental learning truthfulness is more accurately interpreted as 'objective truth' or 'accuracy', in communicative learning as 'honesty', and in emancipatory learning as 'authenticity'. The virtue of 'justice', or fairness, is implied in both communicative and emancipatory learning in that we are concerned with arriving at fair decisions after having considered different points of view. The virtue of courage is most clearly associated with emancipatory learning as calling into question and revising presuppositions involves risk. The development of the virtue of phronesis is essential to both communicative and emancipatory learning (and phronesis will concern us again in Chapter 7). Truthfulness, justice, courage, phronesis and authenticity, I argued, are fundamental to the scholarship of teaching.

However, a sixth virtue, that of 'techne' now also appears to play a role in the scholarship of teaching. 'Techne', as we saw earlier, is associated with instrumental learning. While 'techne' indeed has its part in the scholarship of teaching, it is important to remind ourselves that a practice is 'clearly never just a set of practical skills...' (MacIntyre, 2007, p. 193). A conceptualisation of the scholarship of teaching that is exclusively based on 'techne' diminishes the scholarship of teaching to a set of techniques. By extension, such a view implies that what we should be mainly concerned with is the application of certain means in order to bring about predetermined ends, be this in the process of inquiry into teaching or in the process of teaching itself. Such a view ignores the fact that the scholarship of teaching to a large extent is a *practical* (and not just a productive) activity that involves making moral judgements and engaging in critique. Moreover, engagement in the scholarship of teaching, conceived of as a transformative learning process that is intimately bound up with becoming more authentic, is ultimately aimed at supporting students in their authenticity. Hence we can speak of authenticity *in* and *through* teaching. Helping students develop the capabilities of '*Practical reason; Educational resilience; Knowledge and imagination; Learning dispositions; Social relations and integrity; Respect, dignity and recognition; Emotional integrity, and Bodily integrity*' (Walker, 2006, p. 127) that will support them in attaining their own potential of being is surely not so much a matter of 'techne' than it is of 'phronesis' (and also 'critically inspired phronesis').

Final comment

Critical reflectivity is an essential attribute of scholarship (Andresen, 2000). This chapter focused on the role of reflectivity in the justification of knowledge claims in relation to teaching. I distinguished different functions (content, process and premise) and domains (aims, purposes and goals of education; learning and student development; curricula and pedagogies) of reflection. To reflect, in essence, means to think carefully about something, to examine knowledge claims or simply to carry out an inquiry. Although inquiries can be either formal or informal, what really matters in the end is not the degree of how formally we engage in the inquiry but how deeply we engage in the reflective process underpinning the inquiry. I also distinguished between two types of teacher knowledge (experience-based and theory-based/research-based). Critically reflective engagement in teaching (or 'the scholarship of teaching') is always informed by experience-based knowledge and extends this knowledge. Often the scholarship of teaching is also informed by theory-based/research-based knowledge and at times it even extends this knowledge. Finally I distinguished three forms of learning associated with the scholarship of teaching (the instrumental, the communicative and the emancipatory) and showed how these help us cultivate the virtues that are internal to practices.

Arendt (2003) emphasised the need for humans 'to stop and think' and to train the imagination to go 'visiting'. Such visiting of different possible viewpoints is fundamental to inquiry and critical reflection. This means that we take an interest in the happenings around us, engage in dialogue, feel a responsibility to inform ourselves, and, after careful consideration of alternative viewpoints, stand up for what we believe to be true. This is the mark of authenticity and it is what critical engagement in the scholarship of teaching essentially is about. In the next chapter I will turn to the linkages between critical engagement in the scholarship of teaching and students' learning and development. Arguing principally from a critical theory position, I will demonstrate that the challenges associated with moving towards greater authenticity include recognising power relations and overcoming hegemonic assumptions and that these challenges are the same for teachers and students.

Chapter 6

Recognising power

Introduction

Much of the previous chapter focused on the internal reasoning processes of academics, a freeing of minds that brings about awareness of alternatives to our habitual ways of thinking about teaching and learning. In this context we encountered Mezirow's (1991) distinction between three distinct functions of critical reflection (reflection on content, process and premise), three different forms of learning (instrumental, communicative and emancipatory) and two types of reframing (objective and subjective reframing). The purpose of Chapter 5 was to illustrate what 'critical reflectivity', an essential attribute of scholarship (e.g. Andresen, 2000; Glassick *et al.*, 1997), might look like in the context of university teaching. Drawing on Mezirow (1991), I suggested that critically reflective engagement in the scholarship of teaching may lead to two kinds of transformative learning: the transformation of specific assumptions, expectations or beliefs we hold with respect to teaching and learning and/or the more profound transformation of broad frames of reference or meaning perspectives. The former occurs when through content or process reflection these specific assumptions turn out to be invalid; the latter occurs when we become aware of 'distorted' premises or core presuppositions that underlie what we think, feel and do. Critical reflection on premises or core presuppositions involves emancipatory learning, which leads us to envisage alternatives to our present ways of understanding. When our premises or core presuppositions are transformed, such emancipatory learning liberates us from constraints previously held assumptions had placed on our options of how we experience and engage with the world. Implied in the argument was that such a reframing of premises involves a process of becoming more *authentic*.

In Chapter 5 I also showed how critically reflective inquiry into matters of teaching and learning helps to cultivate the virtues that authentic engagement in the scholarship of teaching entails. These virtues, employed and exercised through the process of critical inquiry, I argued with MacIntyre (2007), connect us with the internal goods or values of the social practice we call 'the scholarship of teaching'. The goods or values that we come to appreciate through our participation in this social practice include the enjoyment, achievement or satisfaction we experience by:

- inquiring into significant questions in relation to teaching and learning;
- deepening our understanding of these issues;
- growing into ourselves and becoming critically aware of the inner motives that guide us in this work;
- doing what is in the important interests of students; and thus
- contributing to the betterment of teaching and learning, and, by extension, to a fairer and more compassionate world (see Table 4.1).

In Chapter 2 I had argued that the essential purpose of the scholarship of teaching is to serve the important interests of students. Calling on the work of Habermas, Heidegger, Nussbaum and Sen, I interpreted 'important interests' as those fundamental human needs that must be satisfied for humans to flourish. From this premise I concluded that serving the important interests of students is a key function of education, a moral obligation, and, at heart, a social justice issue. I further argued that the students' fundamental interests can be captured in the notion of 'authenticity'. In the same chapter I also outlined what it might look like when students move towards greater authenticity, drawing on the three perspectives considered in this book – the existential, the critical and the communitarian – thereby emphasising the multidimensional meaning associated with the notion of authenticity.

In this present chapter I would like to draw a closer link between the notion of critical reflectivity and the essential purpose of the scholarship of teaching. Revisiting this purpose works to remind us that what we ultimately aim for is not just freedom from 'distorted' assumptions in relation to teaching and learning but emancipatory *practices* that serve the important interests of students. Emancipatory or liberatory practices, therefore, refer to those teaching approaches that foster the students' authenticity. Given the above considerations, we might then also say that engagement in the scholarship of teaching implies that both teachers and students become implicated in a process of transformative learning. Transformative learning, in essence, is a process of questioning and critique, of redefinition and reconstruction, in short a process of moving towards greater authenticity.

While the previous chapter offered an illustration of the different functions of reflection (on content, process and premises), the present chapter concentrates on critical *self*-reflection on premises (i.e. core presuppositions) and draws more firmly on the critical theory tradition. The focus is still on academics' engagement in the scholarship of teaching but I also show what it looks like when students engage in critical self-reflection, as it is *their* authenticity that we are ultimately concerned with. Argued from the critical theory tradition, teachers and students experience the same two interrelated challenges. One is learning to recognise how relations of power can distort experiences. The other is learning to recognise and challenge 'so-called hegemonic assumptions'. Hegemonic assumptions are practices and beliefs we embrace without realising that these same assumptions work against our own interests in the long term (Brookfield, 2000, 2005). I suggest that unacknowledged power relations are pervasive in higher education and also affect our teaching and the learning of students. To be clear, my point in this chapter is not to suggest that authentic engagement with the scholarship of university teaching is *exclusively* about critiquing ideologies. Nor do I intend to argue that students' growing into their authenticity is *exclusively* a matter of them learning to engage in ideology critique. My reason for now adding a more politicised (i.e. *critical*) view of critical reflection to our previous discussion is that power is always and inevitably present, although its presence is rarely acknowledged. Recognising the subtle ways in which power operates and legitimises certain ideas and practices over others can therefore enrich our engagement with the scholarship of teaching. Moreover, critical theory's central concern with both critiquing and improving the world brings to the fore another vital theme of this book, namely that through authentic engagement in the scholarship of teaching we work towards greater social justice and equality *in* and also *through* higher education. These observations now require some elaboration. In developing my case that critical theory can helpfully inform the scholarship of teaching, I will review some of the previous arguments made in this book and show their connections. I shall begin by revisiting what we have come to understand about student authenticity in Chapter 2, drawing also on some of the concepts introduced in the previous chapter.

Authenticity in relation to students revisited

Each of the three perspectives on authenticity discussed in Chapter 2 – the *existential*, the *critical* and the *communitarian* – is concerned with the *being* of the student. This *being* perspective is different from the 'correspondence view' of authenticity (Splitter, 2009). As I pointed out in the Introduction and in subsequent discussions, although clearly different, the 'being' conception of authenticity and the 'correspondence' conception of authenticity are not incompatible. The principal challenge for teachers espousing a 'correspondence view' of authenticity is how to make learning tasks *correspond* most closely to problems students might encounter in the 'real world', or those tackled by actual scientists or scholars in the field, and how to promote students' intellectual mastery of these learning tasks. The principal challenge for teachers espousing a 'being' conception of authenticity is how to help students grow into their authenticity thereby achieving their own full potential of being. As was summarised in Table 2.1, promoting the authenticity of students implies helping students realise the importance of learning for themselves (Entwistle, 2009; Entwistle & McCune, 2009) and grasping a subject in their *own* way (Kreber, 2009). For this to happen the subject needs to be perceived as meaningful and relevant so that students are able to make connections between what they are learning and their personal lives. Pedagogical practices associated with the correspondence view include involving students in what we might call 'authentic conversations' about the subject, such that they learn the ways of thinking and practising distinctive to this field, debate issues that scientists or scholars still grapple with, and come to appreciate why these issues are important and how they matter to their personal lives. It would seem then that there is some overlap in the pedagogical practices employed by advocates of the 'being' and 'correspondence' conceptions of authenticity. However, as we saw in Chapters 1 and 2, authenticity has also more profound meanings attached to it, which the existential, critical and communitarian perspectives bring to the surface.

Students who grow into their authenticity do not only come to know more, but they come to know differently than they did before. As they become 'disencumbered' from other voices (Barnett, 2007) they become authors of their own lives (Baxter Magolda, 1999). Self-authorship entails not only that students develop intellectually but also that they gain in personal and relational maturity. Moving towards greater authenticity entails that students develop an awareness of their own unique possibilities, including envisaging alternatives to their present ways of meaning-making. This requires that they develop an awareness of how the beliefs, habits and expectations they have acquired, or their present views on what is possible for them, might have limited their choices up to now. The existential and critical perspectives thus suggest that fostering students' authenticity involves encouraging students to engage in critical reflection and critical *self*-reflection. In addition, and as suggested by the communitarian perspective, fostering authenticity means helping students understand themselves as members of a wider social community towards which they feel a commitment and responsibility.

Another key difference between the learning associated with the 'being' conception of authenticity and the learning associated with the 'correspondence' conception is that between subjective and objective reframing. The 'being' conception, by definition, is associated with *subjective reframing*, stimulated by critical *self*-reflection on assumptions (Mezirow, 1998). Central to this process of subjective reframing is becoming aware of how assumptions or core presuppositions that were uncritically assimilated at an earlier age have powerful consequences for how we think, feel, perceive and act in the present. Learning in the context of the 'correspondence' conception is likely to lead to a deeper understanding of the issues the students are studying, in that it challenges their preconceptions of a problem or how a problem is to be solved. However, such learning is typically not intended to encourage consideration of 'how habits of expectations (meaning perspectives) affect reflective thought – as in problem posing – or how reflective thought might affect them – as in consciousness raising or psychotherapy' (Mezirow, 1991, pp. 101–102). Put differently, learning that is broadly associated with the 'correspondence' conception is mostly about *objective reframing*, rather than *subjective reframing*. Objective reframing leads to a deeper learning of subject matter, unquestionably a vital goal of higher education. We are reminded of the mature university student Rita (see Chapter 2) who learns to think and write according to the conventions of literary criticism. Subjective reframing is involved when students relate what and how they are learning to who they are, and who they are becoming. Rita experiences subjective reframing when she questions why higher education is really important to her and, as a result of this process, eventually discovers her own voice and envisages new possibilities for herself. We might say that subjective reframing is about 'becoming', objective reframing is about 'enhancing one's knowledge'. When students move towards greater authenticity in the context of higher education both forms of reframing are implicated in this process, but subjective reframing is central.

Subjective reframing as critical *self*-reflection

An example of students' subjective reframing and, therefore, of a change in meaning perspective or personal core presuppositions, is offered by Perry's (1970) observations of how undergraduate students change their epistemic assumptions. Epistemic assumptions refer to the beliefs we hold about the nature, limits and certainty of knowledge. Perry's research led him to conclude that there are four broad stages (divided into nine positions) of intellectual development, each characterised by specific assumptions students hold about the nature, limits and certainty of knowledge. As students move through the four stages (Dualism, Multiplicity, Relativism and Commitment) they develop increasingly more sophisticated assumptions about what knowledge is, where it is located and how it is justified. Comparable findings were reported in the research programmes of Baxter Magolda (1992) and King and Kitchener (1994). For example, Perry's first stage, Dualism (or 'received knowledge') is characterised by the following three assumptions students hold: first, all problems are solvable; second, there are either right or wrong answers to these problems; and third, experts have the right answers and if they do not it is just a matter of time before they will. The fourth stage, Commitment (or 'constructed knowledge'), by contrast, is characterised by very different assumptions: first, knowledge depends on reasoned argument or evidence; second, there are no right or wrong answers as such but problems need to be considered within the contexts in which they arise; and third, knowledge itself is constructed through reflection and reference to the knowledge of others as well as one's own experience.

Perry's model suggests that the intellectual stage a student has reached serves as a frame of reference or filter for how experiences are interpreted. Each stage, therefore, is characterised by personal core presuppositions informing the student's epistemic meaning perspective. Notwithstanding the criticism that can be levelled against linear stage models such as Perry's (for alternatives see, for example, the work of George Vaillant or Paul Baltes as reviewed in Bee, 2003), there are still important insights to be gained from this research. Students who believe, for example, that first, knowledge is a matter of having opinions, second, all of us have the right to our own opinion and third, all opinions, therefore, are equally valid (assumptions associated with Perry's second stage of intellectual development, Multiplicity) will have trouble in academic learning situations where they are expected to construct and present an actual argument and make their reasoning processes explicit. There is some evidence also that students whose thinking processes are characteristic of the higher stages of the Perry model are more likely to adopt deep approaches to learning (e.g. Entwistle & Ramsden, 1983).

Apart from the influences epistemic assumptions exert on academic learning, our epistemic assumptions also influence how we make sense of the world more generally. For example, individuals whose thinking is characterised by either Dualism or Multiplicity are more likely to accept uncritically what they hear on the radio or see on television, let alone the prejudices and ill-informed opinions of those with whom they associate. Moving towards greater authenticity involves coming to appreciate that knowledge is constructed, contextual and based on reasoned arguments and/or evidence.

I used Perry's model of intellectual development (i.e. epistemic cognition) as just one *example* of how we might think of a meaning perspective. However, the epistemic assumptions we hold are not the only filters we habitually apply in the process of giving meaning to our experiences. In his earlier work Mezirow (1991) originally distinguished three different meaning perspectives. These included next to the *epistemic* meaning perspective, also the *psychological* and the *socio-cultural/linguistic* meaning perspectives. These three meaning perspectives are broadly related to the various theoretical traditions that inform Mezirow's theory of transformative learning examined in the previous chapter. Knowledge of Gould's (1978) work on psychotherapy led him to identify the psychological meaning perspective. This meaning perspective is associated with any thoughts, feelings and perceptions we have developed regarding our self-confidence, self-efficacy, self-concept, and so forth. It is easy to see how students' psychological meaning perspective plays a crucial role in how they experience learning situations and how it will affect their academic aspirations. I will provide just two examples. Stefanie experiences strong anxiety in class discussions because during her first year at university she internalised a view of herself that she is not as capable or intelligent as her peers. Everyone else in her social theory and literature courses sounds like Judith Butler or Michel Foucault; it makes her feel really stupid. She feels she is better off not to pursue a graduate degree, and avoids choosing more advanced courses during her undergraduate degree, even though she actually is interested in the topics on offer. In response to earlier events Pascal internalised the view that he is not a good public speaker and that people will not take him seriously. He approaches oral exams, presentations to groups and class discussions with considerable anxiety. In many public speaking situations he gets nervous, is not able to concentrate well and then not able to articulate clearly and demonstrate his understanding, which leads to frequent misjudgement of his knowledge of the material. Moving toward greater authenticity for both Stefanie and Pascal would involve becoming aware of and confronting these 'distorted' views and then replacing them with beliefs about themselves that do not hinder but support their moving towards greater authenticity. This is not to say that this would be easy, in either case!

In identifying the *socio-cultural/linguistic* meaning perspective Mezirow was inspired by critical theory, principally the work of Freire (1970), Gramsci (1971) and Habermas (1983). This meaning perspective is associated with the various beliefs, expectations and ways of justification that we 'learn' as being true or morally desirable through our interactions with the various communities of which we are a part. This meaning perspective is involved, for example, when students pick up the implicit rules of how to conduct themselves in a class discussion or lecture, which forms of discourse are legitimate and which ones are not, when to talk and when to let others talk, and even which arguments are acceptable and which are not. Just as with the other two meaning perspectives, students enter university with a particular socio-cultural/linguistic meaning perspective already in place through which they filter and interpret their new experiences. Assumptions students hold about issues such as race, class, gender, age, religion, disability, sexual orientation and any other social dimensions of difference are also associated with this meaning perspective. From a critical theory perspective, racism, homophobia, Islamophobia, and other forms of bigotry, for example, are understood as uncritically assimilated assumptions and beliefs about what is right or wrong.

As should be obvious, the socio-cultural/linguistic meaning perspective affects students' learning experiences in higher education just as much as the psychological and the epistemic. In addition, we need to keep in mind that the students' learning experiences in higher education are affected not only by their *own* socio-cultural meaning perspective but also by those of other students and staff. How the socio-cultural/linguistic meaning perspectives held by dominant others can lead to marginalisation of students and prevent them from growing into their authenticity is helpfully portrayed by D'Andrea and Gosling (2005) who observe:

> Students who are marginalized within society and their universities by virtue of their race, gender, age, religion, sexual orientation or disability, can feel that the vast apparatus of the dominant traditions and conventions of their subject gives them no space to develop a position of their own without being penalised. The experience of higher education for students from minorities can feel oppressive and disempowering...
>
> (D'Andrea & Gosling, 2005, pp. 32–33)

The epistemic, psychological and socio-cultural/linguistic meaning perspectives may exert a powerful influence on student learning in higher education. More recently, Mezirow (2000) identified three further meaning perspectives, the moral–ethical, the philosophical and the aesthetic, and if we think about it long enough we might come up with even more (for example, is it conceivable that students' attitudes and feelings towards digital technologies could be viewed as a distinct frame of reference that influences how they make meaning of their university experience?). What all these meaning perspectives have in common is that they serve as frames of reference, or perceptual filters, by which we interpret our world. Of course, separating our personal view or outlook on the world neatly into discrete meaning perspectives is artificial and meant for analytical purposes only. Nonetheless, the instructive point about all this is that each of these individual perspectives (or our combined 'general outlook on the world', if you prefer) might be characterised by 'distortions' in the underlying presuppositions which 'limit our options and our rational control over our lives but have been taken for granted or seen as beyond control' (Mezirow, 1991, p. 87). Moving towards greater authenticity then is importantly always a matter of *subjective reframing*, of revising one's personal frames of reference, or meaning perspectives, although it also includes objective reframing.

Engaging in the scholarship of teaching and promoting students' authenticity

I proposed earlier that students' authenticity should be recognised as a universal (although not the only) aim of higher education on the grounds of it being a natural and fundamental interest for each and every person, and that, therefore, it is a moral obligation of educational institutions to serve this interest. While the aim is universal, I now wish to highlight that the approaches we might take in order to invite students into their authenticity, of necessity, will be rooted in attention to particularity. By this I mean that *how* to serve the important interests of students (or how to encourage authenticity) will always be a matter of finding out what becoming more authentic implies for this particular student, in the context of this particular class, course, programme, or university. In Chapter 2 I argued that we can get a hold on the 'important interests of students' by consulting the philosophical literature that is concerned with identifying what makes a human life worth living. I suggested that this approach was preferable over both asking the students what they *perceive to be* their important interests and us determining these interests *for* them. When it comes to the practical question of how to promote the students' authenticity, however, the literature is of limited use and it becomes imperative that we listen to the students' voice – after all, how students experience their learning and the learning environments we offer is evidently a question only the students can answer. Involving students in the scholarship of teaching *by listening to them* then becomes an imperative. Not only does listening to students help us ask better questions about how to make our practices more conducive to their learning and development but it also serves to encourage students to reflect on their own assumptions and their personal ways of meaning-making.

Listening to students may take on the form of students becoming partners in formal pedagogical inquiries, as in the example of Chris and her colleagues (see the preamble to this book), who collaborated with students to study the implementation and impact of a curriculum change initiative in their department. By actually working *with* students, rather than only collecting data *from* students, Chris and her colleagues offered their students the opportunity to become more aware also of their own learning and possibilities. The study Chris and her colleagues carried out is an example of what engagement in the scholarship of teaching may look like, but other forms of engagement are possible. Whenever our critically reflective inquiries are directed at how students make sense of their learning experiences and how we can support them in their learning and development, we are involved in the scholarship of teaching. Essential to our engagement in this social practice is not that it is carried out as formal teacher-led research. Instead what is essential can be expressed as two points: first, that the inquiry serves the important interests of students (i.e. it is aimed at fostering the *students' authenticity*) and second, that we ourselves engage in a critical questioning of assumptions and core presuppositions, as discussed in the previous chapter, that supports us in our *own* striving for *authenticity*. I now want to argue that, although moving towards greater authenticity is not exclusively about critiquing ideology, authenticity is not really possible without ideology critique. This, of course, is the same argument Adorno levelled against Heidegger (see Chapter 1). It is the critical theorists' (and critical postmodernists') concern with power and ideology critique that I turn to next. Understanding how power works also allows us to develop a deeper insight into the *critical* perspective on authenticity. In the discussion that follows we will recognise some of the themes already encountered earlier in this book.

A critical theory perspective on the scholarship of university teaching

My intent here is not to offer a comprehensive overview of work that fits evenly within the critical theory tradition, nor is my purpose to discuss the origins of critical social analysis. Fortunately others have done this enormous task for us already (e.g. Brookfield, 2005; Geuss, 1981; Held, 1980). All I really want to do is to point to the meaning of 'ideology', and the related notion of 'hegemony', as I consider both concepts to offer helpful tools for interpreting how dominant ideas and practices in university teaching and learning come to be. In doing so, I will mainly draw on the work of Stephen Brookfield.

Ideology and ideology critique

Brookfield (2005) explains that 'Critical theory is grounded in an activist desire to fight oppression, injustice, and bigotry and create a fairer, more compassionate world' (p. 10). It 'springs from a distinct philosophical vision of what it means to live as a developed person, as a mature adult struggling to realise one's humanity ...' (p. 27). Critical theory does not only criticise the status quo but also attempts to develop a vision of a world that is more democratic and fair. Tierney and Rhoads (1993) describe the major purpose of critical theory as 'aiding marginalized individuals and groups in realizing how relations of power have structured subjectivity in such a way as to limit their potential and understanding of their life's circumstances and ultimately their ability to act self-reflectively' (p. 322).

The three core assumptions that inform the critical theory tradition include: first, our societies are characterised by social inequality and discrimination; second, it is through dissemination of dominant ideology that these inequalities are reproduced; and third, understanding how ideology works is essential for effecting change (Brookfield, 2005). But how might we understand the notion of ideology?

Ideology is a contested notion interpretable in a variety of ways. In the critical theory tradition, ideology refers to 'the broadly accepted set of values, beliefs, myths, explanations, and justifications that *appears self-evidently true*, empirically accurate, personally relevant, and morally desirable to a majority of the populace' (Brookfield, 2005, p. 41, emphasis added). Ideologies thus remind us of Mezirow's meaning perspectives, as they are the 'broadly accepted beliefs and practices that frame how people make sense of their experiences and live their lives' (Brookfield, 2005, p. viii). The principal purpose of ideology is to 'convince people that the world is organised the way it is for the best of all reasons' (p. viii) and 'works in the best interest of all' (p. ix). Critical theory then is naturally concerned with revealing and contesting ideology, or with ideology *critique*. How might we understand this notion?

The chief purpose of ideology critique is 'to provide people with knowledge and understandings intended to free them from oppression' (Brookfield, 2001b, p. 11). Through ideology critique we realise that 'what strikes us as the normal order of things' is 'a constructed reality that protects the interest of the powerful' (p. 16). Moreover, we also become aware of how we at times collude in our own oppression as 'we learn to love our servitude' (Brookfield, 2005, p. 93). This aspect of ideology, often, following Gramsci (1971), referred to as hegemony, describes the phenomenon of people coming to happily support the beliefs and practices that actually work against their own interests. We are not coerced into these ideas and practices that actually hurt us; they are not forced upon us against our will. We *consent* to them and they become part of who we are. Brookfield (2005) perhaps again says it best: 'The cruelty of hegemony is that adults take pride in learning and acting on the beliefs and assumptions that work to enslave them' (p. 45). Underlying critical theory is a notion of critical reflection that is highly politicised.

Brookfield (2005) argues that to reflect critically means to be 'able to identify, and then to challenge and change, the process by which a grossly iniquitous society uses dominant ideology to convince people this is a normal state of affairs' (p. viii). In an earlier book he also points out that while critical reflection does lead to the uncovering of premises, that is, of paradigmatic, super-ordinate or core presuppositions, this structural element (the depth in reflection) is not the fundamental distinction between critical reflection and other forms of reflective action. Imperative to *critical* reflection, he contended, is first, that we 'understand how considerations of power undergird, frame and distort' (Brookfield, 1995, p. 8) our experiences and second, that we recognise how assumptions and practices we have adopted because they seem to make our (professional) lives easier might 'actually work against our long-term interests' (p. 8).

As briefly touched on in the previous chapter, although Mezirow is influenced by Habermas's (1983) theory of communicative action, he does not consistently argue from the core assumptions of Habermas's revised critical theory (e.g. Clark & Wilson, 1991; Collard and Law, 1989). Mezirow holds more generally that critical reflection is a questioning of premises (as well as of content and process). Nonetheless, already in the early 1980s, Mezirow wrote that emancipatory learning 'involves . . . helping the learner identify real problems involving reified power relationships rooted in institutionalized ideologies which one has internalized in one's psychological history' (Mezirow, 1981, p. 18). It is this kind of learning that he later associates with the transformation of a social–linguistic/cultural meaning perspective (Mezirow, 1991). The socio-cultural/linguistic meaning perspective, as we saw earlier, is associated with the various expectations, beliefs, prejudices, and justifications that we learn as being true or morally desirable through interacting with others. Reflecting critically on this meaning perspective involves becoming aware of how we came to think that these expectations, beliefs, prejudices, and justifications are self-evidently true. This in turn implies unmasking the relations of power that were implicated in us accepting these beliefs as true. Mezirow's view of critical reflection, therefore, is broader than Brookfield's. It is broad enough to accommodate ideology critique but it is not limited to ideology critique.

Mezirow (1981, 1998) talks about institutionalised ideologies, such as taken-for-granted social, political, economic or ecological systems (we might also refer to these as external ideologies). However, ideologies can also be construed as a set of beliefs that is learned within particular social contexts; these social contexts being undergirded by power relations that legitimise certain ways of thinking and acting over others. One could now take the position, as does Brookfield (2000, 2001b, 2005), that *all* learning happens in a social context, and that these contexts are never free of power. A separation into critical self-reflection as ideology critique and critical self-reflection where we do not consider power, strictly speaking, does not really hold then. We are always already implicated in social contexts characterised by power relations. Although there is something very valuable about students and staff reflecting on their psychological assumptions (e.g. 'I am not good enough for graduate studies') and their epistemic assumptions (e.g. 'my opinion is as good as yours') – as through reflection on these assumptions we might overcome distortions in these 'domains' – from a critical theory position we would not consider overcoming these distortions as incidents of 'emancipation'. Emancipation requires that we become aware of how relations of power played a role in how we accepted such assumptions as being true to begin with. In other words, we are only ever really free of distortions if we also consider our socio-cultural/linguistic assumptions, thereby engaging in ideology critique. To make the distinction between Brookfield and Mezirow even clearer, Mezirow sees ideology critique as one form that critical self-reflection may take; Brookfield sees it as the form critical self-reflection must take.

Ideologies are acquired through social learning at the workplace, just as they are acquired through social learning in the classroom, programme, peer group or family, to list just a few obvious examples. Moving towards greater authenticity, for teachers and students, then also involves becoming aware of power relations and how these influence what they consider to be true and morally desirable. Following Brookfield (2001b), I suggest that critical engagement with the scholarship of teaching includes that academic teachers 'recognise the predominance of ideology in their everyday thoughts and actions' and 'challenge ideology that serves the interest of the few against the well-being of the many' (p. 20). If the purpose of the scholarship of university teaching is also to promote greater justice *in* (and *through*) higher education, engagement in ideology critique is an imperative.

To briefly summarise the main arguments made in this chapter thus far we can say, first, that in order to promote student learning and development we need to listen to students' assumptions and their personal ways of meaning-making; second, authenticity without *critical self*-reflection (or ideology critique) is, in actuality, not possible; third, in their striving for authenticity students and teachers face the same two challenges (recognising power relations and identifying hegemonic assumptions); and fourth, by paying attention to ideology and power we are more likely to work towards creating greater social justice *in* (and *through*) higher education. In the next section of this chapter I will offer some concrete illustrations of what recognising ideology might mean, for teachers and students respectively.

Recognising ideological and hegemonic assumptions

Teachers

To start with, let us look at some examples of assumptions that might appear 'self-evidently true' to teachers. These might include:

1 If students don't engage, either by not coming to class or by not participating in class, my responsibility ends right there – the students have to take some responsibility for their learning!
2 When I use the discussion rather than the lecture method I spread power evenly.
3 Learning contracts and learning journals encourage students to find their own voice.
4 As someone deserving to teach at this institution I need to be able to answer all the questions students have.
5 Autonomous or independent learning should be a goal of higher education.
6 A curriculum based on the experiences of the majority of students will be to the best interest of all students.

7 Students from Confucian Heritage Cultures think less critically than their Western peers.

8 Standards must be the same for all students as this is only fair.

9 The only literature that usefully informs the scholarship of teaching is the psychologically based literature on learning.

10 The scholarship of teaching is teacher-led pedagogical research.

11 A style of teaching that is suitable for Philosophy cannot possibly work in Chemistry.

12 I cannot learn anything valuable about teaching from colleagues in other disciplines.

13 Students do not want to think hard.

I suggest that each of these apparently 'self-evident truths' is a potential candidate of ideology, and many more examples could be added. This means that I understand them as ideologically based assumptions that we take to be true or right, that are disseminated and/or reinforced through the mechanisms of power that characterise the particular work environments of which we are a part. Questioning these assumptions would involve becoming aware of how power works and how it influences our consciousness. There is not the space to explore the ideological character of all of these examples but I shall discuss a few of them. The first assumption 'If students don't engage, either by not coming to class or by not participating, my responsibility ends right there – -the students have to take some responsibility for their learning' is reinforced by popular books on teaching that highlight the importance of learner responsibility. The idea that students are responsible for their learning is then adopted, for example, by institutional teaching and learning strategy documents. Such views become ideological when they are accepted uncritically. Surely students need to feel responsible for their learning but when students are not engaged we should perhaps also be reminded of D'Andrea and Gosling's (2005) observation that 'The experience of higher education for students from minorities can feel oppressive and disempowering...' (pp. 32–33). The reason students are not engaged might be, as D'Andrea and Gosling suggest, that 'the vast apparatus of the dominant traditions and conventions of their subject gives them no space to develop a position of their own without being penalised...' (pp. 32–33). Making sure that students do not feel oppressed and disempowered in this way is very much our responsibility.

Books and conferences on teaching in higher education celebrate the practices mentioned in the second and third examples as progressive and empowering of students. However, a teacher whose intent it is to encourage students to think for themselves, by employing learning journals, electronic discussion forums, face to face discussions or portfolios, might in fact inadvertently promote students' dependence on authority. It is not that these practices are inherently bad, or less desirable than those where the expert is clearly visible (as is the case in a lecture); the point is rather that we should not assume that power has gone away in these situations. Brookfield (2001a), drawing on Foucault (1980), observes that there are no power-free zones and that power only shifts in often unpredictable ways. When students feel that their work is being monitored, this can lead to a kind of self-disciplining which finds expression in the student's desire to give the teacher what he or she wants to hear. Students then become expert performers. What appears as the students' own voice may in reality be the voice the student thinks the teacher is waiting for. In formal educational settings such as universities where students are being formally assessed by their teachers it may not be possible to circumvent this problem entirely; nonetheless, it is then all the more important to be aware of these interactions. We might also want to remind ourselves that discussions, in particular, serve the interests of those who are extraverted (see Chapter 2). They also serve the interest of those who already come with the cultural capital that allows them to quickly pick up on and then perform in the accepted or desired ways. Foucault (1980) discusses regimes of truth which, I suggest, also function in university seminars (as well as university committee meetings) and thus influence learning and teaching. Foucault argues that:

> each society has its regime of truth, its 'general politics' of truth; that is, the types of discourse which it accepts and makes function as true; the mechanisms and instances which enable one to distinguish true from false statements, the means by which each is sanctioned; the techniques and procedures accorded value in the acquisition of truth; the status of those who are charged with saying what counts as true.
>
> (Foucault, 1980, p. 133)

For some students, and not only those from non-Western cultures, participating in class discussions where they have to reveal parts of themselves without a chance to first observe and get a feel for what is expected is nothing less than an ordeal. While we might still see value in students learning to participate in such a social setting, it is important to be aware that not everybody feels safe in discussions. It then takes a very skilled and reflective teacher, who is alert to the challenges this involves for individual students and can respond appropriately, to create more inclusive spaces. What it means to foster the authenticity of 'student A' may be very different from what it means for 'student B', as these students may be positioned entirely differently in terms not only of the cultural capital they have acquired but also in terms of race, class, gender, sexual orientation, disability, faith or any other social dimension of difference. My intent in this section has been to identify the ideological character of some of the assumptions we might hold about teaching and learning. It is the notion of hegemonic assumptions that I will turn to next.

Brookfield (1995) offers four examples of hegemonic assumptions that critically reflective teachers are aware of. Viewing *teaching as a vocation*, the first of Brookfield's examples, is a hegemonic assumption as it can lead to burn-out and self-destruction. We are told, and happily embrace the view, that teaching, for very plausible reasons, is a vocation and not just a job that pays the bills. Everyone around us is doing their very best and, of course, we know it is only fair that we do so too. At the same time resources are shrinking, classes are getting bigger, more international students need supervision, and demands for external research funding continue to rise while such funding is getting harder to secure. We are proud of it when we work fifteen-hour days and feel we have not pulled our weight if we are not utterly exhausted by eight o'clock at night. Yet, what we are really doing, Brookfield argues, is 'proving' that underfunded institutions can work properly, while we suffer serious consequences to our health and social well-being, thereby serving the needs of powerful others.

Related to the first assumption is Brookfield's second example, which is that *good teachers meet everyone's needs*. After all, this is what good teachers do, don't they? We hear it everywhere – we are here to meet the needs of students. However, we are setting ourselves up for being demoralised from the start, as it is, of course, clearly impossible to meet everyone's need! Moreover, trying to do so is also pedagogically unsound. As discussed in Chapter 2, serving the important interests of students is often very different from meeting the students' felt/ expressed needs. The assumption that we should respond to learner needs, according to Brookfield, serves the interests of those who believe that educational institutions should be run as a capitalist economic system where we develop and market a desirable product (i.e. respond to what students want or ask for) and compete for students and income.

The third hegemonic assumption Brookfield discusses is that we take it for granted that *there is a ready-made answer out there to the problem I'm experiencing* in my teaching. Essentially, this assumption has negative consequences as ready-made solutions are (unsuccessfully) applied to the particular contexts of our practice, which end up harming students and ourselves. The hegemonic character of this assumption lies in the fact that by believing that we need solutions that others have developed for us we serve the interests of those others who accumulate power, prestige and financial gain from developing these 'answers'.

The final assumption Brookfield discusses is the notion that *good teachers get perfect ratings on teaching evaluations*. A critically reflective teacher realises, Brookfield argues, that given the diversity of students and the complex nature of higher levels of learning, such student ratings of instruction are very hard to interpret. Receiving mixed ratings should be the logical outcome in a group of diverse learners and beating oneself up over not receiving perfect ratings is, therefore, unjustified. Exclusive use of student ratings of instruction can also cause an unhealthy popularity contest among colleagues, as those with the highest ratings are the most popular and get celebrated. Brookfield observes that reliance on student ratings of instruction serves the needs of those who are charged with making decisions about others (for example, in relation to tenure and promotion where teaching needs to be taken into account) with little time to spare to consult on more meaningful alternatives.

Each of these four assumptions serves the interests of the powerful and is ultimately self-destructive and demoralising to the teacher. At least three of these assumptions also work against the students' important interests. We can see this being the case most readily with the 'Meeting expectations/or felt needs' assumption. But similarly, the view that 'Good teachers get perfect ratings on teaching evaluations' can lead to teachers catering to the expressed needs of students, which, ultimately, can be damaging to students in the long term. The notion that 'There is a ready-made answer out there to the problem I'm experiencing' can also hurt students in the long run. The students' interests, I will argue in the next chapter, are not served by generic solutions but by practical wisdom exercised in particular situations. The latter implies listening to what and how students think and how they experience their learning.

Let us next look at some of the assumptions that might appear 'self-evidently true' to students.

Students

Examples of assumptions that students might take for granted could include:

1   Learning means to absorb the content delivered in lectures, through lecture notes, and assigned reading/study material.
2   If I do not do well in the first year, I have no right to be here.
3   In order to know how well I did I need to know how I compare to others.
4   It's good to have more students and teachers from other cultures but they should conform to what the norm is around here.
5   I need to write down as much as I can of what the lecturer says and memorise it.
6   In classes where I did not end up with pages of written notes I cannot have learned very much.
7   The only person who can assess my work is the teacher.
8   I cannot learn much from my peers.
9   I don't mind students from other cultures being here but I don't see what I can learn from them.
10   Teachers should keep their political and social views to themselves.
11   The teacher is pushing his agenda when he refers to 'his partner' all the time.
12   She does not know the material well otherwise she would have given us the answer.
13   I don't care what sexual orientation, faith or whatever people identify with as long as they don't talk about it in public.

Some of these assumptions are similar to those Perry (1970) and Baxter Magolda (1992) identified in students who demonstrated epistemic cognition characterised by either Duality or Multiplicity. In the light of the previous discussion, we can construe all of the above examples as ideologically based assumptions, beliefs, expectations and justifications that have been learned socially through the particular teaching practices and learning environments we provide, which are undergirded by certain mechanisms of power. These views take on a hegemonic character when students do not notice that such assumptions actually can cause them great harm in the long term and serve the interests of only a few powerful others. Let us explore some of these assumptions in greater depth.

The assumption that 'Learning means to absorb the content delivered in lectures, through lecture notes and assigned reading/study materials' could be hegemonic to the extent that it is loosely linked to the view that learning in higher education is a commodity that can be packaged and sold. The lecture, lecture notes, and reading/study materials are provided against a fee and learning occurs as a result of that transaction. Ultimately this assumption further advances the interest of those who believe that universities should be run as capitalist economic systems. The assumption works against the students' interest in the long term as they miss out on recognising that meaningful learning involves becoming 'disencumbered' (Barnett, 2007) from other voices and thinking for oneself rather than absorbing material. The second example, 'If I do not do well in the first year, I have no right to be here' is ideological, as these views are disseminated by programmes making it very clear to students that the first year will be very hard, that university is different from school, and that only the fittest will survive. Making it deliberately hard for students to progress beyond the first year and keeping only the top students means that these programmes are more likely to end up with good retention and completion numbers in the final years. This serves the interests of administrators who need to demonstrate publicly the quality of their teaching in a competitive higher education environment. Students to some extent collude in their own oppression by accepting as just a system of unfair selection that serves the interests of the powerful. Students who do not progress to the second year internalise the belief that they are simply 'not good enough', not 'university material', which is likely to lower their self-esteem and future academic aspirations. Those who do progress to the next year internalise the belief that they need to compete against others, which ultimately works against their interests, as key to authenticity is not the individual pursuit of private ends but recognition of our mutual interdependence.

The third example 'In order to know how well I did I need to know how I compare to others' is hegemonic in the sense that it serves a system which allocates rewards (for example, jobs, scholarships, or admission to Graduate School) on the basis of grade point averages (GPAs) and classified degrees. As in the previous example, students are encouraged to compete against each other rather than to collaborate, and the resulting individualism constrains their authenticity. The fourth example 'It's good to have more students and teachers from other cultures but they should conform to what the norm is around here' is ideologically based, in that principally economically driven internationalisation strategies, which neglect other important dimensions of internationalisation such as intercultural learning, work to produce such beliefs and attitudes. The assumption is also hegemonic in that as long as students hold these views it serves the interests of the institution, which feels no pressure to change and can continue accruing resources in terms of international staff and students without having to invest too much in return. Students holding these views also end up harming themselves, as they miss out on opportunities of widening their horizons by learning from students and staff from other cultures.

Furthering the students' authenticity through our engagement in the scholarship of university teaching demands that we *listen to the assumptions, views, expectations, beliefs and justifications* by which students make sense of the world. Some of these assumptions are those that they hold about themselves (associated with Mezirow's psychological meaning perspective), others those that they hold about the nature, certainty and limits of knowledge (associated with Mezirow's epistemic meaning perspective), and again others that involve their thoughts and opinions on social and political issues. All of these assumptions have been learned socially in contexts characterised by certain relations of power that legitimatise these assumptions and de-legitimatise others. These socially learned views can be understood as regimes of truth, or ideologies, that they (and we) rarely feel compelled to question.

But is this not indoctrination?

Some readers might feel that this concern with 'ideology critique' and 'emancipation' takes us too far away from the actual purposes of university teaching and the scholarship of teaching specifically, the latter typically understood as examining how best we can support students in developing a deep understanding of the subject matter. My response to such observations is that the scholarship of university teaching clearly is about helping students understand the subject matter at a more sophisticated level. Helping them work through difficult subject-specific concepts will often lead students to transform their previous ways of making sense of the discourses of the field they are studying. The notion of 'threshold concept acquisition' captures this learning well (Meyer & Land, 2006). Threshold concepts refer to the fundamental ideas underpinning a given discipline or subject. Unless students grasp these concepts the deeper meaning or logic of the subject will remain concealed from them. By coming to terms with a so-called 'threshold concept', students undergo not just a shift in how they *understand* the material, but the experience of negotiating a threshold concept may involve a 'transformation of personal identity, a reconstruction of subjectivity' (Meyer & Land, 2006, p. 7). By grasping a subject at a deeper level and thus making the knowledge their own, the process of learning shifts from a purely cognitive (or cognitive and socio-cultural) process to one that is also ontological. Not only the students' knowledge but their sense of self is changed as a result of the learning. Nonetheless, this (subjective) reframing, as understood by Meyer and Land, occurs in relation to particular concepts associated with the subject matter (i.e. physics, economics, history, etc.). While such reframing in response to the process of threshold concept negotiation is extremely important in higher education, the point I have been arguing in this book is that this kind of 'subject-centred' transformative learning cannot be all that higher education is concerned with if it is to make a difference in this world. Transformative learning, as discussed in this and the previous chapter, also has a broader meaning.

As we saw in the Introduction, Barnett (2004b) proposed that universities should see their role principally as cultivating in students dispositions such as 'carefulness, thoughtfulness, receptiveness, resilience, courage and stillness' (p. 258), and enact 'a pedagogy of human being' (p. 247). Surely such dispositions are needed in order to confront the difficult subject-specific concepts whose grasp is required in order to succeed in academia; however, such dispositions are also needed to deal with the complexities and challenges of our times more generally. In Chapter 2 we saw that Barnett (1990) also argued that a 'genuine higher learning is subversive in the sense of subverting the student's taken-for-granted world, ... It is disturbing because, ultimately, the student comes to see that things could always be other than they are' (p. 155). This seeing that 'things could be other than they are', I want to argue, goes beyond the student's learning and understanding of subject matter.

Baxter Magolda and Terenzini (1999) argue that not only intellectual maturity but also personal and relational maturity are prerequisites for students to cope with uncertainty and complexity in the spheres of work, citizenship, and continued learning throughout life. Similarly, Nussbaum (1997, 2010) comments that the purpose of higher education is to develop democratic and empathetic citizens with the capacity to address the problems of our times. Proponents of the capabilities approach to higher education pedagogies (e.g. Walker, 2006) emphasise that many of our social problems are those of inequality, where certain groups of the population are deprived of the opportunity to recognise and live their full potential. Students, therefore, should acquire capabilities such as *practical reason, emotional integrity, respect, dignity and recognition*, and *knowledge and imagination* (Walker, 2006), as developing these is in both their own interests and that of our larger society.

I suggest that none of the above authors would deny that helping students understand the subject matter at a deep level is a critical function of higher education teaching. However, teachers in higher education vary in how narrowly or broadly they conceive of the functions or purposes of higher education teaching. For some the purpose of teaching is exclusively about helping the students acquire a deep understanding of the subjects they teach. At times this position is argued on ethical grounds in a sense that it is claimed that anything that goes beyond teaching the subject would be a form of indoctrination. As students learn to think critically within the discourses of the discipline, so goes the argument, they will develop the critical capabilities they need in order to take a personal stance on issues and make a contribution to the world. These teachers might still see value in the notion of authenticity but understand it more narrowly. They would agree with some of the aspects of student authenticity I discussed in Chapter 2 and reviewed in this present chapter, but clearly not all.

Others, myself included, are inclined to view the purposes of higher teaching more broadly. They would argue that universities are also places for students to develop personally and relationally. They would suggest that higher education should provide opportunity for students to grow into their authenticity in a broader sense, thereby realising 'the ways dominant ideology limits and circumscribes what (they) feel is possible in life' (Brookfield, 2005, p. 8). Providing such opportunity could involve helping students become aware of various forms of bigotry or helping them recognise that academic learning is enhanced by learning with others rather than competing against their peers, for example. These colleagues would concede that they teach from an explicit value position but would strongly refute the charge of indoctrinating students. They would argue instead that what they are really doing is freeing students from indoctrination that ensues whenever ideologically based assumptions are being left unquestioned. The narrow view of the purposes of university teaching focuses on acquiring a deep understanding of the discipline. The broader view, by definition, is inclusive of acquiring a deep understanding of the discipline but considers the students' critical examination of their epistemic, socio-cultural/linguistic and psychological meaning perspectives as equally important.

Conclusion

My argument in this chapter was that teachers and students are both implicated in a process of transformative learning and thus face the same kinds of challenges. By learning to recognise, through critical *self*-reflection, how power distorts consciousness (ideology) and how some assumptions we readily embrace are actually harmful to us and serve the interests of powerful others (hegemony) we can create greater social justice *in* and *through* higher education. In order to foster these transformative learning processes in ourselves we need to pay attention to our own assumptions. In order to foster these transformative learning processes in students we need to listen to individual students and thus get a sense of what their assumptions are.

Engagement in the scholarship of teaching involves promoting the students' authenticity by fostering in them a questioning, inquiring and self-critical disposition, a process of critical reflection and critical *self*-reflection, or of objective and subjective reframing. Moving towards greater authenticity is not exclusively a matter of engaging in ideology critique; however, there is no truly 'authentic being' without considering how consciousness is affected by social situation, and thus relations of power. In the next chapter I shall argue that if authentic engagement in the scholarship of university teaching means that we listen to students' *assumptions, views, expectations, beliefs and justifications* then there might be something problematic about the view that the scholarship of teaching is an 'evidence-based practice'.

Chapter 7

Challenging the notion of the scholarship of teaching as an evidence-based practice

Introduction

I have taken the position in this book that engagement in the scholarship of university teaching means that both academics and students are implicated in a process of critical reflection and critical *self*-reflection on assumptions, which opens the path to transformative learning and thus supports their move towards greater authenticity. How and whether this position can be squared with the conception of the scholarship of teaching as 'an evidence-based practice' is the issue I shall explore in this chapter. The value of 'evidence-based' approaches to educational policy development and practice has been debated widely and its underlying ideology critiqued (e.g. Clegg, 2005). However, perhaps precisely because the notion of evidence-based practice has not gone unchallenged, it is intriguing to observe that many advocates of the scholarship of teaching embrace the notion with notable enthusiasm (e.g. Ginsberg, 2010; O'Brien, 2008; Perry & Smart, 2007). Thus, I believe that there is value in deliberating the notion of evidence-based practice in the context of the scholarship of teaching.

My intent is to bring to the surface some of the problems that arise when the notion of 'evidence-based practice' is interpreted too narrowly. Specifically, I shall argue in this chapter that a narrow interpretation is based on an instrumental rationality, which 'essentially (is) concerned with means and ends, with the adequacy of procedures for purposes more or less taken for granted and supposedly self-explanatory' (Horkheimer, 1974, p. 3). The problem with instrumental rationality is that it is inherently conformist. It thereby ignores the fact that the scholarship of university teaching is, importantly, also concerned with deliberating how to achieve greater equality and social justice *in* and *through* higher education, matters which cannot be adequately addressed on the basis of an instrumental rationality. A view of the scholarship of teaching as an 'evidence-based practice', if this is too narrowly conceived, also ignores that it is a practice in which we are personally invested through the specific judgements we make as professionals working in concrete contexts. The notion of 'evidence-based practice' suggests that research can tell us 'what works' (e.g. Davies, Nutley and Smith, 2000). Since strategies are offered as tried and tested, there is no requirement on our part to reflect on which strategies to employ to support student learning, and questions regarding aims and purposes do not even arise. Readers may object that this is not what evidence-based practice means in relation to the scholarship of teaching, that we are certainly not blind followers of prescribed technique but astute interpreters of research, and that the preceding portrayal is at best a caricature of a concept long recognised as being open to a range of interpretations (e.g. Hammersley, 2007). In this chapter I shall take a careful look at what we mean by 'evidence'. I will consider what types of questions an evidence-based approach encourages us to take up, and whether, and if so how, our understanding of evidence might be broadened so as to intentionally encourage a wider range of questions for inquiry. Inquiry, I suggest, ought to be aimed at exploring not only the effectiveness but also the value or desirability of what we do *in* and *through* higher education.

Building on Chapters 5 and 6, I will show that justifying knowledge claims through critically reflective inquiry may take on the form of generating evidence of 'what works' in particular contexts; however, justifying knowledge claims may, indeed should, also take on the form of generating reasoned arguments that allow us to make moral judgements (see Fenstermacher, 1994). In addition, and following from this first observation, I shall argue that these two forms of justification of knowledge claims stand in a particular relationship to one another. The questions 'What does it mean?' and 'Is this right?', and related sub-questions such as 'Who gains, who loses, by which mechanisms of power?', 'Is this desirable?' and 'What can be done?' (see Flyvbjerg, 2001, p. 162), at all times ought to precede the question 'And does it work?'. Additionally, while in Chapter 5 my concern was to show that critically reflective engagement in the scholarship of teaching involves justifying our own knowledge claims, I now want to recognise that as part of this process we also mediate the claims that are being put forward as justifications of good practice by others.

In the next section I will review relevant literature on evidence-based practice, highlighting in particular the arguments that critics have raised against a narrow interpretation of this concept. As a way into this discussion I recall a conversation I had with a colleague some time ago that brings to the fore some of the problematic issues with the notion of the scholarship of teaching as an evidence-based practice. Eventually, I will distinguish two fundamentally different meanings of evidence-based practice in relation to teaching and show how these link up with the particular interpretation of the scholarship of university teaching offered in this book. My basic conclusion is that evidence matters but our sense of what constitutes evidence in the scholarship of teaching needs to be broadened.

The trouble with 'evidence-based practice'

In recent years it has become popular to add the words 'and learning' to the original expression 'scholarship of teaching'. The longer title, 'scholarship of teaching *and learning*' (abbreviated by the acronym SOTL), is seen to reflect the widely celebrated shift from a so-called 'teaching paradigm' to a 'learning paradigm' in higher education pedagogy (e.g. Barr & Tagg, 1995; Tagg, 2003). In essence, what distinguishes the 'teaching paradigm' from the 'learning paradigm' is that the former is described from the perspective of teachers and/or institutions while the latter is described from the perspective of learners. Notions such as *student success* rather than *student access*, and *students constructing knowledge* rather than *teachers transferring knowledge*, are seen to characterise the 'learning paradigm'. The articulation of the 'learning paradigm' also led to an awareness of the need for thoughtful alignment of the various components of the learning environment and the influence of this environment on student learning.

Although the emphasis on student learning may attract many academics to 'SOTL', I suggest this emphasis does carry with it the risk of paying inadequate attention to the professional learning that the scholarship of teaching demands of academics engaged in this work. Nicholls (2005) similarly observed that one difficulty with the scholarship of teaching is that it has not been sufficiently grounded within the learning of academics, arguing that 'scholarship begins where learning begins' (p. 44). This brings to mind an experience I had a couple of years ago when I was invited to give a talk at a conference in the United States for which I had chosen the title 'Why we need the "Scholarship of teaching" for making good educational judgements'. One conference participant approached me after the session to let me know that I had missed the boat entirely as SOTL was not about teaching but about learning. My effort to explain to him that the very notion of teaching, to me, involved making a positive difference to the learning of students, and assuring him that I (really!) did not mean to suggest that teaching is necessarily based on a teacher-directed pedagogy, left him unimpressed. After some more discussion the conference participant suggested to me that I change my terminology as it was 'inappropriate for a conference like this', adding that I clearly was not aware of the shift from the teaching to the learning paradigm that had taken place years ago!

It dawned on me that for this colleague 'teacher', and also 'teaching', were dirty words and as long as I continued using them I would continue to offend his pedagogical sensibilities. More importantly, however, it became apparent to me that this conference participant could not square my comments on the importance of academics being reflective about their teaching and wider educational ideals with his own conception of what the scholarship of teaching and learning was all about. He suggested to me that I change my talk around and discuss instead the reflection of students, insisting that 'it's them who have to learn how to reflect!'. What this colleague made me realise are two things. First, I now think it makes little sense to talk about the professional learning that engagement in the scholarship of teaching entails on the part of academics without at the same time drawing linkages to the learning we hope students will engage in. In my talk I had exclusively discussed the need for critical reflection (and self-reflection) on the part of teachers, making only occasional reference to the general aim of serving the important interests of students. I also did not spend much time unpacking the meaning of 'important interests'. I now am aware that I was telling only part of the story. I certainly agree with my colleague that students, too, should be encouraged to reflect and now think that this side of the story also needs telling. But something else occurred to me. My colleague's comment that the ideas I had presented were 'inappropriate for a conference like this', puzzling as it appeared to me initially, is entirely intelligible once one adopts the perspective of 'SOTL' as an 'evidence-based practice'; that is, a process by which we either obtain and/or apply the research evidence that has been shown to improve student learning.

The problem of course rests with how notions of evidence and application are being interpreted. Research (or as I referred to it in Chapter 5, theory-based/research-based knowledge about teaching) can and *should* inform teaching. A narrow conception of evidence-based practice, however, is founded on an instrumental rationality that assumes that research evidence once applied to practice will bring about predictable results. When instrumental rationality reigns, it becomes unnecessary for teachers to reflect on their actions. Available evidence is interpreted as a foregone conclusion. Strategies are offered as 'tried and tested' and questions regarding the desirability of actions, purposes and goals do not crop up. Rather than being conceived of as an activity that depends crucially on teachers' capacity and willingness to be reflective, SOTL is interpreted as an activity of gathering (and/or implementing) so-called evidence about which strategies will offer predictable results. Rather than being a practice in which we are personally invested through the specific judgements we make as individual professionals working in concrete contexts, SOTL is construed as an impersonal activity and in this sense an '*a*-reflective' or perhaps non-reflexive one. Nicholls (2005) argued that 'objectivism', observable in situations when we distance or disconnect ourselves from the phenomenon we want to understand, may be the underlying cause for what she calls the 'fear factor' (p. 85) that real engagement with teaching and learning might entail for many academics. This 'fear factor' might be the cause for the resistance that can at times be observed towards understanding oneself as a learner of teaching. Nicholls further suggests that 'isolation and objective consideration of teaching and learning is by far the easier option' and adds 'particularly when framed through an individual's discipline base' (p. 85).

Certainly, SOTL is a term that I have employed myself in earlier writing and many colleagues who use it hold a much broader view than the one I portrayed and criticised above. My point, I should emphasise, is not to argue against adding the word 'learning' to the phrase 'the scholarship of teaching' (after all, the resulting acronym is much better than either 'SOT' or 'SOFT'); rather I want to draw attention to what is lost with an overly narrow interpretation that focuses exclusively on the learning of students and an interpretation of evidence viewed from an instrumental rationality. I, therefore, agree with McLean (2006) that 'there is an urgent need to go beyond . . . narrow, technical rational definitions of evidence-based practice' (p. 93).

In line with Biesta (2007), I would thus like to argue that there are two serious reservations that can be brought against the notion of evidence-based practice. The first reservation is that the discourse of evidence-based practice does not invite questions about the desirability of the ends towards it is directed (let alone the means), but is concerned solely with the effectiveness of means for predetermined ends. Specifically, Biesta (2007) commented that such a discourse leads us to lose sight of the fact that 'The most important question for educational professionals is not about the effectiveness of their actions but about the potential educational value of what they do, that is, about the educational desirability of the opportunities for learning that follow from their actions' (p. 10). The second reservation is that the concern with prediction and control underlying evidence-based practice is an attempt to escape from the inevitable complexities, frailty, contingencies and unpredictability of human action (Arendt, 1958). I will say more about this in the next section where I shall introduce two contrasting interpretations of evidence-based practice. We have already encountered the first of these; the second, I suggest, serves to enrich the scholarship of teaching.

Two different versions of evidence-based practice

Following Elliott (2005), we can distinguish two different versions of evidence-based practice in relation to teaching. According to the first version, the evidence we are concerned with is the instrumental effectiveness of the strategies we use in order to achieve certain learning outcomes. According to the second version, the evidence we are concerned with rests in the ethical consistency between our strategies or processes and educational aims. I will discuss each version separately.

Instrumental effectiveness of strategies used to achieve certain learning outcomes

This view of the nature of the evidence is widespread and, as we saw above, is also alive and well in discourse on the scholarship of teaching. It is a view associated with the idea that 'research should provide decisive and conclusive evidence that if teachers do X rather than Y in their professional practice, there will be a significant and enduring improvement in outcome' (Hargreaves, 1997, p. 413). A few years after making this statement Hargreaves softened his position somewhat, suggesting that evidence-*informed* practice might be a more appropriate expression given that research findings should inform but not displace the teacher's own professional judgements. Specifically he elaborated that:

> to avoid any implication that teachers or educational policy makers should not, in making decisions, take account of (i) the quality and strength of the research evidence and (ii) the contextual factors relating to that decision, we should, I suggest, speak of *evidence-informed*, not evidence-based, policy or practice.
>
> (Hargreaves, 1999, p. 246)

However, Elliott (2005) observed that, although Hargreaves altered his language over the years, the assumptions he holds of how educational research findings ought to relate to the practice of teaching have not really changed. He characterised Hargreaves's version of evidence-based (or informed) practice 'as a means of improving teaching as a form of technical control over the production of learning outcomes' (Elliott, 2005, p. 558).

The basic presupposition underlying this view of evidence-based practice is that it is possible to identify, through scientific research, which methods are most effective in bringing about certain ends. When practitioners raise concerns that these studies ignore the particular contexts in which they work, the usual answer is that we can solve this problem by doing more scientific research. As more and more studies take contextual factors into consideration, typically as 'variables' to be studied more systematically, so goes the argument, we will eventually overcome the problem of insensitivity to particularity. The problems with this view were highlighted by Schwandt (2005), who observed:

> Deciding whether one is doing the right thing and doing it well in educating a student requires more than an ability to implement evidence-based curricula for teaching knowledge and skills.... It requires decision-making methods that are inescapably characterized by simultaneous attention to the particulars of the situation ... and to a host of considerations having to do with values, interests, habits, beliefs, traditions, and so forth that make decisions about how best to educate (at least in a democracy) inveterately untidy, contested, corrigible, and case specific. This practical character of deliberating educational means and ends cannot be made to go away by increasing the rigor, pace, or reach of science-based thinking.
>
> (Schwandt, 2005, p. 296)

Schwandt realises that the question of the right course of action to take in particular teaching contexts is not always answerable on the basis of scientific research, no matter how sophisticated the research, because scientific thinking is simply not suited to answer certain questions. Perhaps more to the point, within the framework of scientific thinking certain questions simply do not arise. Similarly, Biesta (2007) argues that the discourse of evidence-based (read science-based) practice does not leave room for questions about the purposes and goals of our educational endeavours. Cranton (1998) considers instrumental or scientific approaches to learning about teaching to be limited because they do not take into account individual characteristics of students and teachers, do not address the goals of education, ignore the complexity and unpredictability of human communication, and are not sensitive to changes in social and organisational cultures. Dunne (1993) likewise argued that the extent to which a teacher can achieve what he or she sets out to achieve cannot be predicted. Drawing directly on Hannah Arendt (1958), he commented:

> this resonance – or the degree to which his [sic] action strikes a responsive chord in others who will co-operate with it and carry it along toward some

completion – is always a happening as well as an achievement. It may well be forthcoming but it is not something that can be reliably counted on or guaranteed; even if it has happened for him (sic) with some regularity in the past, there still remains an element of hazard about each new occasion on which it is actualized.

(Dunne, 1993, p. 93)

Recognition of the unpredictability of human action led Biesta (2007) to conclude that educational research cannot tell us *what works* – it can only tell us *what worked*. Power to influence is then a 'potentiality in being together . . . not an unchangeable, measurable, and reliable entity' (Arendt, 1958, p. 200), a point also acknowledged by MacIntyre (2007) who remarked that 'Our social order is in a very literal sense out of our, and indeed anyone's, control. No one is or could be in charge' (p. 107).

The above arguments are difficult to accept for those of us who want to believe in the capacity of research to offer rules for future actions and teaching effectiveness. Cranton (1998) argued that it is natural for us to want to be able to predict and control our environment but added: 'The more we come to understand teaching and learning, however, the more we realise that it is neither entirely under our control nor subject to established principles. Perhaps becoming a scholar of teaching starts with this understanding' (p. 14). According to Nixon (2008), authentic action on the part of teachers implies that we are perceptive of the actual and unique needs of varying groups of learners. This requires resisting instrumentalist approaches to teaching that claim that the needs of our students can be met by following a certain set of means, thereby ignoring the contingency, particularity and variability of teaching and learning. Nixon's observation fits well with our discussion in Chapter 6. If it is the purpose of the scholarship of teaching to promote the students' authenticity, that is, a process of reframing based on critical reflection and critical *self*-reflection on assumptions, then listening to students' unique needs is an imperative. Knowing what strategies to use in particular situations to help students learn and develop is an important aspect of the scholarship of teaching; yet, deciding what to do in particular situations cannot ever be based exclusively on evidence yielded from studies on 'what works' (or as Biesta would say, 'what *worked*'). In Chapters 4 and 5 we encountered the virtue of 'phronesis' or practical wisdom. Revisiting and exploring the nature and role of phronesis in the context of teaching is useful as part of this present discussion.

Aristotle showed that the knowledge needed in the realm of *praxis* or human affairs is of an entirely different kind than that required for production or making things (Thomson, 1976). Phronesis is the knowledge relevant for *praxis*. Bowman (2002) explains that the person who acts phronetically is someone who, as a result of experience, is particularly able to perceive, within a concrete situation, an indeterminate number of potentially relevant factors; who is able to recognise among these the ones that are especially important and who is able to select, from among all the possible ways in which he or she could act, the one that is most appropriate for the situation at hand. To act phronetically, therefore, means to accurately assess a given situation and make an appropriate decision, while abandoning the security offered by rules and regulatives for the sake of meeting 'the other' in his or concrete uniqueness. It is by developing phronesis that we become more accepting of working with insecurity and unpredictability so characteristic of large aspects of the scholarship of teaching. Flaming (2001) discussed the value of phronesis in the context of nursing practice, arguing that a professional field like nursing (or we might instead say teaching) is misconceived when thought of as a research-*based* (or evidence-*based*) practice. To be clear, the point is not that knowledge from research is not relevant for professional practice; the argument is that professional action should not just be wholly determined by information from research, tradition or authority but that professionals should always deliberate the applicability of research findings within the specific contexts in which they work. Intuitive, experience-based, ethical and personal ways of knowing are just as important for professional practice.

Importantly then, phronesis, or good judgement, is not uninformed by theoretical and systemised knowledge. As Dunne and Pendlebury (2003) make clear, one of the critical functions of phronesis is precisely to facilitate the mediation between the universal and the particular. Phronesis is:

> an ability to recognize cases, or problems of this kind (which are precisely of *no* clearly specified kind) and to deal adequately with them. A person of judgement respects the particularity of the case – and thus does not impose on it a procrustean application of the general rule.
>
> (Dunne and Pendlebury, 2003, p. 198, emphasis in original)

This position is echoed by Hansen (2007), who argues that while 'the wise thing to do in a teaching-student-relation can seldom-if ever-be deduced from general rules and prescriptions or methods but has to be sensed in the situation in a more experienced and intuitive way' (pp. 15–16), one of the key roles of phronesis is to mediate between theory and the particulars of the situation. Norris (2001) likewise observed that the only way that educational theories can be expected to enrich teaching practice is not as situational or context-specific problem-solving strategies that can be applied in a recipe-like fashion but instead as general models which teachers need to adapt to their specific context. Whether and how a certain theory applies to a teacher's given situation is a question that only those who know the particulars of the situation can answer. I suggest it is the virtue of phronesis, both employed and exercised in the process of critical reflection and self-reflection, that allows teachers to answer this question. To act authentically in teaching, and as scholars of teaching, then involves investing one's *self* in one's actions. I have to decide and take responsibility for my actions in the light of uncertainty and contingency. I cannot hide behind any 'evidence-based' rules or algorithms, although I consider research findings in my decision.

In making a case for a second version of evidence-based teaching Elliott draws on the by now classic work of educational thinkers Richard Peters and Lawrence Stenhouse, writing in the 1960s and 1970s, respectively. It is this second version I will turn to next.

Ethical consistency of teaching strategies and educational ends

In this version of evidence-based practice the concern lies not in instrumental effectiveness but 'in the extent to which teaching strategies are ethically consistent with *educational* ends' (Elliott, 2005, p. 570, emphasis in original). Commenting on what he means by educational ends or aims, Peters proposed that a person is never educated 'in relation to any specific end, function, or mode of thought' (Peters cited in Elliott, 2005, p. 562). These specific competences would constitute training not education. True educational ends or aims, according to Peters, should not be confused with purposes that are extrinsic to education, such as the employability of students or the economic growth or productivity of the community. Aims that are intrinsic to what it means to become educated are best understood as 'the transformation of a person's way of seeing the world in relation to him or herself' (Elliott, 2005, p. 562). This notion of what it means to become educated, understood as a qualitative transformation in one's general perspective or outlook on life, chimes well with the idea of student authenticity that we have been concerned with throughout this book. Peters's intent in identifying the aims which are intrinsic to becoming educated was 'to clarify the minds of educators about their priorities' (Peters cited in Elliott, 2005, p. 562). The many daily judgements teachers need to make should be consistent with the overall aim of helping students acquire a transformed way of 'seeing the world in relation to themselves'. This argument that educational priorities, or overall aims, should offer guidance for teachers' actions is also reminiscent of the notion of a *horizon of significance* we encountered earlier in this book.

As I discussed in Chapter 2, horizons of significance refer to our socially constructed ideals of what it means to do 'good' and act professionally as academic teachers. Following Grimmet and Neufeld (1994), I suggested that doing 'good' as a teacher means to serve the important interests of students. Since it is in the students' important interests that they grow into their authenticity, I further argued that inviting the students into their authenticity should be a universal aim of higher education teaching. The assumptions that inform the capabilities approach to higher education pedagogies (e.g. Walker, 2006) resonate especially well with this overall aim. Developing the capabilities of '*Practical reason; Educational resilience; Knowledge and imagination; Learning dispositions; Social relations and integrity; Respect, dignity and recognition; Emotional integrity*, and *Bodily integrity*' (p. 127), offers students the opportunity to choose a life they have reason to value (Nussbaum & Sen, 1993) and thus provides the foundation for students to become authentic. It is through critical reflection and critical *self*-reflection on assumptions, or objective and subjective reframing, that students might develop the above capabilities and thus move towards greater authenticity. In Chapter 2 I made some practical suggestions for how to promote the authenticity of students. The underlying argument was similar to that offered by Peters: it is the aims of education that define what counts as worthwhile educational processes and the aims and processes must be ethically consistent. For Peters, as for Carr (2000), the aims and processes of education are therefore not externally, contingently or causally related, as in a traditional means–ends model based on instrumental rationality, but the processes (or means) are internally, logically or constitutively related to the aims (or ends). Importantly, the means are never neutral but always influence the ends. In response to these considerations Elliott (2005) concludes that the most appropriate role of educational research is then not to discover causal links between strategies and learning outcomes but 'to investigate the conditions for realising a coherent educational process in particular practical settings' (p. 564).

Citing Stenhouse, Elliott makes clear that 'the problems selected for inquiry are selected because of their importance as educational problems; that is, for their significance in the context of professional practice' (Stenhouse cited in Elliott, 2005, p. 570). Stenhouse argued that as teachers follow a research-based approach to their teaching, they ought to base their decisions on the two kinds of evidence just outlined: the ethical consistency between strategies and aims *and* the instrumental effectiveness of the strategies employed. Together these two constitute 'actionable evidence'. Importantly, what is shown to be instrumentally effective must also be shown to be ethically consistent. Evidence that meets only the first criterion is an insufficient basis for teaching practice. Hence, engaged in pedagogical inquiry in the form of context-bound case studies on their own teaching, teachers may adopt a variety of different methods of inquiry in establishing 'actionable evidence'. So while Hargreaves conceives of the role of educational *research as a basis for practice*, Stenhouse sees *practice as a basis for research* (Elliot, 2005). This distinction, we saw in Chapter 3, also underlies different conceptualisations of the scholarship of university teaching. In the next section I will reconnect with the 'scholarship of teaching literature' and show how the observations made above link up with the particular interpretation of the scholarship of teaching developed in this book.

Experience-based and theory-based/research-based knowledge in the scholarship of teaching

In Chapter 3 we saw that different conceptions of the scholarship of university teaching (or the scholarship of teaching and learning, if you prefer) intersect with how the relationship between research and practice is understood (Menges & Weimer, 1996; Perry & Smart, 2007; Richlin, 2001). Although Menges and Weimer (1996) and Perry and Smart (2007) conceptualise the 'scholarship of teaching' slightly differently, they seem to share the view that *research on teaching* should be the *basis for practice*. In other words, they suggest that formal research carried out in settings other than the one in which we teach offers us guidance or insights for our own teaching. I would imagine that both Menges and Weimer (1996) and Perry and Smart (2007) assume that in the process of engaging with the research evidence of others, or, we might say, with the knowledge claims of others, teachers ask themselves 'How, if at all, is this research evidence relevant and how might it inform my practice?'.

Richlin (2001), we saw in Chapter 3, seems to espouse the view that *practice* should be *a basis for research*, as advocated, for example, by Stenhouse (1983) and Cochran-Smith and Lytle (1993). What Richlin seems to be saying is that our own particular teaching context – that is, our own courses, programmes or departments, with our own students – is what needs to be understood better and hence should become the basis for research. However, Richlin (2001) also emphasises that before teachers should embark on any research on their practice they should first engage with the research evidence of others, that is, the knowledge claims of others, so that they can build on this evidence. Again, the question that teacher-researchers need to ask is 'How, if at all, is this existing research evidence relevant and how might it inform my practice *and* my research'?. So in essence Richlin holds both views: *practice* should be *a basis for research on teaching* and *research on teaching* should be a *basis for practice*.

There are two points I want to hold on to here: first, common to all three perspectives (Menges and Weimer, Perry and Smart, and Richlin) is the idea that research can deliver answers that can guide us in our teaching practice; second, engagement in the scholarship of university teaching always involves some form of engagement with the knowledge claims of others. However, this engagement, as intimated in the introduction to this chapter, I now want to stress, is best understood as a mediation of theory-based/research-based knowledge with experience-based knowledge, which is different from presupposing that research can offer (or must offer) evidence of 'what works'!

In Chapter 5 I interpreted the scholarship of teaching as critically reflective inquiry into the various practices, policies, processes, aims and purposes associated with university teaching and learning. This reflective inquiry can be engaged in either formally or informally. Taking a critically reflective inquiring approach to teaching and learning, I suggested in the Introduction, is an obligation on the part of all academics, for we all have a professional responsibility to approach our teaching with the same level of curiosity, knowledge and care as we would for the other aspects of our academic work. However, I do not hold the view that all academics must engage in *formal* reflective inquiry. Formal inquiry, or research, when motivated by the goods that are internal to this social practice, has much value (a point discussed in Chapter 5 and one I shall return to in the next chapter); however, to repeat an earlier observation, it is the nature and depth of the reflective processes underpinning the inquiry, not the level of the formality by which we engage in the inquiry, that open the path to authenticity.

The informal inquiries we engage in are informed by and add to our experience-based knowledge. Experience-based knowledge includes both the knowledge we hold as individuals and our shared wisdom of practice (Weimer, 2006). The formal inquiries some of us engage in are, obviously, also informed by and enrich our experience-based knowledge but in addition they are informed by public, codified or theory-based/research-based knowledge and contribute to this knowledge. Importantly, although such knowledge is often regarded to be more robust and valid than experience-based knowledge, Fenstermacher (1994) argued that experience-based knowledge is also legitimate knowledge as long as its underlying knowledge claims are justified. In Chapter 5 we saw that Fenstermacher (1994) proposed that in the realm of informal inquiry, leading to experience-based or *practical* knowledge, the justification of knowledge claims may occur through either the use of evidence or reasoned argument. In the realm of formal inquiry, leading to theory-based/research-based knowledge, the justification of knowledge claims, so Fenstermacher had argued, occurs through the use of evidence. To my mind the distinction Fenstermacher draws here between evidence and reasoned argument does not really hold. The reasoned conclusions reached through the careful and systematic interpretation of various sources of data, as portrayed in the story of Chris and her colleagues in the preamble to this book, is also a form of evidence. Evidence is not be restricted to statistical evidence generated through large-scale controlled experimental or quasi-experimental studies, as advocated by some proponents of 'evidence-based practice'. Writing about the different methodological approaches that are possible in the scholarship of teaching, when construed as formal inquiry, McKinney (2007) and Hutchings (2000) take a similar position. When we justify our knowledge claims through critical reflection and critical self-reflection on assumptions, we develop reasoned arguments that constitute evidence. This is the case irrespective of whether these inquiries are engaged in formally or informally.

Closing the loop: the role of evidence in justifying our claims to knowledge on how to serve the important interests of students

The three knowledge domains that are relevant to engagement in the scholarship of teaching include: knowledge about educational aims, purposes and goals; knowledge about student learning and development; and knowledge about curricula and pedagogies (see Figure 5.1). Engagement in the scholarship of teaching implies the justification of knowledge claims through critical reflection and critical self-reflection in each domain. The justification of knowledge claims may involve instrumental, communicative or emancipatory learning (Table 5.1). In the previous chapter I argued that if the purpose of the scholarship of teaching is to serve *the important interests of students*, and this is recognised as fostering the students' *authenticity*, then it follows that we need to find out what becoming more authentic implies for particular students. Engagement in the scholarship of teaching, therefore, requires *listening to how students think*; that is, listening to how they make sense of the world. This includes listening to how students experience their learning and how they perceive their learning environments. By getting a sense of the assumptions, views, expectations, beliefs and justifications by which students make sense of their world we are in a position to ask better questions about how to make our practices more conducive to their learning and development. This in turn implies finding ways that will encourage students to reflect on their own assumptions and their personal ways of meaning-making. Listening is similar to Arendt's notion of 'visiting'. It involves imagining what a situation looks like from another person's perspective and developing an understanding for the standpoints of others. How does this understanding of what the scholarship of teaching (and learning) *is*, or *could be*, relate to the previous discussion of evidence-based practice?

Drawing on Peters and Stenhouse (as discussed in Elliott, 2005), I suggest that engagement in the scholarship of teaching implies that we reflect, first, on the value or desirability of educational ends (i.e. the aims, purposes and goals of university teaching), second, on the ethical consistency between our means (strategies) and ends, and, only third, on whether the means bring about desired ends. The notion of educational ends and means can be mapped onto the three knowledge domains in teaching. The *ends* obviously refer to the knowledge domain '*educational aims, purposes and goals*' (see Figure 5.1). However, ends also include the forms of '*learning and student development*' we expect students to engage in for the realisation of these aims, purposes and goals. This second knowledge domain we might also think of as 'concrete ends', while the first knowledge domain can be conceived of as 'principal ends'. The *means* refer to the third knowledge domain, *curricula and pedagogies* (including specific teaching and assessment strategies).

In Chapter 5 I offered several examples of reflective questions that can be asked for each of the three knowledge domains, distinguishing questions that consider how we describe or frame the problem (content reflection) from those that focus on how we solve the problem (process reflection) and those that examine underlying presuppositions (premise reflection). The purpose was to show how we engage in the justification of knowledge claims in each of these domains through different forms of reflection and kinds of learning (see Table 5.1). I now want to argue that these questions, and the knowledge domains they represent, actually stand in a particular relationship to one another (see Table 7.1). In developing this argument I start with three observations. First, I observe that our educational aims, purposes and goals (principal *ends*) and the forms of learning and student development these demand (concrete *ends*) need to be desirable. Second, I observe that the principal and concrete *ends* must also be internally and ethically consistent with the curricula and pedagogies we employ (*means*). And third, I observe that only if the ends and means are ethically consistent does it make sense to explore whether the curricula and pedagogies (*means*) are effective in bringing about the desired ends. In establishing the ethical consistency between our educational (principal and concrete) ends and the means we employ when working with particular students, we draw on the virtue of 'phronesis'. In establishing the

Table 7.1 The relationship between ends and means in university teaching

Principal/universal ends	Concrete ends	Means
A: Aims, purposes and goals of university teaching	B: Forms of learning and student development	C: Curricula and pedagogies we employ
Concrete reflective questions (1) What is it that we hope to achieve?	*Concrete reflective questions* (2) What are the assumptions, views, expectations, beliefs and justifications by which students presently make sense of the world? (4) Are we successful with how we support students in questioning these assumptions?	*Concrete reflective questions* (3) How can we help students question these assumptions?
Generic thematic questions	*Generic thematic questions*	*Generic thematic questions*
On content:	On content:	On content:
• What are the aims, purposes and goals of my (our) teaching, in relation to this particular class or course or programme but also in relation to higher education in general?	• What do I (we) expect or demand of students in terms of the learning that they need to master? • What are the challenges for different students? • What are their present ways of knowing and being and what are the ones that they need to develop?	• What curricula and pedagogies are needed to support students in their learning and development?
On process:	On process:	On process:
• How do I (we) know that these are good aims, goals and purposes? • How meaningful are these aims, goals and purposes?	• How do I (we) know that these ways of knowing and being are important? • How well do I (we) support students in developing these ways of knowing and being? • Who is doing well, who is not doing well?	• How do I (we) know that these curricula and pedagogies (and specific teaching and assessment strategies) we decided on are good ones? • How good am I (are we) at implementing them?

(*Continued*)

Table 7.1 (Continued)

Principal/universal ends	Concrete ends	Means
On premises:	On premises:	On premises:
• Why did I (we) decide on these aims, goals and purposes? • Are they equally relevant for all learners? • What might be other possibilities/ alternatives?	• Why do I (we) believe these ways of knowing and being are important? • Are they equally relevant for all learners? • Do all learners have an equal chance to develop them? • Why do I (we) expect learners to behave in these particular ways? What might be other possibilities/ alternatives?	• Why did I (we) decide on these curricula and pedagogies? • What considerations were driving these decisions? • How inclusive are these curricula and pedagogies? • Are they appropriate for all students? • What might be other possibilities/ alternatives?
1. Ensure desirability of ends Drawing on the virtue of 'phronesis'		
2. Ensure ethical consistency between means and ends Drawing on the virtue of 'phronesis'		
to achieve ends Drawing on the virtue of 'techne'		3. Ensure effectiveness of means

effectiveness of means (curricula and pedagogies) for bringing about certain ends (forms of learning and development), we draw on the virtue of 'techne'. Hence, both 'phronesis' and 'techne' are important in the scholarship of teaching but I would like to stress that 'techne' is in the service of 'phronesis', or put differently, that 'phronesis' informs 'techne' (see also Squires, 1999).

If the goal is to foster in students critical reflection and critical self-reflection on assumptions so as to invite them to grow into their authenticity, what might be some of the questions critically reflective teachers could pose about their practice, and how do these relate to the knowledge domains and kinds of learning introduced earlier? The general or thematic questions introduced in Chapter 5 are still relevant. However, critically reflective teachers might consider additional more concrete questions including:

1   What is it that we hope to achieve here?
2   What are the assumptions, views, expectations, beliefs and justifications by which students presently make sense of the world?

3   How can we help students question these assumptions?
4   Are we successful with how we support students in questioning these
     assumptions?

The first two questions, I suggest, address the knowledge domains of 'aims,
purposes and goals' and 'learning and student development', respectively. The
third question addresses the knowledge domains of 'curricula and pedagogies'.
The fourth question addresses the knowledge domain of 'learning and student
development'. The key issue in the remaining part of this chapter is to clarify
what drawing on and contributing *evidence* means in this context (see Table 7.1).

Revisiting Habermas's distinction between three different kinds of knowledge
is helpful at this stage as it also offers a broader conceptualisation of 'evidence'.
As we saw in Chapter 5, in his early work, Habermas (1971) distinguished three
knowledge-constitutive interests which develop within the social media of work,
language and power: the technical (an interest in controlling and predicting the
environment); the practical (an interest in arriving at shared understandings and
getting along with one another); and the critical (an interest in developing or
becoming empowered). These interests give rise to certain forms of science (or
processes of knowing), with their corresponding domains of knowledge. A technical interest gives rise to the empirical–analytical sciences which lead to 'objective truth'. The practical interest gives rise to interpretative science which leads to
an understanding of what is considered 'right' in the light of the norms that are
accepted within a certain social context. The critical interest is associated with a
critical social science and leads to emancipation, that is, freedom from oppression
and ideology, and gives rise to 'truthfulness'.

The basic idea is that subjecting all forms of knowing to one and the same form
of rationality is inappropriate. These three domains and processes of knowing
have also been associated with instrumental, communicative and emancipatory
learning (Mezirow, 1991), respectively (see Table 5.1). The four concrete reflective questions introduced earlier can now be allocated to these different forms of
learning. The first two (see also Table 7.1) fall into the realm of communicative
learning, the third into the realm of emancipatory learning and the fourth within
the realm of instrumental learning.

All three forms of learning identified by Mezirow are therefore relevant to the
scholarship of university teaching. As part of the scholarship of teaching we want
to know 'What are the assumptions, views, expectations, beliefs and justifications
by which students presently make sense of the world?'(see question 2). In relation to this, we also want to inquire into 'What is it that we hope to achieve' (see
question 1), and explore whether this 'is right' and whether our strategies and
aims are meaningful and *desirable* (communicative learning). We might ask is it
right that we expect students to participate in discussion groups. Is it right to
challenge students' conceptions? In other words, in dialogue with colleagues we
want to come to an understanding of what we hope to achieve in and through
higher education and what pedagogies would be consistent with identified aims,

purposes and goals. In dialogue with students, and importantly, by listening to students, we want to get a sense of how they think and make sense of their experiences. Communicative learning falls within the second understanding of evidence-based practice discussed earlier. It is based on a practical interest and inspired by the virtue of 'phronesis'. Here we explore the ethical consistency between our means and ends.

However, ethical consistency, albeit critically important, is not enough. We also want to know how *effective* the teaching approaches are that we employ in particular situations (instrumental learning). To this effect we might ask 'Does it work?' or 'Are we successful with how we support students in questioning their assumptions?' (see question 4). This learning is based on a technical interest and inspired by the virtue of 'techne'. It addresses the first meaning of evidence-based practice discussed earlier.

In addition, we want to know whether certain practices we employ might inadvertently privilege or disadvantage certain individuals or groups. Within this context we might ask 'How can we help these particular students question their assumptions?' (see question 3). This question is based on a critical interest and is informed by the virtue of a critically inspired phronesis (Table 5.1). The pursuit of the critical interest entails tracing the origins of our own justifications, expectations, norms, values and traditions that have evolved within our community, and exploring alternatives to these. The question that concerns us is 'Why did we ever think that things need to be done this way – might there be alternatives?', an example of emancipatory learning.

In summary, engagement in the scholarship of teaching involves asking not only 'Does it work?' but also 'Is it right?' (or 'What are we doing it *for*?'). In addition engagement in the scholarship of teaching involves seeking to understand *for whom* it works, for whom *not*, in what contexts, and *why*, and acting on these insights. As noted in the introduction to this chapter, questions such 'Who gains – who loses, by which mechanisms of power?', 'Is this desirable?' and 'What can be done?' (see Flyvbjerg, 2001, p. 162) at all times ought to precede the question 'And does it work?'.

Existing research-based knowledge, or the knowledge claims of others, can be helpful in guiding our thinking about some of these questions but research cannot give us all the answers. Critical reflection on practice, therefore, always involves a process of mediation of the claims that are being put forward as justifications of good practice by others. We might say that engagement in the scholarship of teaching involves us being evidence-*aware* or evidence-*informed*, as both these terms acknowledge explicitly that the 'evidence' produced by research does not determine but only informs the decisions professionals make (Biesta, 2007). Moreover, in determining the desirability of our educational aims, the traditional research literature again is of only little help. As noted earlier in this book, it is the philosophical literature that can offer better guidance on value questions. The prevailing view that the most important knowledge about university teaching (along with expertise in the subject matter) comes from the psychology of learning and instructional design (see Introduction) is therefore clearly erroneous. As far as our own generation of evidence or justification of knowledge claims through reasoned arguments is concerned, this can be a matter of either formal or informal inquiry. There are a wide range of approaches, quantitative and qualitative, available to us in the formal study of content, process and premise reflection questions. However, given that authenticity requires also subjective reframing through critical *self*-reflection, and not just objective reframing, purely instrumental approaches to research, or scientific studies, by themselves, are not conducive to promoting authenticity. In terms of informal inquiry, evidence or reasoned arguments are generated through observations of students, dialogue with students, colleagues, administrators, policy makers and so forth, and a felt sense of empowerment. Such evidence is perhaps similar in nature to Patti Lather's (1986) notion of catalytic validity in formal critical inquiry/research, which refers to the degree to which research moves those it studies to transformative action.

Conclusion

A narrow interpretation of the scholarship of teaching as an 'evidence-based practice' (and/or as studies that offer evidence of 'what works', which then is to be directly applied to practice) ignores the fact that the scholarship of teaching is a practice that takes place in contexts characterised by unpredictability, complexity and contingency, and hence calls for the professional's personal judgements. The validity claim against which instrumental studies of 'what works' are judged is that of '*objective truth*', associated with the empirical–analytical sciences. I suggested that the dominant discourse of a narrowly defined evidence-based practice founded on an instrumental rationality is an ideology, leading us to emphasise questions of 'what works' at the expense of those addressing the desirability of our aims and means, and the ethical consistency between means and ends. Indeed, Carr (2000) made the point that 'Education is at heart a moral practice which is deeply implicated in values and conflict of value – rather than a technological enterprise directed towards the efficient achievement of agreed ends' (Carr, 2000, p. 76). Included in any consideration of value or desirability, I suggest, have got to be questions that ask 'Desirable for whom?', 'For whom not?', 'In what contexts?', and 'Why?'. While studies of 'what works' (or, as Biesta argued, 'what worked') are important, the scholarship of teaching is enriched through explorations that are located within the interpretive and critical sciences, adhering to the validity claims of '*rightness*' and '*truthfulness*' (or authenticity), respectively. Rather than conceiving of the scholarship of teaching as an 'evidence-based practice', I argue that the scholarship of teaching is a critically reflective, evidence-informed and moral practice. I intimated that equating the scholarship of teaching with research on teaching, or *formal inquiry*, is also an ideology that a critical perspective would encourage us to challenge. But this is the issue to be taken up in the following chapter.

Chapter 8

Going public

Introduction

'Making public' is widely accepted as the distinguishing feature of scholarship (e.g. Andresen, 2000; Huber & Hutchings, 2005; McKinney, 2007, 2012; Richlin & Cox, 2004; Shulman, 2000). In this chapter I will review some of the traditional reasons for why we think going public is important. My intent, however, is to offer a reinterpretation of what 'making public' in the scholarship of teaching might entail and Hannah Arendt's (1958) tripartite categorisation of the *vita activa* (the life of action and speech) and Jürgen Habermas's (1983) validity claims offer me helpful conceptual tools for this final task.

Arendt's analysis of the human condition and the intersections of her work with Habermas's much later theory of communicative action are powerful theoretical frameworks to consider in our understanding of what it means to 'go public'. As was the case with MacIntyre's (2007) notion of a social practice discussed in Chapter 4, I propose that turning to theory can be immensely helpful for understanding the very practical matter of public engagement with the scholarship of teaching. Brookfield (2005) likewise observes that 'theory is useful to the extent that it provides us with understandings that illuminate what we observe and experience' (p. 5). With respect to *critical theory* specifically, he comments that it is useful to the extent 'that it helps us understand not just how the world is but also how it might be changed for the better' (p. 7) and similarly 'to the extent that it keeps alive the hope that the world can be changed to make it fairer and more compassionate' (p. 9). I was first inspired to explore the contributions Hannah Arendt's work could make to our understanding of the scholarship of teaching through a paper by David Coulter (2004) from the University of British Columbia, which was shared at the First Annual Conference of the International Society for the Scholarship of Teaching and Learning at Indiana University, Bloomington. Although at that time described as a work in progress, Coulter's paper included a tantalising discussion of Arendtian action, focusing on her concept of judging, comprising both 'visiting dialogue' (or we might say 'narrative imagination') and thinking (or we might say 'reflection'). Coulter proposed that true scholars are public intellectuals who practise both 'visiting' and thinking and thereby engage with others critically. One way they do this, Coulter argued, is through their teaching; however, he made clear that 'teaching', when understood as engagement, refers not just to the teaching of specific classes or courses but goes beyond to include engagement with the wider community. As scholars engage in this wider form of teaching, they can be seen as public intellectuals who practise their freedom. In making this point Coulter is inspired by Edward Said (1994) who commented that public intellectuals are people:

> whose whole being is staked on a critical sense, a sense of being unwilling to accept easy formulas, or ready-made clichés, or the smooth, ever-so-accommodating confirmations of what the powerful or conventional have to say, and what they do. Not just passively unwilling, but actively willing to say so in public.
>
> (Said, 1994, p. 17)

It is this broader sense of what it means to 'go public' with our teaching that I would like to draw on in this chapter. I basically pick up the discussion where Coulter's paper ended. Going public, I argue, is of necessity linked to questions of social justice and equality *in* and *through* higher education. Scholars of teaching construed as public intellectuals, hold a sense of professionalism that is oriented not just to questions of what works and what one is *supposed* to do but 'why one does it and who benefits from it' (Said, 1994, p. 83). In line with the position taken in this book, I suggest that the scholarship of teaching needs to be linked to public engagement with ethical considerations, specifically the question of what we think we are committed to in the scholarship of teaching and what we consider its purpose to be. Defining ourselves around such commitments and purposes, or 'horizons of significance', I argued in Chapter 3, is part of developing a new sense of professionalism as academics (e.g. Brookfield, 1990; Nixon *et al.*, 2001), and hence an integral aspect of the scholarship in which we are engaged. Building on the previous chapter, I propose that a narrowly interpreted evidence-based approach to the scholarship of teaching is associated with a public review against the validity claim of 'truth', rather than those of 'rightness' and 'truthfulness' by which we judge knowledge in the ethical realm of human activity (Habermas, 1971, 1983). I further suggest that traditional notions of peer review, favour a concept of scholarship as *work* rather than as *action* (Arendt, 1958). Broadening our understanding of the scholarship of teaching as *action* would address hitherto neglected validity claims and emphasise the linkages between scholarship and public engagement. These observations, concepts and their relationships now require some elaboration. Prior to this discussion, I shall briefly review how other commentators on the scholarship of teaching typically interpret the meaning and purpose of 'making public'.

Making the scholarship of teaching public

In a widely cited article Shulman (2000) proposed that 'we develop a scholarship of teaching when our work as teachers becomes public, peer-reviewed and critiqued. And exchanged with members of our professional communities so they, in turn, can build on our work' (p. 50). McKinney (2007) helpfully observes that 'notions of making public and of peer review are socially constructed; they vary by time or history, context, and the groups involved in defining them' (p. 84). She then goes on to note that just what counts as making public is construed differently across a range of disciplines and institutions. However, she adds that within the academy, traditional peer-reviewed articles and presentations are the most highly regarded ways of making one's work public. Given this privileging of traditional over alternative forms of making one's work public, McKinney then offers useful advice on how to share one's scholarship of teaching work through journal articles, presentations and web-postings. More recently, McKinney (2012) takes a more radical view, adding that it is important to make greater use of 'public/press interviews, newsletters, web representations, performances, readings, videos, and structured conversations' (p. 2). In terms of structured conversations specifically, she argues that formal seminars where we come to together to 'share and discuss local or other appropriate SoTL results' (p. 2) might be ways of enhancing what we do presently to make our work public.

Similarly, Hash (2005) observes that while different genres and venues help to reach different audiences:

> only the critical and collaborative examination of that work can determine whether it is useful to others. To that end, the mechanisms and forums for exchanging and reviewing teachers' work across groups, organisations, and contexts also have to be developed.
>
> (Hash, 2005, p. 11)

Ideas of going public and engaging in critique are central also to the notion of the 'teaching commons', which Huber and Hutchings (2005), in the introduction to their Carnegie Foundation report on the scholarship of teaching, describe as 'a conceptual space in which communities of educators committed to inquiry and innovation come together to exchange ideas about teaching and learning' (p. x).

The observations by Shulman, McKinney and Hash, as well as Huber and Hutchings, suggest that the reason we consider making our pedagogical inquiries public is twofold: first, we see value in exchanging what has been learnt from various inquiries, as others may become inspired to use some of it in order to improve the learning and development of their students; second, we believe that through a process of public peer review we can assess the quality of what has been learned. While I agree with these points on a general level, I do, at the same time, observe that the academy seems to have happily bought into the assumption that unless our knowledge about teaching is shared and made public in a similar way to how research is shared and made public, it is not really considered worthwhile knowledge at all. Foucault's (1980) notion of regimes of truth encountered in the previous chapter leads us to question why certain ideas of what the scholarship of teaching *is* apparently come naturally to the forefront in discussions on its meaning within the academy. Despite Boyer's (1990) intention to challenge the undervaluing of teaching, we can still observe, with apologies to Orwell, that the scholarship of discovery is more equal than the other domains of scholarship, particularly teaching. For it to count for something, the scholarship of teaching has to resemble research; that is, it has to be carried out as formal inquiry and be published in ways that the academy (and its various subcultures) considers legitimate. This is the regime of truth that characterises the academy. Moreover, even in cases when less traditional ways of publicising our work are proposed, such as websites and structured dialogue, there is an understanding that our inquiries should offer evidence of 'what works', or should show how the evidence generated by others was useful in bringing about certain results. What we usually stress in our conversations of what it means to go public is that the results that are shared should then be *useful* for improving practices. Quality is equated with usefulness. This, I want to argue, is another aspect of the prevailing regime of truth. If there is no clear sense resulting from our inquiries that 'if teachers do X rather than Y in their professional practice, there will be a significant and enduring improvement in outcome' (Hargreaves, 1997, p. 413), the work is not really deemed very valuable.

There is clearly much value in inquiries that explore 'what works' (or what worked) in particular contexts, and also in the careful consideration of how the results obtained by others might be useful for our own context (in the previous chapter I discussed this form of reflection as the *mediation* of research-based/ theory-based knowledge). However, as I discussed in that chapter as well, the problem is that within this discourse of 'what works' questions regarding the value or desirability of our efforts are not routinely raised. We might also say that we observe the hegemony of 'utility' over 'meaningfulness'. We do need utility, but the utility we strive towards should be informed by what we consider to be meaningful. What I would like to argue in this chapter, therefore, are four points. First, we need to appreciate the value of public exchanges about our formal *and* informal inquiries and encourage these; second, these exchanges need to consider both the value or 'meaningfulness' of our efforts as well as their utility; third, going public should be a way of working towards greater social justice *in* and *through* education; fourth, going public requires being critical and is an integral aspect of what it means to become more authentic. Hannah Arendt's work helpfully informs each of these points.

Scholarship and the 'vita activa'

Arendt (1958) divides human activity into *labour*, *work* and *action*. She asserts that labour and work occur principally in private spaces but that action occurs publicly. *Labour* is linked to human survival and refers to the cyclical, repetitive and continuous process of meeting the needs of the moment. The products of labour do not last very long but are needed for immediate consumption. Essentially, labour refers to the activity whereby humans react to the necessity of the demands of nature. As labour takes care of basic needs, it is a prerequisite for humans to be able to engage in the other two activities. We can easily see how the notion of labour plays out in university teaching. Courses need to be prepared, revised and taught to new groups of incoming students each year, their learning needs to be nurtured and assessed, and course quality assurance procedures adhered to. Once one group of students leaves, a new semester begins with a new group of students and the cyclical process continues. Teaching in many ways is labour. Because labour occurs in the sphere of the private, it is perhaps more diffi-cult to associate the notion of labour with the scholarship of teaching. However, the scholarship of teaching can be interpreted as either *work* or *action*.

In contrast to labour, *work* is geared towards gaining control over and separat-ing from nature (Arendt, 1958). Rather than being cyclical, work has a clear beginning and end and is characterised by using appropriate means so as to pro-duce certain predetermined ends. The thinking underlying the activity of work is therefore that of 'techne', defined by a means–ends rationale. Work is associated with producing things, such as tools, that are permanent and can be used and reused. It produces stable structures that instil a sense of security and confidence in light of the unpredictability of nature. According to Arendt, work is important as it generates a safe space for humans to live. Just like labour, work is also a rather private activity. Although the products of fabrication are traded in the public sphere, Arendt suggests that they are still produced in private by the master builder and the purpose of the exchange is to serve principally private not public interests.

The scholarship of teaching resembles the activity of *work* in that it is associated with developing outputs that can be used, reused, shared and built upon (e.g. Shulman, 2000). These outputs typically include articles and conference papers (although some would include in this list web-postings and the development of innovative teaching artefacts that others can draw on). Although publicly shared, conference papers and journal articles serve a principally private interest if they are developed to satisfy external demands (e.g. institutional requirements for publi-cations) or to satisfy one's own internal needs (e.g. writing another book or arti-cle brings me personal rewards). Of course, the same publications *can* serve a public interest, but the distinguishing feature then is an authentic motivation to enhance teaching by doing what is in the important interests of students.

In Chapter 4, following MacIntyre, we said that serving the important interests of students, that is, the students' authenticity, is one of the important internal goods to be gained from our engagement in the scholarship of teaching. Other internal goods included the enjoyment, achievement or satisfaction we experi-ence by inquiring into significant questions relating to teaching and learning, deepening our understanding of these issues, growing into ourselves and becom-ing critically aware of the inner motives that guide us in this work, and eventually contributing to the betterment of teaching and learning, and, by extension, the world we live in (see Table 4.1). The scholarship of teaching is also associated with the activity of work because many (but clearly not all) of the questions the scholarship of teaching is concerned with are informed by an instrumental rationality. The key issue is how to make teaching and learning more effective, and investigations often attempt to offer solutions on how best to control the outcomes of teaching and learning through the implementation of certain strategies. When these investigations are made public, the criterion by which they are judged, in the process of peer review, is that of 'objective truth' (see Table 5.1). In other words, what is accepted as evidence is that which can be judged as being 'true' according to the methods and criteria of the empirical–analytical sciences.

I have already made reference to Habermas's work in previous chapters but his work is also relevant to this present discussion of what it means to 'go public' in the scholarship of teaching, given the close linkages Habermas draws between reflectivity and public engagement. Habermas (1983) suggests that there are different discourses, which are associated with the processes and domains of knowing discussed in his earlier work (Habermas, 1971). The theoretical discourse is concerned with claims to 'truth', the practical discourse with claims to 'rightness' and the aesthetic discourse with claims to 'truthfulness' (or 'authenticity'). On the one hand, adherence to these established discourses with their disciplined methods of inquiry is immensely useful as they assist us in continuously testing (or *con*testing) the validity claims underlying our assertions (see also Dewey, 1991); on the other hand, however, these same discourses may be conceived of as cultural traditions themselves and hence, at least in principle, are open to critique with respect to their adequacy for informing decisions in particular contexts.

As we saw in Chapter 5, Brookfield (2000) provides a good example of such a critique in the domain of instrumental learning (theoretical discourse) when he suggests that critical reflection might involve understanding how the scientific method itself was socially and politically created and how it came to hold its present status in our minds; basically moving the discussion into the realm of practical discourse and *subjective reframing*. In some instances, then, we are able to redeem validity claims by referring to accepted ways of constructing knowledge (for example, the sciences and their claims to 'truth'). In other instances the premises underlying how a problem is defined are heavily contested and reaching consensus is not a straightforward matter. Most complex problems affecting individuals and society, including how to promote student success in education and identifying the key responsibilities of higher education, are not solvable through 'science' alone but require the consideration of moral implications. As noted in the previous chapter, a purely instrumental rationality is inherently conformist (Horkheimer, 1974), as within it important questions regarding the value or desirability of our practices do not arise. This is why I argued that our understanding of what counts as 'evidence' in the scholarship of teaching needs to be broadened, as in most serious discussions all validity claims ('truth', 'rightness' and 'truthfulness' or 'authenticity') would seem important and need to be considered (see also Table 5.1). Arendt's notion of *action* is particularly valuable in further developing this argument. I will first describe what Arendt means by *action* and then discuss how *action* can inform how we understand going public in the scholarship of teaching.

Arendt views *action*, which she derived from Aristotle's notion of 'praxis', as fundamental to politics. Action refers to people practising their freedom to share their opinion in public and thus engage with the opportunity of renewing the world. Specifically, she argues that 'in acting and speaking, men show who they are, reveal actively their unique personal identities and thus make their appearance in the human world' (Arendt, 1958, p. 179). Action is thereby different from behaviour, which she associates with the expected responses of people in a mass society (akin to 'das *man*' or 'the *they*', Heidegger, 1962). In *action* a person takes a stance and discloses *who* he or she is. There is a clear parallel between Arendt's understanding of action and Guignon's (2004) sense of authenticity. Guignon refers to being authentic as the process of getting clear for oneself what one's deliberations lead one to believe and then honestly and fully expressing this in public places.

Arendt also argues that action is based on two conditions, those of plurality and natality. Plurality refers to the fact that as humans we are all equal, in the sense that we are all part of the human species and share a common world; yet, each of us is also unique and distinct from all others. Natality refers to the fact that with each person who was brought into the world there is the chance of a new beginning. This chance of a new beginning is offered each time a person participates in *action*, where 'the unexpected can be expected from him' (Arendt, 1958, p. 178). Natality, for Arendt, was the 'essence of education. Because all newcomers bring with them the possibility that the world might be reinvigorated, natality is a source of social hope' (Levinson, 2001, p. 13). Natality points to both the unpredictability of human action and the possibility for change. According to Arendt (2007), the key purpose of education was for teachers to make it possible for students to act on the future differently and renew the common world. By recognising the views of others with whom we share our world, by 'going visiting', as Arendt (2003) says, we try to imagine what the situation looks like from the point of view of others. In Chapter 2, we saw that one way to foster students' willingness to contribute to social justice and invest themselves in the significant questions facing our humanity is by promoting their 'narrative imagination' (Arendt, 2003; Greene, 1995; Nussbaum, 1997, 2010). Narrative imagination refers to the capacity or disposition to consider a situation from the perspective of someone different from oneself. Being able to do that, I suggested, is an important aspect of what it means to become authentic. Of course, not only the authenticity of students but also the authenticity of teachers hinges on the capability for narrative imagination. Being able to show compassion for the student who is struggling, particularly in an area I myself did not, or would not, find difficult given my unique positioning, requires my capacity for imagining what a situation is like for someone very different from myself.

Action as public engagement

Interpreted through the lens of *action*, the scholarship of teaching takes on a much broader meaning than is typically attributed to it and the idea of 'going public' is inseparable from the intention of creating a better world in which to learn, teach and live. This would include sharing findings from formal inquiries into teaching and learning at conferences, through web-postings and academic journals. However, the scholarship of teaching interpreted as action would also take up bigger issues that are a concern for society as a whole: for example, what are the aims and purposes of higher education (and the scholarship of teaching in particular); what qualities and dispositions do we hope students participating in higher education will graduate with and to what purpose do we hope they will employ these; who has access to certain types of higher education and who does not; what is participating in higher education like for different people; who gains, who loses, and why?

Arendt's influence on Habermas is apparent in the compatibility of their ideas, which, I propose, are both equally helpful for analysing the scholarship of teaching. For Arendt (1958) *action* involves both words and deeds, and is directly linked to speech. Recognising that human consciousness is largely shaped by language and that ideology, therefore, is systematically distorted communication, Habermas (1983) proposes that we need universal standards by which any speech act could be held accountable in terms of the validity claims it makes (i.e. truth, rightness, and truthfulness). A true consensus would be maintainable in an environment of ideal speech conditions; these would include:

> (i) no one capable of making a relevant contribution has been excluded, (ii) participants have equal voice, (iii) they are internally free to speak their honest opinion without deception or self-deception, and (iv) there are no sources of coercion built into the process and procedures of discourse.
>
> (Bohman & Regh, 2011, electronic source)

In the case that conditions are not ideal, and they rarely are, doubt could be cast on what has been accepted as the 'consensus' and could be revealed as a form of ideology. Arendt's *action*, too, does not only involve stating one's opinions freely and publicly but is an invitation to others to question the claims to validity underlying one's arguments.

In reference to both Arendt and Habermas I would like to make two points at this stage. First, the scholarship of university teaching is enriched when formal inquiries are informed not only by the empirical–analytical but also the interpretive and, importantly, the critical sciences (e.g. Carr & Kemmis, 1986). Second, when interpreted as *action*, the scholarship of teaching is enacted not just in such formal inquiries but also in the public dialogue that ensues from posing certain critically reflective questions in the first place. Through such dialogical encounters we engage in the public questioning of validity claims with the purpose of reaching agreement and insight on important matters related to teaching and learning. This public dialogue, I want to emphasise, is not just a way of going public with our inquiries but is, by itself, a form of inquiry.

I would assume that something along these lines is also what both McKinney (2012) and Hash (2005) have in mind when they argue that we need to create more spaces where we can share, discuss and critically examine our work. Ideally, the ideas, questions and controversies that arise from these public dialogical encounters across different views will inform future inquiries into teaching and learning, and the insights gained from these inquiries we will, in turn, share at the next public forum so that they continuously feed into our community discussions. I am extending the argument made by Patricia Cross (2005, keynote address delivered to the American Association of Higher Education in 1998) that we might do better to consider research findings as the start of our conversations into teaching and learning rather than as the conclusion. Specifically she commented:

> If we are to take learning seriously, we need to know what to look for (through research), to observe ourselves in the act of lifelong learning (self-reflection), and to be much more sensitively aware of the learning of the students that we see before us every day. At present, I think we are prone to consider research findings as the conclusion of our investigations into learning. We might do better to think of them as the start of our investigations.
>
> (Cross, 2005, electronic version)

To be clear, when the scholarship of teaching is interpreted as *action* the validity claims that are at stake are not exclusively, or principally, those of 'truth' but also, and importantly, those of 'rightness' and 'truthfulness'. In the previous chapter we also saw that this alters what counts as evidence. Evidence is not just what research has shown to 'work', but also that which we recognise as right and truthful in contexts of dialogue across differences. Critically reflective inquiry in the scholarship of teaching then means more than carrying out a formal study – it means to engage publicly with these same issues so that different perspectives can be heard and debated. This dialogue in itself is informal critical inquiry, in that we engage in the various forms of reflection discussed in previous chapters. It is through such dialogical encounters that we question our current practices and ask what can be done to make them more inclusive and help all students to flourish. These questions, I had argued earlier, are at the heart of the scholarship of teaching.

Habermas's (1983) main thesis, that through communicative action it is possible to arrive at knowledge where the only power at work is that of the better argument, has not remained unchallenged. Many educators have criticised this view for putting too much emphasis on the verbalisation of rational arguments and for ignoring other more subtle ways in which power operates. This position is often associated with the work of Foucault (1980), a name typically placed within the postmodern tradition, but as Tierney and Rhoads (1993) and Brookfield (2005) observe, he is more appropriately labelled a 'critical postmodernist'. According to Tierney (1993) critical postmodernism seeks to fuse 'critical theory's advocacy for empowerment and the development of voice for the oppressed people ... with the postmodern notion of difference' (p. 10). Foucault and Habermas hold different assumptions about how power, and by extension ideology, works. Foucault (1980) believes that there are no power-free zones. In Chapter 6 we saw that Brookfield (2005) is taking a similar position, arguing that power is exercised in multiple ways even in educational practices that on the surface might appear democratic. Ideal speech conditions change the power game but do not eliminate power. Real criticality, critical postmodernists would argue, involves trying to 'separate out, from the contingency that has made us what we are, the possibility of no longer being, doing, or thinking what we are, do, or think' (Foucault, cited in Flyvbjerg, 2001, p. 103). By showing how certain understandings of situations have evolved, by showing that they are the way they are not by necessity and, therefore, could be otherwise, we can open up new possibilities for being and acting. While it is important to point out these postmodern challenges to Habermas's theory of communicative action, these views are compatible with, rather than contradictory to, the basic notion of critique at the heart of Habermas's project and the point of this discussion. Moreover, Arendt's notion of *action* emphasises plurality and dialogue across differences so as to broaden one's views by considering and possibly incorporating those of others. This dialogue across differences is essential for establishing a collective or shared purpose. In a similar vein, and with direct reference to higher education, McLean (2006), as we saw earlier, helpfully observes that 'What is essential is that relevant actors come to agreement about what counts as good pedagogy, for what purposes and what is to be done to make it happen' (p. 126).

Conclusion

The scholarship of teaching understood as *action* thus involves not only the formal inquiries we undertake into matters of teaching and learning but also the inquiry-oriented public dialogue among diverse stakeholders. These include colleagues from our own departments and disciplines but also colleagues from other disciplines, as well as policy makers, parents, politicians and, importantly, students. Everyone participating in this dialogue is uniquely positioned along various dimensions of difference, and the point of the dialogue is not just to share insights and findings but also to disclose and debate diverse points of view about educational matters. Understood this way, the very purpose of 'going public' is to be encouraged, and to encourage others, to reflect even more carefully on matters of profound importance to students and our world. As MacIntyre (1987) once remarked 'one can only think for oneself if one does not think by oneself' (p. 24). True reflectivity, a core attribute of scholarship, therefore requires a public sphere where debate against certain standards of justification can take place. A view of the scholarship of teaching as *action* is also firmly linked to the aims and purposes (the *ends*) of higher education and not just its processes or strategies (the *means*). These aims and purposes include creating a better world *in* and *through* higher education.

Chapter 9

Concluding comments

Rather than offering a summary of how the book's main argument unfolded I will restrict myself in this concluding chapter to just a few final observations on some of the points that have been raised. In Chapter 2 I developed the first central point of this book, which was that academics who engage in the scholarship of university teaching authentically are motivated by a desire to serve the important interests of students. Linked to this was the second central point of this book, namely the assertion that what is in the important interests of students is precisely their own growth towards greater authenticity. I substantiated this assertion through reference to philosophical literature that is chiefly concerned with identifying our most fundamental human interests (e.g. Habermas, 1971; Heidegger, 1962; Nussbaum, 2000; Nussbaum & Sen, 1993). I concluded that promoting students' authenticity is a social justice issue. Once we realise this, it follows that it is imperative that we consider carefully what we do in higher education so as to ensure that our practices are fair to all students. It is these considerations that lie behind the observation that promoting the authenticity of students also means to create greater social justice *in* higher education.

Promoting students' authenticity has implications also for creating greater social justice *through* higher education. As I argued in Chapter 1, authenticity has both an internal and external dimension. While authenticity necessarily involves getting in touch with and pursuing one's own inner motives, something equally important to the human condition would be at risk if one were guided exclusively by that which is internal to oneself. Authenticity involves 'self-definition in dialogue' (Taylor, 1991, p. 66). This implies that we strive not only towards our own authenticity but recognise our mutual interdependence and thus support others' striving towards authenticity. Promoting in students the capabilities of *'Practical reason*; *Educational resilience*; *Knowledge and imagination*; *Learning dispositions*; *Social relations and integrity*; *Respect, dignity and recognition*; *Emotional integrity*, and *Bodily integrity'* (Walker, 2006, p. 127), therefore, could support not only the students' own flourishing but contribute to a reduction of the many problems and inequalities facing our societies as students employ the capabilities they developed for the sake of supporting the authenticity of others (e.g. Nixon, 2011; Walker, 2010). Already a decade ago, Cortese (2003) shared the disturbing

involves 'being unwilling to accept easy formulas, or ready-made clichés' (Said, 1994, p. 17) and being oriented not just to questions of what works and what one is supposed to do but 'why one does it and who benefits from it' (Said, 1994, p. 83). As we engage in critically reflective inquiries on teaching and learning we draw on and further develop the virtues of courage, truthfulness, justice, phronesis and authenticity.

Critically reflective inquiries into 'What works?', 'What is to be done?' *and* 'Why do it?' hold the greatest promise to empower the scholarship of teaching. These questions not only serve to create better teaching and better learning but, so I wish to think, a fairer, more compassionate and sustainable *world*.

References

Adams-Webber, J. R. (1979). *Personal construct theory: Concepts and applications.* New York: Wiley.

Adorno, T. (2003). *The jargon of authenticity* (originally published by Suhrkamp Verlag in 1964). London: Routledge.

Allen, M. N., & Field, P. A. (2005). Scholarly teaching and scholarship of teaching: Noting the difference. *International Journal of Nursing Education Scholarship, 2*(1), Article 12.

Altbach, P. G. (2007). *Tradition and transition: The international imperative in higher education.* Rotterdam, the Netherlands: Sense Publishers.

Andresen, L. W. (2000). A usable, trans-disciplinary conception of scholarship. *Higher Education Research and Development, 19*(2), 137–153.

Arendt, H. (1958). *The human condition.* Chicago: University of Chicago Press.

Arendt, H. (2003). *Responsibility and judgment* (edited with an introduction by Jerome Kuhn). New York: Schocken Books.

Arendt, H. (2007). The crises in education (previously published in *Between Past and Future*, London: Faber & Faber, 1961). In R. Curren (Ed.), *Philosophy of education: An anthology* (pp. 188–192). Oxford: Blackwell.

Argyris, C., Putnam, R., & McLain Smith, D. (1985). *Action science: Concepts, methods, and skills for research and intervention.* San Francisco, CA: Jossey-Bass.

Arnason, V. (1994). Towards authentic conversations: Authenticity in the patient–professional relationship. *Theoretical Medicine, 15*(3), 227–242.

Ashenden, S., & Owen, D. (1999). *Foucault* contra *Habermas: Recasting the dialogue between genealogy and critical theory.* London: Sage.

Ashwin, P., & Trigwell, K. (2004). Investigating staff and educational development. In D. Baume, & P. Kahn (Eds), *Enhancing staff and educational development* (pp. 117–131). London: Falmer Press.

Asmar, C. (2004). Innovations in scholarship at a student-centred research university: An Australian example. *Innovative Higher Education, 29*(1), 49–66.

Astin, A. W., & Astin, H. S. (2006). Foreword. In A. W. Chickering, J. C. Dalton, & L. Stamm (Eds), *Encouraging authenticity and spirituality in higher education* (pp. vii–xi). San Francisco, CA: Jossey-Bass.

Atkinson, M. (2001). The scholarship of teaching and learning: Reconceptualizing scholarship and transforming the academy. *Social Forces, 79*(4), 1217–1230.

Baggini, J. (2005). *What's it all about: Philosophy and the meaning of life.* Oxford: Oxford University Press.

Carr, W., & Kemmis, S. (1986). *Becoming critical: Education, knowledge and action research.* London: Falmer Press.

Cattell, R. B. (1963). Theory of fluid and crystallized intelligence: A critical experiment. *Journal of Educational Psychology, 54,* 1–22.

Chickering, A. W., Dalton, J. C., & Stamm, L. (2006). *Encouraging authenticity and spirituality in higher education.* San Francisco, CA: Jossey-Bass.

Clark, M. C., & Wilson. A. L. (1991). Context and rationality in Mezirow's theory of transformational learning. *Adult Education Quarterly, 41*(2), 75–91.

Clegg, S. (2005). Evidence-based practice in educational research: A critical realist critique of systematic review. *British Journal of Sociology of Education, 26*(3), 415–428.

Cochran-Smith, M., & Lytle, S. (1993). *Inside outside: Teacher research and knowledge.* New York: Teachers College Press.

Colby, A., Ehrlich, T., Beaumont, E., & Stephens, J. (2003) *Educating citizens: Preparing America's undergraduates for lives of moral and civic responsibility.* San Francisco, CA: Jossey-Bass.

Collard, S., & Law, M. (1989). The limits of perspective transformation: A critique of Mezirow's theory. *Adult Education Quarterly, 39*(2), 99–107.

Collini, S. (2012). *What are universities for?* London: Penguin Books.

Cooper, D. E. (1983). *Authenticity and learning: Nietzsche's educational philosophy.* London: Routledge & Kegan Paul.

Cortese, A. (2003). The critical role of higher education in creating a sustainable future. *Planning for Higher Education, 31*(3), 15–22.

Coulter, D. (2004). *Using the scholarship of teaching to foster educational judgment.* Paper presented at the First Annual Conference of the International Society for the Scholarship of Teaching and Learning Bloomington, Indiana State University, October 22.

Cranton, P. (1996). *Professional development as transformative learning.* San Francisco, CA: Jossey-Bass.

Cranton, P. (1998). *No one way: Teaching and learning in higher education.* Toronto: Wall & Emerson.

Cranton, P. (2001). *Becoming an authentic teacher in higher education.* Malabar, FL: Krieger.

Cranton, P. (Ed.) (2006a). *Authenticity in teaching.* New Directions for Adult and Continuing Education, No. 111. San Francisco, CA: Jossey-Bass.

Cranton, P. (2006b). Integrating perspectives on authenticity. In P. A. Cranton (Ed.), *Authenticity in teaching* (pp. 83–89). New Directions for Adult and Continuing Education, No. 111. San Francisco, CA: Jossey-Bass.

Cranton, P. (2011). A transformative perspective on the scholarship of teaching and learning. *Higher Education Research and Development, 30*(1), 75–86.

Cranton, P., & Carusetta, E. (2004). Perspectives on authenticity in teaching. *Adult Education Quarterly, 55*(1), 5–22.

Cross, K. P. (1990). Teachers as scholars. *AAHE Bulletin, 43*(4), 3–5.

Cross, K. P. (2005). What do we know about students' learning and how do we know it? Center for Studies in Higher Education, University of California, Berkeley. Paper CSHE, 7,05 presented at the AAHE National Conference on Higher Education, Atlanta, Georgia, March 24, 1998. Available at: http://cshe.berkeley.edu/publications/docs/ROP.Cross.7.05.pdf (accessed 18 March 2012).

Cross, K. P., & Steadman, M. H. (1996). *Classroom research: Implementing the scholarship of teaching.* San Francisco, CA: Jossey-Bass.

Cuthbert, R. (2011). Is SOTL special and precious, or too special and precious? *SRHE News*, (5), 1.

D'Andrea, V., & Gosling, D. (2005). *Improving teaching and learning in higher education: A whole institution approach*. Maidenhead, UK: Society for Research into Higher Education and Open University Press.

Dall'Alba, G., & Barnacle, R. (2007). An ontological turn for higher education. *Studies in Higher Education, 32*, 679–691.

Davies, H. T. O., Nutley, S. M., & Smith, P. C. (Eds) (2000). What works? *Evidence-based policy and practice in the public services*. Bristol, UK: Policy Press.

Dewey, J. (1991, originally published in 1910). *How we think*. Buffalo, NY: Prometheus Books.

Diamond, R. M. (1993). Changing priorities and the faculty reward system. In R. M. Diamond, & B. E. Adam (Eds), *Recognising faculty work: Reward systems for the year 2000* (pp. 5–23). New Directions for Higher Education, No. 81. San Francisco, CA: Jossey-Bass.

Dillard, C. (2006). *On spiritual strivings: Transforming an African American woman's academic life*. New York: State University of New York Press.

Dirks, A. L. (1998). The new definition of scholarship: How will it change the professoriate? Published online by author, Bridgewater, MA. Available at: http://webhost. bridgew.edu/adirks/ald/papers/skolar.htm (accessed 15 August 2011).

Dirkx, J.M. (2006). Authenticity and imagination. In P. A. Cranton (Ed.), *Authenticity in teaching* (pp. 27–39). New Directions for Adult and Continuing Education, No. 111. San Francisco, CA: Jossey-Bass.

Dunne, J. (1993). *Back to the rough ground: 'Phronesis' and 'techne' in modern philosophy and in Aristotle*. Notre Dame, IN: University of Notre Dame Press.

Dunne, J., & Pendlebury, S. (2003). Practical reason. In N. Blake, P. Smeyers, R. Smith, & P. Standish (Eds), *The Blackwell guide to the philosophy of education* (pp. 194–211). Blackwell Philosophy Guides. Oxford: Blackwell.

Eagleton, T. (2007). *The meaning of life: A very short introduction*. Oxford: Oxford University Press.

Egerton, M. (2002). Higher education and civic engagement. *The British Journal of Sociology, 53*, 603–620.

Elliott, J. (2005). Making evidence-based practice educational. *British Educational Research Journal, 27*(5), 555–574.

Elton, L. (1992). Research, teaching and scholarship in an expanding higher education system. *Higher Education, 46*(3), 252–268.

Elton, L. (2000a). Turning academics into teachers: A discourse on love. *Teaching in Higher Education, 5*(2), 257–260.

Elton, L. (2000b). Dangers of doing the wrong thing righter. HAN Conference Proceedings, January, pp. 7–9. Hogeschool van Arnhem en Nijmegen.

Entwistle, N. (1988). *Styles of learning and teaching: An integrated outline of educational psychology for students, teachers and lecturers*. London: David Fulton.

Entwistle, N. (2009). *Teaching for understanding at university: Deep approaches and distinctive ways of thinking*. London: Palgrave Macmillan.

Entwistle, N. J., & McCune, V. (2009). The disposition to understand for oneself at university and beyond: Learning processes, the will to learn and sensitivity to context. In L.-F. Zang, & R. J. Sternberg (Eds), *Perspectives on the nature of intellectual styles* (pp. 29–62). New York: Springer.

Hansen, F. T. (2007). Phronesis and authenticity as knowledge for philosophical praxis in teacher training. *Paideusis – Journal of Canadian Philosophy of Education, 16*(3), 15–32.

Hargreaves, D. (1997). In defence of research for evidence-based teaching: A rejoinder to Martyn Hammersley. *British Educational Research Journal, 23,* 141–161.

Hargreaves, D. (1999). Revitalizing educational research: Lessons from the past and proposals for the future. *Cambridge Journal of Education, 29*(2), 239–249.

Harland, T., & Pickering, N. (2011). *Values in higher education teaching.* New York; Routledge.

Harvey, L. J., & Myers, M. D. (1995). Scholarship and practice: The contribution of ethnographic research methods to bridging the gap. *Information Technology & People, 8*(3), 13–27.

Hash, T. (2005). Introduction. In T. Hatch, D. Ahmed, A. Lieberman, D. Feigenbaum, M. Eiler White, & D. H. Pointer Mace (Eds), *Going public with our teaching: An anthology of practice.* New York: Teachers College, Columbia Press.

Hatton, N., & Smith, D. (1995). Reflection in teacher education: Towards definition and implementation. *Teaching and Teacher Education, 11,* 33–49.

Healey, M. (2000) Developing the scholarship of teaching through the disciplines. *Higher Education Research and Development, 19,* 169–189.

Healey. M. (2003). The scholarship of teaching: Issues around an evolving concept. *Journal on Excellence in College Teaching, 14*(1/2), 5–26.

Healey, M. (2005). Linking research and teaching exploring disciplinary spaces and the role of inquiry-based learning. In R. Barnett (Ed.), *Reshaping the university: New relationships between research, scholarship and teaching* (pp. 30–42). Maidenhead, UK: McGraw-Hill and Open University Press.

Healey, M. (2011). *Linking research and teaching: A selected bibliography.* Available at: http://www.mickhealey.co.uk/resources (accessed 5 September, 2011).

Heidegger, M. (1962). *Being and time* (translated by J. Macquarrie and E. Robinson). London: SCM Press (original work published in 1927).

Held, D. (1980). *An introduction to critical theory: Horkheimer to Habermas.* Berkeley, CA: University of California Press.

Henkel, M. (2005). Academic identity and autonomy in a changing policy environment. *Higher Education, 49*(1), 155–176.

Herrington, J., Oliver, R., & Reeves, T. C. (2003). Patterns of engagement in authentic online learning environments. *Australian Journal of Educational Technology, 19*(1), 59–71.

Herteis, E. M. (2006). The scholarship of teaching and learning. *Reflections and Directions.* Teaching and Learning at the University of Guelph, pp. 4–8. Available at: http://www.tss.uoguelph.ca (accessed 15 September 2012).

hooks, b. (2003). *Teaching community: A pedagogy of hope.* New York: Routledge.

Horkheimer, M. (1974). *Eclipse of reason.* New York: Continuum.

Hounsell, D. (2011). Graduates for the 21st century: Integrating the enhancement themes. Institutional activities. Synthesis of work of the theme 2010–2011. QAA paper graduate attributes. Available at: http://www.enhancementthemes.ac.uk/docs/resources/synthesis-of-work-of-the-theme-2010-2011-end-of-year-report-dai-hounsell.pdf (accessed 19 December 2011).

Hounsell, D., & Anderson, C. (2009). Ways of thinking and practicing in biology and history: Disciplinary aspects of teaching and learning environments. In C. Kreber (Ed.), *The university and its disciplines* (pp. 71–84). New York: Routledge.

Hoyle, E. (1975). Professionality, professionalism and control in teaching. In V. Houghton, R. McHugh, & C. Morgan (Eds), *Management in education: The management of organisations and individuals* (pp. 314–320). London: Ward Lock Educational in association with Open University Press.

Huber, M., & Hutchings, P. (2005). *The advancements of learning: Building the teaching commons.* The Carnegie Foundation Report on the Scholarship of Teaching and Learning. The Carnegie Foundation for the Advancement of Teaching, San Francisco, CA: Jossey-Bass.

Huber, M., & Hutchings, P. (2008). Placing theory in the scholarship of teaching and learning. *Arts and Humanities in Higher Education, 7,* 229–244.

Huber, M., & Morreale, S. P. (2002). Situating the scholarship of teaching and learning: A cross-disciplinary conversation. In M. Huber, & S. P. Morreale (Eds), *Disciplinary styles in the scholarship of teaching and learning: Exploring common ground* (pp. 1–24). Carnegie Foundation for the Advancement of Teaching and the American Association for Higher Education.

Hughes, J. H. (2006). The scholarship of teaching and learning: A Canadian perspective. *Teaching and Learning in Higher Education, 42.* The newsletter of the Society for Teaching and Learning in Higher Education (STLHE). Available at: http://www.stlhe.ca/wp-content/uploads/2011/06/STLHE-Newsletter-42-2006-Winter.pdf (accessed 12 August 2011).

Hutchings, P. (2000). *Opening lines: Approaches to the scholarship of teaching and learning.* Menlo Park, CA: The Carnegie Foundation for the Advancement of Teaching.

Hutchings, P. (2004). The scholarship of teaching and learning in the United States. *Presentation at the International Society for the Scholarship of Teaching and Learning Conference,* October 2004, Bloomington, Indiana. Available at: http://www.issotl.indiana.edu/issotl/04/hutchings.pdf (accessed 25 August 2011).

Hutchings, P. (2007). Theory: The elephant in the scholarship of teaching and learning. *International Journal for the Scholarship of Teaching and Learning, 1*(1). Available at: http://academics.georgiasouthern.edu/ijsotl/2007_v1n1.htm (accessed 8 August 2011).

Hutchings, P., Huber, M. Y., & Ciccone, A. (2011). *The scholarship of teaching and learning reconsidered: Institutional integration and impact.* The Carnegie Foundation for the Advancement of Teaching. San Francisco, CA: Jossey-Bass.

Hutchings, P., & Shulman, L. S. (1999). The scholarship of teaching: New elaborations, new developments. *Change, 31*(5), 10–15. Available at: http://www.carnegiefoundation.org/elibrary/scholarship-teaching-new-elaborations-new-developments (accessed 29 August 2011).

Inlow, G. (1972). *Values in transition: A handbook.* New York: Wiley.

Jankowicz, D. (2004). *The easy guide to repertory grids.* West Sussex: Wiley & Sons.

Jarvis, P. (1992). *Paradoxes of learning: On becoming an individual in society.* San Francisco, CA: Jossey-Bass.

Jung, C. G. (1971). *Psychological types.* Princeton, NJ: Princeton University Press.

Kahane, D. (2009). Learning about obligation, compassion and social justice. In C. Kreber (Ed.), *Internationalizing the curriculum in higher education* (pp. 49–60). New Directions for Teaching and Learning, No. 118. San Francisco, CA: Jossey-Bass.

Kahn, P. E., Young, R., Grace, S., Pilkington, R., Rush, L., Tomkinson, C. B., & Willis, I. (2006). *The role and effectiveness of reflective practices in programmes for new academic staff: A grounded practitioner review of the research literature.* Higher Education Academy,

Macfarlane, B. (2007). It's more than a stand-up routine. *Times Higher Education*, 23 November. Available at: http://www.timeshighereducation.co.uk/story.asp?storyCode= 311237&sectioncode=26 (accessed 29 August 2011).

MacIntyre, A. (1987). The idea of an educated public. In G. Haydon (Ed.), *Education and values: The Richard Peters lectures* (pp. 15–36). Institute of Education, University of London.

MacIntyre, A. (2007). *After virtue: A study in moral theory* (3rd ed.). London, Duckworth.

McKinney, K. (2002). The scholarship of teaching and learning: Current challenges and future visions. Remarks presented at the Ceremony to Install the Cross Chair in the Scholarship of Teaching and Learning at Illinois State University. Available at: http://www.sotl.ilstu.edu/crossChair/sotlFuture.shtml (accessed 11 April 2011).

McKinney, K. (2007). *Enhancing learning through the scholarship of teaching and learning: The challenges and joys of juggling*. Bolton, MA: Anker Publishing.

McKinney, K. (2012). Making a difference: Application of SoTL to enhance learning (invited essay). *Journal of the Scholarship of Teaching and Learning, 12*(1), 1–7.

McLaughlin, T. H. (2003). Teaching as a practice and a community of practice: The limits of commonality and the demands of diversity. *Journal of Philosophy of Education, 37*(2), pp. 339–352.

McLaughlin, T. H., & Halstead, J. M. (1999). Education in character and virtue. In J. M. Halstead, & T. H. McLaughlin (Eds), *Education in morality* (pp. 132–163). London: Routledge.

McLean, M. (2006). *Pedagogy and the university: Critical theory and practice*. London: Continuum Studies in Education.

Malpas, J. (2003). Martin Heidegger. In R. C. Salomon, & D. L. Sherman (Eds), *The Blackwell guide to continental philosophy* (pp. 143–162). Oxford: Blackwell.

Mann, S. (2001). Alternative perspectives on the student experience: Alienation and engagement. *Studies in Higher Education, 26*(1), 7–19.

Mazutis, D., & Slawinski, N. (2008). Leading organizational learning through authentic dialogue. *Management Learning, 39*(4), 437–456.

Menges, R. J., & Weimer, M. & Associates (Eds). (1996). *Teaching on solid ground: Using scholarship to improve practice*. San Francisco, CA: Jossey-Bass.

Merton, R. K. (1973). *The sociology of science: Theoretical and empirical investigations*. Chicago: University of Chicago Press.

Meyer, J. H. F., & Land, R. (2006). Threshold concepts: An introduction. In J. H. F. Meyer, & R. Land (Eds), *Overcoming barriers to student understanding: Threshold concepts and troublesome knowledge* (pp. 3–18). London: RoutledgeFalmer.

Mezirow, J. (1981). A critical theory of adult learning and education. *Adult Education, 32*, 3–24.

Mezirow, J. (Ed.). (1990). *Fostering critical reflection in adulthood*. San Francisco, CA: Jossey-Bass.

Mezirow, J. (1991). *Transformative dimensions of adult learning*. San Francisco, CA: Jossey-Bass.

Mezirow, J. (1998). On critical reflection. *Adult Education Quarterly, 48*, 185–198.

Mezirow, J. (2000). Learning to think like an adult: Core concepts of transformation theory. In J. Mezirow (Ed.), *Learning as transformation: Critical perspectives on a theory in progress* (pp. 3–33). San Francisco, CA: Jossey-Bass.

Newman, F., King, M., & Carmichael, D.L. (2007). Authentic instruction and assessment. *Common standards for rigor and relevance in teaching academic subjects*. Available at: http://www.smallschoolsproject.org/PDFS/meetings/auth_instr_assess.pdf (accessed 7 August 2011).

Newman, F. M., Marks, H. M., & Gamoran, A. (1996). Authentic pedagogy and student performance. *American Journal of Education*, *104*, 280–312.

Nicholls, G. (2005). *The challenge to scholarship: Rethinking learning, teaching and research*. New York: Routledge.

Nietzsche, F. (1883). *Also sprach Zarathustra: Ein Buch fuer Alle und Keinen (Thus spoke Zarathustra)*. Chemnitz, Germany: Verlag von Ernst Schmeitzner.

Nixon, J. (2004). Education for the good society: The integrity of academic practice. *London Review of Education*, *2*(3), 245–252.

Nixon, J. (2007). Excellence and the good society. In A. Skelton (Ed.), *International perspectives on teaching excellence in higher education* (pp. 23–53). New York: Routledge.

Nixon, J. (2008). *Towards the virtuous university: The moral bases of academic practice*. New York: Routledge.

Nixon, J. (2011). *Higher education and the public good: Imagining the university*. London: Continuum.

Nixon, J. (2012). *Interpretive pedagogies for higher education: Arendt, Berger, Said, Nussbaum and their legacies*. London: Continuum.

Nixon, J., Marks, A., Rowland, S., & Walker, M. (2001). Towards a new academic professionalism: A manifesto for hope. *British Journal of Sociology of Education*, *22*(2), 227–244.

Noddings, N. (2003a). *Caring: A feminine approach to ethics and moral education* (2nd ed.). Berkeley, CA: University of California Press.

Noddings, N. (2003b). Is teaching a practice. *Journal of Philosophy and Education*, *37*(2), 241–251.

Norris, S. P. (2001). The pale of consideration when seeking sources of teaching expertise. *The American Journal of Education*, *108*(3), 167–196.

Norris, S. P., & Ennis, R. H. (1989). *Evaluating critical thinking*. Pacific Grove, CA: Midwest Publications.

Nussbaum, M. (1986). *The fragility of goodness: Luck and ethics in Greek tragedy and philosophy*. New York: Cambridge University Press.

Nussbaum, M. (1997). *Cultivating humanity: A classical defense of reform in liberal education*. Cambridge, MA: Harvard University Press.

Nussbaum, M. (2000). *Women and human development: The capabilities approach*. Cambridge: Cambridge University Press.

Nussbaum, M. (2004). *Upheavals of thought*. Cambridge: Cambridge University Press.

Nussbaum, M. (2010). *Not for profit: Why democracy needs the humanities*. Cambridge: Cambridge University Press.

Nussbaum, M. (2011). *Developing capabilities*. Cambridge: Cambridge University Press.

Nussbaum, M. (2012). Recoiling from reason: Review of MacIntyre, Whose justice? Which rationality. In *Philosophical interventions: Reviews 1986–2011* (Chapter 4, pp. 53–68). Oxford: Oxford University Press.

Nussbaum, M., & Sen, A. (Eds). (1993). *The quality of life*. Oxford: Clarendon Press.

Oakley, F. (1996). *Scholarship and teaching: A matter of mutual support*. American Council of Learned Societies Occasional Paper No. 32. Available at: http://archives.acls.org/op/32_Scholarship_and_Teaching.htm (accessed 15 August 2011).

Stenhouse, L. (1983). *Authority, education and emancipation: A collection of papers.* London: Heinemann.

Sternberg, R. (1985). *Beyond IQ: A triarchic theory of intelligence.* Cambridge: Cambridge University Press.

Sternberg, R. (1990). Wisdom and its relations to intelligence and creativity. In J. Sternberg (Ed.), *Wisdom, its nature, origins, and development* (pp. 142–159). Cambridge: Cambridge University Press.

Steutel, J. W. (1997). The virtue approach to moral education: Some conceptual clarifications. *Journal of Philosophy of Education, 31*(3), 395–407.

Tagg, J. (2003). *The learning paradigm college.* Bolton, MS: Anker Publishing Co.

Taylor, C. (1991). *The ethics of authenticity.* Cambridge, MA: Harvard University Press.

Thomson, J. A. K. (1976). *The ethics of Aristotle: The Nichomachean ethics.* London: Penguin Books.

Tierney, W. G. (1993). *Building communities of difference: Higher education in the twenty-first century.* Westport, CT: Bergin and Garvey.

Tierney, W. G., & Rhoads, R. A. (1993). Postmodernism and critical theory in higher education: Implications for research and practice. In J. C. Smart (Ed.), *Higher education: Handbook of theory and research, 10* (pp. 308–344). New York: Agathon Press.

Trigwell, K., Martin, E., Benjamin, J., & Prosser, M. (2000). Scholarship of teaching: A model . *Higher Education Research and Development, 19*(2), 155–168.

Trilling, L. (2006). *Sincerity and authenticity.* Cambridge, MA: Harvard University Press (original work published in 1972).

University of Edinburgh (2011). College of Science and Engineering Learning and Teaching Strategy 2011–2013. Available at: http://www.ed.ac.uk/schools-departments/science-engineering/staff/learning-teaching (accessed 30 April 2012).

University of Ulster (2008). Teaching and Learning Strategy 2008/09–2012/13. Available at: http://www.ulster.ac.uk/tls/tls2008-13.pdf (accessed 30 April 2012).

Vannini, P. (2007). The changing meanings of authenticity: An interpretive biography of professors' work experiences. *Studies in Symbolic Interaction, 29,* 63–90.

Vu, T. T. (2012). *Investigating authentic assessment for student learning in higher education.* Unpublished doctoral (PhD) thesis. University of Queensland.

Vu, T. T., & Dall'Alba, G. (2011). Becoming authentic professionals: Learning for authenticity. In L. Scanlon (Ed.), *'Becoming' a professional: An interdisciplinary analysis of professional learning* (pp. 95–108). Dordrecht, the Netherlands: Springer.

Walker, M. (Ed.). (2001). *Reconstructing professionalism in university teaching: Teachers and learners in action.* Buckingham, UK: Society for Research into Higher Education and Open University Press.

Walker, M. (2004). Pedagogies of beginning. In M. Walker, & J. Nixon (Eds), *Reclaiming universities from a runaway world* (pp. 131–146). Maidenhead, UK: Society for Research into Higher Education and Open University Press.

Walker. M. (2006). *Higher education pedagogies: A capabilities approach.* Maidenhead, UK: Society for Research into Higher Education and Open University Press.

Walker, M. (2009). 'Making a world that is worth living in': Humanities teaching and the formation of practical reasoning. *Arts and Humanities in Higher Education, 8*(3), 231–246.

Walker, M. (2010). A human development and capabilities 'prospective analysis' of global higher education policy. *Journal of Education Policy, 25*(4), 485–501.

Weimer, M. (1997). Assumptions that devalue university teaching. *International Journal of Academic Development, 2*(1), 52–59.

Weimer, M. (2006). *Enhancing scholarly work on teaching and learning: Professional literature that makes a difference.* San Francisco, CA: Jossey-Bass.

Wenger, E. (1998). *Communities of practice: Learning, meaning and identity.* Cambridge: Cambridge University Press.

Williams, B. (2004). *Truth and truthfulness: An essay in genealogy.* Princeton, NJ: Princeton University Press.

Wittgenstein, L. (1953). *Philosophical investigations.* G. E. M. Anscombe, & R. Rhees (Eds.), (translated by G. E. M. Anscombe), Oxford: Blackwell.

Zeichner, K. (1986). Preparing reflective teachers: An overview of instructional strategies which have been employed in pre-service teacher education. *International Journal of Educational Research, 2*(5), 565–575.

Zimmerman, M. (1986). *The development of Heidegger's concept of authenticity: Eclipse of the self* (Revised ed.). Athens, OH: Ohio University Press.